PIECES
— *of* —
SOUND

PIECES
— *of* —
SOUND

German
Experimental Radio

Daniel Gilfillan

 University of Minnesota Press
Minneapolis • London

The University of Minnesota Press gratefully acknowledges the financial assistance provided for the publication of this book from the School of International Letters and Cultures and the College of Liberal Arts and Sciences at Arizona State University.

Chapter 1 was previously published as "Media Experiments: Kempowski's *Bloomsday '97* and Tanaka's *Prométhée numérique*" in *"Was das nun wieder soll?" Von Im Block bis Letzte Grüße. Zu Werk und Leben Walter Kempowskis,* ed. Carla Damiano, Jörg Drews, and Doris Plöschberger (Göttingen: Wallstein, 2005), 207–19. Chapter 3 previously appeared as " 'Don't Touch That Dial': Designing a Collaborative Radio in 1950s West Germany," *Explorations in Media Ecology* 4, no. 3–4 (2005): 247–64. Chapter 4 was previously published as "Radio Art, Documentary, and the Sounds of Displacement: Paunović's *Other Voices — Echoes from a Warzone,* Vienna/Belgrade April 29, 1999," *Modern Austrian Literature* 38, no. 3–4 (2005): 65–84.

The work of Alfred Andersch was printed with the permission of Diogenes Verlag AG. Copyright Alfred Andersch and Diogenes Verlag AG Zürich. Alfred Andersch's work was published in 2004 by Diogenes Verlag AG.

Published by the University of Minnesota Press
111 Third Avenue South, Suite 290
Minneapolis, MN 55401-2520
http://www.upress.umn.edu

Library of Congress Cataloging-in-Publication Data

Gilfillan, Daniel
    Pieces of sound: German experimental radio / Daniel Gilfillan
      p. cm.
    Includes bibliographical references and index.
    ISBN 978-0-8166-4771-2 (hc: alk. paper) – ISBN 978-0-8166-4772-9 (pb: alk. paper)
    1. Experimental radio programs – Germany – History and criticism. 2. Radio broadcasting – Germany – History – 20th century. I. Title.
    PN1991.8.E94G55 2009
    791.44'611 – dc22

                                          20090011519

Printed in the United States of America on acid-free paper

The University of Minnesota is an equal-opportunity educator and employer.

14   13   12   11   10   09   10 9 8 7 6 5 4 3 2 1

For my mother, Marlene,
and her unwavering support
and in loving memory of my father,
Gilbert Gilfillan

Contents

Acknowledgments

A book may be written in isolation, but it is never written alone. *Pieces of Sound: German Experimental Radio* was a long time in the making, starting with the seed of an idea planted while I was a graduate student at the University of Oregon that I began to cultivate after my arrival at Arizona State University. Numerous trips to research archival holdings and to Germany and Austria to interview artists and critics during the past several years have added to the excitement and rigor of bringing this study together. I thank many people and institutions for providing research assistance, moral and emotional encouragement, intellectual camaraderie, and financial support.

I thank Helga Schreckenberger at the University of Vermont and Karla Schultz at the University of Oregon, whose intellectual insight, patience, and good spirits have accompanied me throughout my graduate studies and into my professional academic career. Several other teacher-scholars contributed to my own development as a scholar: Wolfgang Mieder, David Scrase, Veronica Richel, and Dennis Mahoney awoke in me an unending interest in German studies, while Susan Anderson, Jan Emerson, Kenneth Calhoon, John Lysaker, and Aletta Biersack helped to shape that interest further into a critical understanding. I found engaged listeners and discussants in my colleagues at Arizona State: I must thank in particular Holly Cashman and Cora Fox for their unfailing willingness to listen to my excitement, my discouragement, and my endless worrying about the development of arguments in the manuscript, and for discussions about the minute details of an argument or a sentence I wished to craft. Hyaeweol Choi, Juliann Vitullo, Markus Cruse, and Ayanna Thompson have also been friendly readers of various portions of this volume. I received the advice and encouragement of friends and colleagues Jacqueline Vansant and Regina Kecht, who heard selections from this book at professional conferences and read others in greater detail. I am indebted to the editors with whom I had the pleasure to work at the University of Minnesota Press: Andrea Kleinhuber, Richard Morrison, and Jason Weidemann each played a role in helping to shepherd my book through the various stages of publishing, and I deeply appreciate their efforts and assistance.

I am grateful to the College of Liberal Arts and Sciences, the program in Jewish Studies, and the Institute for Humanities Research at Arizona State University for financial support while researching this book. Partial research related to chapter 3 was conducted at Deutsches Literaturarchiv in Marbach a. Neckar, Germany, with the assistance of a German Academic Exchange Service grant. My participation in a Fulbright German Studies Seminar in the summer of 2004 and an NEH Summer Institute in the summer of 2006 offered me travel to Germany and Austria for rewarding intellectual experiences and networking opportunities with German and American scholars. I was able to parlay these trips into extended stays to conduct archival research and interviews, for which I thank Friedrich Dethlefs at Deutsches Rundfunkarchiv in Wiesbaden and Volkmar Vogt at the Archiv für Soziale Bewegungen in Freiburg im Breisgau for their and their staffs' incredible assistance.

One of the more exciting aspects of my research involved meeting with contemporary radio artists and radio art producers, as well as other scholars and critics of German radio. Here I extend my gratitude and appreciation to Heidi Grundmann, Elisabeth Zimmermann, and Robert Adrian of the Kunstradio project in Vienna for their openness in sharing stories, providing invaluable audio and book materials, and encouraging me to pursue my ideas related to their project. My informal interview with Armin Medosch from Radio Subcom and insightful e-mail exchanges with Atau Tanaka gave me new intellectual and creative energy, as well as access to one-of-a-kind audio and text materials that would have been extremely difficult to locate. Finally, I thank Wolfgang Hagen from Humboldt Universität for his wonderful help in obtaining access to copies of materials by Hans Flesch, and Sabine Breitsameter, professor of media at the University of Applied Sciences Darmstadt and producer of *Audiohyperspace* at the Südwestrundfunk, for her willingness to speak with me during the early stages of this project; she introduced me to the name of Hans Flesch.

Other friends and colleagues offered support at various stages of this project. Prasad Boradkar, Gwyneira Isaac, Jennifer Parchesky, Torin Monahan, David Birchfield, and Philip Bernick gave me comments in relation to a larger collaborative grant project, Engaging Radio, which helped immensely in my conceptualization of this book. Brian Jeffcoat, friend and mentor, has been a solid foundation throughout the writing of this book, and many graduate and undergraduate students have also been supportive. The mentoring process for me is always bidirectional, and the opportunity to work with challenging and motivated students affords me the chance to think about my own work while thinking about theirs. This is the reason I entered this profession in the first place, and with this in mind I have written this book, which I hope will engage discussion among students and colleagues.

Finally, I express my gratitude to my immediate family in Vermont and to my extended ersatz family of friends in Oregon and Arizona. The death of my father in the midst of this project, while emotionally difficult, ultimately made me more determined to complete it. My mother has always been a source of joy and inspiration, and her perseverance helped me to persevere as well. My trips home from the heat of Arizona to the cooler weather of Vermont offered me reflective space to write but also energetic space to relax and have fun with my brothers, sister, nieces, and nephew. I dedicate this book to each of you and also to my dad.

Abbreviations

ANEM Asocijacija nezavisnih elektronskih medija (Association of Independent Electronic Media, Serbia)

BR Bayerischer Rundfunk (Bavarian Broadcasting, Munich)

GEZ Gebühreneinzugszentrale (Central License-Fee Collection Office, Cologne)

HR Hessischer Rundfunk (Hessian Broadcasting, Frankfurt am Main)

KPD Kommunistische Partei Deutschlands (Communist Party of Germany)

NWDR Nordwestdeutscher Rundfunk (Northwest German Broadcasting, Hamburg, 1945–55)

ORF Österreichischer Rundfunk (Austrian Broadcasting, Vienna)

RDL Radio Dreyeckland (Freiburg i. Breisgau)

RFK Reichsfunkkommission (National Communications Commission, Berlin)

RRG Reichsrundfunkgesellschaft (National Radio Company, Berlin)

RVF Radio Verte Fessenheim (Radio Green Fessenheim Alsace/Freiburg i. Breisgau)

SDR Süddeutscher Rundfunk (Southern German Broadcasting, Stuttgart, 1949–98)

SPD Sozialdemokratische Partei Deutschlands (Social Democratic Party of Germany)

SWF Südwestfunk (Southwest Broadcasting, Baden-Baden, 1946–98)

SWR Südwestrundfunk (Southwest Broadcasting, Stuttgart, Baden-Baden, Mainz)

USPD Unabhängige Sozialdemokratische Partei Deutschlands (Independent Social Democratic Party of Germany)

WTB Wolffsche Telegraphenbüro (Wolff Telegraph Office, Berlin)

ZFL Zentralfunkleitung (Central Radio Committee, Berlin)

ZKM Zentrum für Kunst und Medien (Center for Art and Media, Karlsruhe)

Introduction

Who does the air belong to? The air only has
one use value for you, and by means of the
radio it is turned into a commodity; it becomes a
means of transport. Who is then allowed to use
the ether as a means of transport? The ether is
the common property of all people, the public
property of all states. It is about time that the
workers of all countries tend to the air as a
means of transmission, otherwise the air will be
cut off to all the workers' radio transmitters!
— Communication from the
Workers' Radio Club, June 1925

Radio and Artistic Experimentation

Radio has formed an integral but often unnoticed part of the background of everyday life in the twentieth and twenty-first centuries. Located in the borderland between public discourse and private enjoyment, radio can be a device for communication and a medium for artistic practice and experimentation. It may serve as a tool for propaganda or protest, a collector's item, or a site for familial and community building. In addition, a majority of contemporary radio audiences most likely perceives the template-style programming of commercial radio and its broadcasts of news and entertainment as being the only possible types of programming offered by the medium itself. Today, new trends in radio programming, controversies over broadcast content and regulation, technologies such as digital and satellite radio, and convergent practices like web-based streaming audio, Internet radio, and podcasting have brought the long-invisible landscape of radio back into public focus. Radio as a medium, thus, stands at a crucial historical juncture, as these emergent technologies and new modes of broadcast delivery challenge the very definition and function of radio. The radio is a medium that came of age alongside the emergent media environments of film and television, and we would do well to revisit these past moments of intermedial cross-pollination to look for models that inform the radio's current development beside a plethora of networked telecommunications media. *Pieces of Sound* does just that. It considers an array of examples from the contemporary German and Austrian media landscapes to explore the ways in which cultural/artistic radio broadcasting experiments with the metaphors, practices, and interfaces of networked media not only to expand the artistic and communicative possibilities of the medium but also to inform perceptions about the use and direction of these newer telecommunications media. And it tempers this discussion through a concerted examination of acoustical examples from the history of German radio, the attendant media theoretical debates that accompanied the radio's development, and the legislative policies and broadcasting standards that regulated its use. Extending back to German radio's infancy amid the fledgling democracy of 1920s Weimar, moving forward through its implementation in the politico-mythical structuring of National Socialist rhetoric and postwar reorganization as a tool for democratization, and circling around the cultural political landscape that surrounded the formation of the European Union, *Pieces of Sound* approaches artistic practices of experimentation with the radio medium with an eye to understanding how these varied landscapes influenced and continue to impact the cultural politics surrounding the medium.

Many literary and cultural histories of radio broadcasting in Germany focus primarily on the historical development of the *Hörspiel,* or radio play, or literally, an auditory game, as the site where literary imagination and technical innovation come together. In these histories the radio play is viewed as the principal product of the association between artistic expression and radio-specific technology. Yet there exists outside this history equally compelling traces of the experimental, which move beyond the textual limitations of the radio play genre to explore the possibilities of a radio-centered art form based in notions of interactivity, intertextual play and intermedial convergence, and the creation of networked communicative spaces for artistic collaboration. Certainly the radio play figures as an important access point to the frontiers of artistic opportunity within the medium and technology of the radio, but what figures more highly, and what is missing in these cultural histories, are those intriguing moments of critical insight into and experimentation with the semantics and materiality of the radio itself. At its heart *Pieces of Sound* delves past the entertainment veneer of broadcast to discover how sound in any of its representations (as voice, as noise, as text, as detritus) is employed by artists to renegotiate a commodified and regulated notion of radio. To this end, radio artists look for answers to questions such as, How do the practices and structures of radio broadcasts, transmissions, and receptions open up areas of interactivity with the listener, with fellow artists, and with the structures of knowledge and information they distribute? In its traversal of the ether can the structure of a radio wave pick up additional bits of sound that in some way change or enhance the original intent of a broadcast, and if so, what would that sound like? How can long-held beliefs about the economic value of telecommunications for the routing of information be transformed into an intrinsic value for the routing of knowledge? How does the radio initially serve to facilitate notions of local identity and in what ways does local identity itself change vis-à-vis the transformation of the radio medium: as local identity gets caught up in competition (radio advertising), and national patriotism (regulatory practices based in national security), and eventually transforms and possibly disappears as the entanglement of sociopolitical and economic practices converge to create a sense of a world or global market? This notion of an international or global identity combines both the economics of competition and the national narratives of regulation to inform (usurp?) local ideas of culture. Finally, how can the realities of radio commercialization and the arrival of the Internet provide additional models for radio experimentation?

German radio existed long before it became regulated as a medium in 1923. One would have to look back to the latter decades of the 1800s to the work of Hermann von Helmholtz in acoustics, and that of his student Heinrich Hertz with electromagnetic waves, in order to fully capture the science and physics behind what would eventually become broadcast radio. "Nobody listens to radio," writes media theorist Friedrich Kittler. "What loudspeakers or headsets provide for their users is always just radio programming, never radio itself."[1] *Pieces of Sound* looks to those moments in German broadcast radio's short but active history when radio producers were themselves trying to recapture that aura of possibility imbued by the science of acoustics and the physics of electromagnetic frequencies, which had drawn so much excitement within a small but lively community of amateur radio enthusiasts in the period preceding World War I. These levels of anticipation and experimentation with the early iterations of the radio transceiver had become lost behind the economics of information and entertainment that radio had grown into with its regulation as a broadcasting medium, and its retooling as a reception device. Radio experimentation in the early days of broadcasting meant transgressing the limits that had been imposed on the medium by regulation, fearful of unsanctioned broadcasts that would throw governmental sovereignty into question; it meant a slow and deliberate transformation of the airwaves from their role in duplication of content from other media or live venues and toward the introduction of radiophonic art forms that made the practice of broadcasting their focus; and it meant a continued theoretical engagement with issues of sound quality, listener interactivity, receptive versus passive listening, and the role and function of intermediality. These aspects of experimentation with the radio medium would continue to be adapted as the contours of the political and regulatory landscape changed, and as technical advances in recording technologies and in other competitive media changed, but even with these successive modifications to the media landscape, transgressive operating modes, pushing the envelope, and experimentation continued to serve as the artistic response to radio production.

The key to promoting experimental radio forms lies squarely with this issue of access to the technologies of broadcast. Access becomes the nexus point connecting and separating the various broadcasting constituencies: the commercial from the public service broadcasters, and the alternative free radio and subversive pirate broadcasters from those mainstream airwaves funded by public or private commercial monies. And acoustic artists and radio art projects find themselves needing to navigate between the practices and policies or nonpolicies of each. Douglas Kahn writes, "most artists responded to radio only rhetorically, at a distance from the thing that trafficked in distances, because access to the technology was limited, even when it existed."[2] It is also with this question of access that alternative radio practices locate a typology of tactical radio production. Tactical radio production involves strategies that seek in some way to appropriate the more traditional channels of media as relays of consumption, and use them as channels to broadcast less commercially attractive programs, which are often of a documentary or sound artistic nature. Independent radio groups, pirate radio broadcasters, and supporters of noncommercial community/free radio comprise those proponents of an alternative radio practice and find common ground in their quest to exist alongside the more traditional commercial and public radio stations. The aim of these alternative and experimental forms of broadcast involves either the creation of sound-based radio art pieces that engage with social, political, or radio-metacritical topics, the production and dissemination of critical news reporting for activist mobilization, or the provision of an alternative listening experience that weaves local issues and local sounds into the broadcast mediascape. Radio experimentation in the realm of cultural broadcasting and artistic production means the development of new radio genres, the capture and remediation of ambient and found sound, and the piecing together of soundscapes using such techniques as sound montage, live streaming audio feeds, and the transformation of textual thought into vocalized sound. Experimentation with sound benefits from the innate transgressive materiality of its composition. "Sound," according to Brandon LaBelle, "*performs* with and through space: it navigates geographically, reverberates acoustically, and structures socially, for sound amplifies and silences, contorts, distorts, and pushes against architecture; it escapes rooms, vibrates walls, disrupts conversation; it expands and contracts space by accumulating reverberation, relocating place beyond itself, carrying it in its wave, and inhabiting always more than one place; it misplaces and displaces;...sound overflows borders."[3] With respect to the radio medium, experimentation with sound has found fertile ground with the convergence potential offered by the Internet. These interfaces provoke new strategies for perception for exploring sound's relationship to the visual, and for expanding notions of interactivity based in hypermedia models. Alternative and experimental modes of radio practice operate outside conventional boundaries of radio broadcasting. Each situate their raison d'être in the issues of access that commercial broadcasting neglects to address, and they each venture to provide or engage an alternative view, either in the form and type of content they broadcast or in the techniques and strategies they implement.

In the midst of all of these experimental tactics, artistic practices, and theoretical discussions offering insights and know-how for transforming the nature of broadcast, there is the question, To what end? What do these operating modes achieve in their rethinking and retooling of the radio medium? Each period explored in *Pieces of Sound* situates the radio as a device that tonally mediates the economic, political, and cultural threads that run rampant through the sociopolitical fabric of each period: Weimar democracy, National Socialist dictatorship, postwar capitalism, and late twentieth-century globalization. In actively seeking ways to extend the radio beyond the boundaries set up for it in each of these differing climates, practitioners of an acoustic-based radio art provide for new ways of conceptualizing the medium to help support a more transgressive, grassroots approach to understanding the range of alternative potentials that exist for their audiences in contending with the scope and impact of these systems. While the volume at hand is not exhaustive in exploring every major period of German broadcasting history, it does focus on three central historical-technological periods outlined above in order to delimit a broad and varied line of investigation into practices of experimentation within the context of the changing legal and broadcast regulatory landscapes.

Chapter 1 introduces the reader to a matrix of contemporary sound-based experiments that maps the cutting edge interplay between radio and the Internet. The chapter focuses specific attention on the digital sound art piece produced by composer Atau Tanaka, a two-part performance piece occurring via a live online website debuting in February 2002 and a live on-site performance in Karlsruhe, Germany, in March 2002. Commissioned and supported by

Audiohyperspace, a monthly online/on-air program of Germany's Südwestrundfunk in Baden-Baden and the Zentrum für Kunst und Medien (ZKM) in Karlsruhe, *Wiretapping the Beast* offers an intriguing example of German radio's experimentation with the intermedial convergence of sound broadcast and Internet connectivity — the aural spatiotemporality of the radio and the visual, textual, sonic, performative, and haptic interactivity of the Internet. This notion of intermedial convergence is discussed further in relation to the 1930 audio film *Weekend* created by German film director and early media artist Walter Ruttmann, who parlayed his knowledge of the film medium to produce an imageless sound film for broadcast on the radio. The connections between Ruttmann's and Tanaka's innovative interweaving of the radio medium with that of other media points to the long history of experimentation with the radio and to the radio medium's adaptable nature.

The crux of *Wiretapping the Beast* is to detect the extent to which the seamlessness of data transfer so important for the digital economy becomes embodied in the impressions and thought processes that the middle-class techno-workers bring to their own daily lives online and on-screen, and in a sense draws parallels between this new class of worker in the information economy to the creature, beast, Frankenstein's monster, and digital Prometheus that Tanaka simulates in his piece. Drawing on a Western tradition engaged with understanding the human–machine relationship (Mary Shelley, Julien Offray de La Mettrie, Donna Haraway), this project for web, radio, and live performance creates its own version of a human–machine chimera, not from the random information-based noise widespread on the Internet, but rather from the thoughtful input requested of the website's visitors in the form of digital image and sound files submitted as fodder for the on-screen animated creature. A noisy, erratic, and imposing figure, the creature inhabits a narrow space of the browser window, transforming its shape and its song as images and sound files are added as accoutrements for its monstrous dance across the screen. Tanaka's project converses with varying modes of composition: the hypermedia frame of its web-based performance, the DJ-style mix of varying sound inputs as part of its live performance, the parsing of this live performance for radio broadcast, and the studied reflection involved in the arrangement of a sound-based relic for delivery and consumption on compact disc. Not entirely radio or completely live performance, and not only a web-based digital art installation, Tanaka's *Wiretapping the Beast* requires the collaborative efforts of each of these media, and requires as well the interactive input of its audience. What we are left with is a performance piece that stretches the limits of each individual medium that structures the piece and provokes each one to perform beyond an established consumer or standardized idea of what it has been designed to do. While the dynamic network-based database that formed the backbone of the piece helped to capture and archive the range of user input that went into feeding, building, and transforming the online animated creature, the piece itself maintains an impermanence reminiscent of the fleetingness of radio broadcast, which, once out on the airwaves, begins to disappear with each successive utterance.

While the first chapter is situated at the forefront of artistic experiments in digital and sonic telecommunications installations to demonstrate the intermedial play among the individual, yet interreliant, media components (Internet, radio, live performance) active in Atau Tanaka's piece, the second chapter takes readers back to the beginnings of radio broadcasting in Germany in the 1920s. The disjuncture of this move is meant to illustrate the importance of historicizing contemporary artistic and experimental approaches to networked media, since it is through looking to past instances of new technologies and the cultural, political, social, and economic impact they engendered that contemporary approaches to "new" media can be shaped. Yet, unlike the majority of commercial radio broadcast, this is not a unidirectional routing of knowledge from the past to the present; rather this disjunctive move is also meant to highlight the influence of new techniques and new metaphors from the realm of multimedia in reconceptualizing the media landscapes of the past. Chapter 2 tracks the theoretical discussions and practical implementations surrounding the radio as a new communications medium and its impact on cultural and artistic production. Specifically, it explores the radio theoretical and experimental work of Hans Flesch, the first artistic director at Radio Frankfurt from 1924 until his move to Berlin radio in 1929. Flesch's essays and commentaries on radio in 1920s Germany practically litter the pages of Weimar's radio journals, whose number Kate Lacey estimates at 61 by 1930, with a total circulation of 2.5 million.[4]

Of interest to this study are a series of programmatic essays that Flesch wrote in the very beginning years of radio broadcasting, as they demonstrate the issues that he faced with respect to programming, regulation, and industry standards. In particular these essays investigate an early critical engagement with the notion that radio should serve to duplicate content from other media (gramophone albums, newspaper reports) and remediate content from live entertainment venues (concert halls, theater, opera). This prompted Flesch to a metacritical investigation of the technical and media differences between radio and its competitors, the cinema and the gramophone. Following on this, Flesch also writes about the need to move the radio medium away from this role in cultural substitution and create instead a specifically radiophonic art form, one that takes into account those aspects of radio broadcast that make it unique from these other artistic media, specifically looking at the notion of mediation, the impossibility of the radio providing an unmediated listening experience, and the notions of form and creative power in the design of new programs. These programmatic and theoretical aspects are taken up in the exploration of three case studies: the first *Hörspiel* ever broadcast on the German airwaves in 1924, Flesch's own *Zauberei auf dem Sender,* and two additional radio broadcasts, F. W. Bischoff's 1928 *Hallo! Welle Erdball!* and Friedrich Wolf's 1929 *S.O.S....rao rao...Foyn. "Krassin" rettet "Italia"* — locating in them the roots of interactive communication, the ethereality of information, and sound-specific cultures. The mediascape of radio experimentation in Weimar is juxtaposed against a history of German broadcasting leading up to the radio's approval as an entertainment medium in 1923. Along with this history of the medium is an exploration of early broadcast media policies, regulations, and sanctions that marked the radio's growth as a medium and provide a narrative of official radio practice against which these early radio experiments can be read.

Chapter 3 inquires into these practices of artistic radio experimentation begun in the early days of radio in the Weimar Republic and elucidated by Bertolt Brecht in a five-essay series on radio theory. It continues with an investigation of the radio genre designs of Alfred Andersch in the immediate postwar era (1947–59) as an attempt to revive and develop Brecht's ideas for radio after the twelve-year period of National Socialist regulation of radio. Here the volume provides analysis into the official policies and practices regarding radio, looking at radio reforms begun in the latter months of 1932, as well as central speeches by Joseph Goebbels concerning the position of the radio medium in achieving a National Socialist regime. The framework of transition within radio practice, which was prompted by the National Socialist dictatorship, assists in problematizing notions of active, passive, and convivial listening practices, which Andrew Stuart Bergerson's audience studies from communities of listeners in the 1930s also help to elucidate. While Bertolt Brecht's theories for an experimental radio were disrupted by the National Socialist rise to power and Alfred Andersch's designs for a collaborative radio during the postwar 1950s were subsumed and thus diluted by the machinations of West Germany's quick economic recovery, each open the radio up to the possibilities of interactive, audience-centered programming that commercial broadcasts and prevailing technical standards had not yet acknowledged.

As I mention in chapter 2, even though Brecht's radio theoretical work appears within the historic timeline of radio production and experimentation in the latter years of the Weimar Republic, I have chosen to investigate his work in the context of a reformed postwar German radio practice, because his writings in this area are continually invoked by artists and radio practitioners alike for their utopian vision of a freely accessible network of communication based in the structures of radio broadcast. It is in this vein that I see Alfred Andersch's genre designs for postwar radio allowing for a participatory culture to flourish among his listeners. These designs are based in creating a situation of open critical dialogue, which provides a set of mindful, thought-provoking, and reflective approaches to issues of sociopolitical and cultural import to the listening audience. However, Andersch's acknowledgment of the emancipatory potential of the radio medium is tempered by his insights about its subtle role in the cultural political atmosphere of the economic miracle in 1950s Germany. His highly critical commentaries from 1959 serve to illustrate these intricate connections between cultural consumerism, the changing role of art and the artist within the culture industry, and the radio's duplicitous role in substantiating these cultural policies while also being regulated to serve the public good.

The study's fourth and final chapter examines a radio practice that appropriates existing broadcast frequencies, network pathways, and unused telecommunications devices to extend the scope of broadcast possibility to include content often avoided by the stultifying practices of mainstream journalism. This type of tactical media practice functions with an eye to opening the radio up, for establishing points of access to the technologies and frequencies of broadcast normally regulated by the state. In this context, the chapter focuses on the origins of Germany's free radio movement in the 1980s and on two experimental radio art projects from the early and late 1990s produced by the Austrian Kunstradio project. Concurrent with these more tactical strategies to leverage access, the development of a European media policy with the formation and expansion of the European Union was also taking shape. Germany's free radio movement was organized to provide alternative airwave space that would move outside or underneath officially sanctioned programming offered either by government-approved public broadcasting or by private commercial radio. Specifically, this chapter looks at one of the oldest autonomous radio stations in Germany, Radio Dreyeckland (RDL), located in Freiburg im Breisgau and "established" in 1978, which defines itself as a leftist media project — an open broadcast space (both physical and ether-based) in which individuals and groups independently produce cultural, sociopolitical, and educational programs for broadcast. With its roots in the antinuclear protest movement, and encompassing student political demonstrations of the late 1960s, the autonomous radio movement in West Germany serves as a foil for an investigation of a countercultural engagement with the radio medium and tactical/pirate uses of the radio device, and of changes in media policy in the Federal Republic.

The transition from national to European identity, from local to global identity, and the accompanying changes in economic, security, and telecommunications policies anticipating the advent of the European Union in 1992, prompted a two-part series of mobile radio performances by the Austrian performance group Radio Subcom. Their *Europa Report* broadcasts employ tactical and pirate radio practices to focus attention on the dissipation of the internal borders between European Union member states while increasing collaborative efforts on border surveillance through the creation of a centralized and shared data network according to the Schengen agreement. Coverage of the NATO intervention in Serbia and subsequent aerial bombing of Belgrade during the Kosovo conflict in the spring of 1999 is primarily known through the lenses of global media conglomerates like CNN. Yet outside the safety and distance of these visual reports other coverage exists that details the local experience of these events. Located as threads on Internet mailing lists, entries in electronic diaries, and audio streams along radio and Internet channels, this alternative coverage forms the central elements of radio artist Gordan Paunović's live broadcast and CD remix *Other Voices — Echoes from a Warzone*. The analysis of this acoustical art project situates larger questions about wartime identity and mobility within discussions surrounding the changing nature of the self in a globally networked information society. Paunović's piece for live radio broadcast illustrates the changing role of radio in drawing together an array of medial inputs to produce an engaging and thought-provoking documentary in which the personal voices and sounds of war-torn Belgrade are able to be heard. Both of these Kunstradio-supported projects illustrate the ways in which a collaborative artistic space can be formed from within the technologies and techniques of telecommunications media and demonstrate as well how the idea of a globalized telecommunications infrastructure as a backbone of a globalization economy can also be used for a tactics of experimental radio practice. The transgressive power of radio opens up dialogue, establishes collaborative artistic connections, and helps build communities that fall outside the boundaries of a sanctioned notion of broadcast. If anything, the process of artistic experimentation must remain bound up with transgressive practices in order to maintain a position on the forefront, or on the cutting edge. The radio's roles as technical device and as communications medium are caught up within this delicate balance — the navigation it must undertake between advertising revenue based on entertainment value and regulatory policies based in fear of governmental takeover and autonomous thought. Experimentation with the radio as an artistic medium serves as the critical stethoscope to remind, explore, and zero in on this delicate balance.

ONE

Wiretapping the Beast

Radio, Hyperspatiality,
and a New Network for Art

When American modernist painter Jackson Pollock was asked to comment on his unconventional painting technique in a 1951 radio interview, he teased out some intriguing connections between artistic expression and innovations in technological progress:

> My opinion is that new needs need new techniques. And the modern artists have found new ways and new means of making their statements. It seems to me that the modern painter cannot express this age, the airplane, the atom bomb, the radio, in the old forms of the Renaissance or of any other past culture. Each age finds its own technique.[1]

Pollock locates his art directly in the midst of those information networks prevalent in 1950s America and perceives it as a node of experience that expresses visually and texturally the speed of air travel, the minute complexity of the atomic bomb, and the simultaneous ethereality and physical presence of the radio. Some thirty years earlier in 1919/20, German avant-garde filmmaker, animator, and soon-to-be radio artist Walter Ruttmann anticipated these same threads addressed by Pollock when he described the profound cultural growth being experienced in Weimar Germany's burgeoning media landscape in terms of the tempo of the time:

> Telegraph, express trains, stenography, photography, high-speed printing machines — themselves not valued as cultural achievements — bring about a velocity in the transmission of intellectual and cultural ideas never before experienced. Through this rapidity in distribution of public knowledge, a perpetual inundation of material results for each single individual, for whom the old methods of observation and understanding fail. . . . Here lie the reasons for our desperate helplessness vis-à-vis trends in the visual arts. The gaze, which

1

is increasingly relegated to the observation of temporal events, can no longer begin making sense of the fixed, reduced and timeless formulae of painting.[2]

Just as Walter Ruttmann seems to lament the loss of a reflective, timeless gaze for allowing us to make sense of the world around us due to the rapid flow of information as precipitated by innovations in the physical, visual and textual networks of information travel, Jackson Pollock's artworks provide a response to an evermore chaotic system of innovations by patterning a moment of cohesion from the chaos of these "analog" devices. In similar fashion, the multimedia installations of contemporary American-Japanese composer and digital artist Atau Tanaka provoke and expose patterns from within the chaotic global system of convergent telecommunication networks — the digital nexus. This chapter will focus on one specific visual and sound installation for Internet — Tanaka's piece *Frankensteins Netz / Prométhée numérique / Wiretapping the Beast*,[3] which documents one example of German radio's experimentation with the convergence of sound broadcast and Internet connectivity; and which brings German radio one step closer toward reachieving its original design as a transceiver, or two-way communication device. Premiering online, on the airwaves, and live on three continents in February and March 2002, Tanaka's piece combines aural, visual, textual, haptic and performative elements to create a radio-based interactive experience reminiscent of Bertolt Brecht's idea of the transceiver, a concept that we will come back to several times throughout this volume:

> The radio could be the finest possible communications apparatus in public life, a vast system of channels. That is, it could be so, if it understood how to receive as well as to transmit, how to let the listener speak as well as hear, how to bring him into a network instead of isolating him.[4]

Brecht's notion of the transceiver casts radio as a routing medium, as a synchronous communication device that combines the free-flow transmission/reception of two-way radio with the guiding principles of open cultural broadcasting. His description demonstrates the significance of setting the broadcaster/producer and the listener/consumer on the same technical footing by placing radio technology at each of their fingertips and ostensibly allowing for a mutual interchange to occur. Bringing the listener (in this case, the user) into the network, activating them in production as Brecht suggests, is one of the purposes behind Tanaka's performance and installation. Yet it is much more than that. It operates within a rhizomatic structure, itself an ever-changing kaleidoscopic adaptation, coaxed from multiple layers of artistic, literary, user, and programmer interactivity, while navigating and negotiating the various technical parameters and administrative vocabularies assembled by the project's institutional sponsors. What we end up with is an animate, pulsing, and noisy entity that takes its cues from the various information network feeds it receives from the realms of radio, literature, DJ culture, relational database programming, and the middle-class techno-worker.

German radio history has many examples of experimentation. The sound piece by filmmaker Walter Ruttmann, *Weekend* (1930), provides an example of one radio artist who engages with the role of sound as a foundational element in the routine experience of an encountered space.[5] Ruttmann's short experimental piece explores the interface of film and broadcasting technologies through the use of editing, montage, and sound sampling techniques to capture and rearrange the fleeting and oftentimes unnoticed sounds of daily experience. Alfred Braun, radio announcer, reporter, and producer during the Weimar period, defined this technique in relation to radio production using very imagistic and filmic metaphors:

> Acoustical film was the term we used in Berlin . . . for a radio play that through its dreamlike, quickly moving sequence of images gliding, jumping, overlapping each other, alternating between close-ups and distance shots blending in and out, deliberately transferred the techniques of moving pictures to the radio.[6]

Adapting his film editing techniques to sound, Ruttmann (1887–1941) pieced together for radio broadcast a collage of mechanical, spoken word and transactional sound that evokes one weekend in the city of Berlin. The rhythm of the piece is formed by six movements, which chart a particularly modern experience of time through a progression of sounds that move from situations of work to brief moments of leisure. The first movement, referred to as "Jazz der Arbeit" (Jazz of Work), assembles the sounds of typewriters, telephone rings, cash registers, saws, hammers, and dictation. The piece transitions into "Feierabend" (Quitting Time) with the striking of clocks, the knells of factory sirens, and the gradual calming of typewriters to indicate the end of the workday. This is followed by "Fahrt ins Freie" (Journey to the Country), which begins with the sounds of departure: cranks of autos, train whistles, conductors voices; and equally mechanical sounds of arrival. The fourth movement, "Pastorale," includes roosters crowing, birds singing, and the blending of cowbells and church bells to evoke a sense of time outside of the pace of the city. Yet this leisurely pace, these fleeting moments of relaxation, are not able to offset the end of the weekend, signified in the final two movements, which announce the return of the work week and the syncopated rhythms of a time not one's own. Ruttmann's focus on time and the role of montage in adequately representing the nonunity and nonautonomy of temporal space brings to the radiophonic medium an engagement with the immediate that was only beginning to find its way into a radio practice that was ensconced in entertainment and leisure. That *Weekend* foregrounds the mechanical and temporal patterning of daily life, even to the point of capturing the typicality underlying a leisurely trip to the country, is telling for the ways in which radio had begun to develop, and the new intermedial techniques it had begun to use to produce its broadcasts.

By utilizing new technical developments and procedures for incorporating sound into the medium of film, Ruttmann recorded these weekend sounds optically on to film stock, employed the cut/splice editing technique of film, and projected the final version over the airwaves. Here Ruttmann utilized the Tri-Ergon process of optically recording sound waves onto the edges of film stock through a transduction method, which had been in use since the mid-1920s, and employed by radio producers as early as 1928.[7] In 1928 Ruttmann considered the possible interarticulations between the visuality of film and the aurality of radio in a short essay that contextualizes the production of his first sound film, which by all clues can only be determined as the audio-film *Weekend:*

> I am currently busy with the production of my first sound film for the Tri-Ergon studios. The case of this tone film is doubly interesting, since the two most modern achievements overlap on an external level and lead to a comparison between them. My film embraces the German radio and plays on all broadcast stations, in order to be conducted acoustically and visually across

the most beautiful areas of the German Reich. The non-visual radio and the silence of the film are two opposites, which when played against each other approach in another sense the concept of the sound film. The possible proliferation of illusion and fantasy lies with the contrary counterbalancing of sound and image.[8]

The intermedial potential of film and radio, which culminated in this montage work for radio, recalls Ruttmann's earlier film montage *Berlin, Symphony of a Great City* from 1927, which combines the itinerant techniques of the *entfesselte Kamera* (unchained camera) to capture the dynamic, pulsing energies of life in the growing metropolis and the splicing techniques of visual montage to tease out patterns of perception linking the mesmeric transactions of the shop window with the rapid pace of life spiraling out of control.[9] An elucidatory aside: When I encountered Tacita Dean's film installation *Palast* (2005) in the "Constructing New Berlin" exhibition at the Phoenix Art Museum in June 2006, I was immediately struck by the seemingly divergent practices each artist utilized to metaphorically capture an architecturally centered visual and sonic experience of Berlin's cityspace.[10] Where Ruttmann gathers an archive of moving images and sounds to piece together both his film and radio montages and does so with a mobility reflective of the quickly changing economic and media landscape of the city in the late 1920s, it is important to note Dean's decidedly stationary camera techniques to decelerate the equally fast-paced changes affecting the city since the late 1990s. Both artists provide commentary on the transitioning political and economic ideologies of their respective points in history, with Dean's work commemorating the communist vision of a social realist unity as archived in the architectural facades of the *Palast der Republik*[11] as it slips away in the sunset promise of a newfound capitalism and a budding European Union, while Ruttmann's film and radio piece cautiously celebrate the weakening hyperinflation of the early 1920s and the promise of a technologically driven capitalism complete with consumer and worker anonymity, while also drawing attention to the multiple economic, social, political, and ideological contradictions simmering in the urban landscape of Weimar Germany's capital city.

At the time, Ruttmann's media experiments stretched the limits of what was imaginable or sanctioned on broadcast radio. His transference of the visual medium of film into the aural medium of radio anticipated the collaborative and intermedial thrust behind today's marketing and development of convergent media. Sabine Breitsameter, producer and curator of the Südwestrundfunk's (SWR) online acoustic art project *Audiohyperspace: Akustische Kunst in Netzwerken und Datenräumen* (Audiohyperspace: Acoustic Art in Networks and Data Spaces), which commissioned the piece by Tanaka, echoes these ideas in her description of the SWR project:

> The Internet offers to the media as well as to the media artist a new electroacoustic space, abundant with audible live streams, audio on-demand, sound files and increasingly complex interactive audio art. These new possibilities may open up surprisingly new audio "visions" and provoke new strategies of perception. Audio on the Internet has made the boundaries between art, communication and play flexible. This offers a perspective on radio concepts and on radio art designs.[12]

The electroacoustic space proffered by the Internet, as suggested here by Breitsameter, opens up new avenues of acoustic perception — new forays into acoustically mediated visualization — new types of interactive play between traditionally separate media — and new patterns for structuring knowledge and meaning without yielding to a hierarchical primacy of image over sound, or sound over image, of Internet over radio, or radio over Internet. If, as Michael McCauley proposes, convergence is the notion that "once encoded, any digital content — from radio stations, computers, video sources, and so on — is theoretically interchangeable with content produced on other platforms,"[13] then the Internet-based experimental radio art supported by SWR and created by Atau Tanaka expands the definition to maintain a level of independence among each media type, such that interactivity can also occur between image, sound, and text data, while still preserving the specific knowledge structures embedded within each data and media component. Tanaka describes the importance of preserving this heterogeneity in his essay "Composing as a Function of Infrastructure":

> When asked to create a piece for radio and Internet, my response was to seek out a dynamic that would differentiate, not amalgamate, the two media....I was interested to go further than this scenario of one medium duplicating, worse yet being co-opted by, another. I sought to exploit each constituent

medium for qualities particular to its infrastructure and using one as a foil against the other.[14]

While McCauley employs a definition of convergence that focuses on the seamless interchangeability or "plugging in" of digitized content from one media platform (television, radio, newspaper, film, Internet) to another, Breitsameter's vision for *Audiohyperspace* and Tanaka's purpose behind *Wiretapping the Beast* highlight the importance of sustaining the differentiating qualities of the radio and Internet as devices, as well as the traces of materiality encoded within the digitized text, image, and sound components that comprise the multilayered facets of Tanaka's web installation. Within the context of this project, then, the notion of convergence serves as an organizing principle that dismantles itself — not only through Tanaka's desire to maintain the discrete analog qualities of the radio as device within the play between radio and Internet, but also through the effect of digitized web content as a memento to the physical record of text, sound, and photograph.

The same archaeological layering present within any single digitized image, text excerpt, or sound file is also reflected within the three stages of Tanaka's multimedia piece — the launch of the installation's website, a live intercontinental stage performance and simultaneous radio broadcast, and the creation of a final sound mix. This work for radio and Internet was initiated in February 2002 with the announcement and launch of a website known as *The Kreatur.* The project's web component is comprised of three areas, each in its own state of fluctuation. There is a text excerpt region that is switched out every thirty to forty seconds, there is a visitor interface area that blinks in and out of the browser window with no apparent pattern, and finally there is a quasi 3D graphic animation which can either be steered by the visitor or roam freely around the window area prepared for it. Right away we detect an unsettledness to a screen of information that we still have not come to trust as both constant and consistent. The Internet browser window is perhaps one of the original staging areas for convergence, and the transitory nature of data within Tanaka's web installation continues to call this into question. In this instance then, it is not the fixed representation of data on the screen that

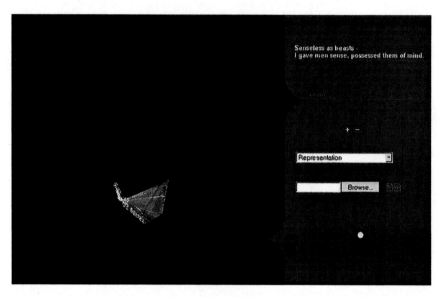

Screen capture from Atau Tanaka's web installation *Wiretapping the Beast* showing the three areas of the installation. www.frankensteins-netz.de. Copyright 2002 Atau Tanaka.

becomes the touchstone of digital art; it is rather the fleeting movement of information and the possibilities for connection that serve to structure meaning in this form of artistic representation. Here we find further echoes to Jackson Pollock:

> The modern artist is living in a mechanical age and we have a mechanical means of representing objects in nature such as the camera and photograph. The modern artist...is working and expressing an inner world — in other words — expressing the energy, the motion, and other inner forces.[15]

We could easily exchange the word "digital" for the word "mechanical" in this quotation and still capture the distinction that Pollock makes between the surface representation of the photograph and the interiority of meaning that drives the artist. Tanaka's project taps into both surface and interiority through the connections within the technical infrastructure of the Internet and radio devices. The interplay between print, visual and sonic textuality, interactivity, and performance fosters these relationships.

Text/Intertext

Situated in the upper right hand corner of the browser window is a text excerpt area. Here provocative passages from a five-work library of texts are randomly displayed in French, German, Japanese, and English: Aeschylus's *Prometheus Bound* (430 B.C.E.), Julien Offray de La Mettrie's *Machine Man* (1747), Johann Wolfgang von Goethe's poem "Prometheus" (1773), Mary Shelley's *Frankenstein* (1818), and Donna Haraway's essay "A Cyborg Manifesto: Science, Technology, and Socialist-Feminism in the Late Twentieth Century" (1985). For the uninitiated visitor, the origin and meaning of these texts remain a mystery, until the curious guest begins exploring. Beyond discovering the sources of the quoted passages, one also begins to discern the complex intertextual trajectories that take shape within this constellation of textual excerpts. When taken as a constellation of ideas, this grouping of excerpts performs any of several possible commentaries on the nature and effect of human–machine interaction, all of which are dependent on any one visitor's depth of knowledge and experience with these individual texts and that person's own ability to draw connections between them. As such, Tanaka's installation creates its own mythos based on the figure of Prometheus, on the character Frankenstein, and on the theoretical imaginings of a human–machine hybrid.

As five discrete texts, each has had an influence either mythically, philosophically, theoretically, poetically, or fictionally on how the relationship between humanity and technology has been perceived at very distinct spatiotemporal moments in Western history. Aeschylus's early tragedy *Prometheus Bound* relates the story of Prometheus, the Titan who stole fire, symbol of creativity and basis for all artworks, from the gods of the new Olympian world order and gave it to humankind — creatures he created from clay in the image of the gods to populate the earth. The Prometheus myth and Aeschylus's rhetorical dramatization of it underscore a rebelliousness in the face of a hierarchical power structure seeking to keep control over knowledge and creation. The Promethean sharing of information, in contrast to a unilateral sovereignty over the mysteries of the natural realm, bears with it a propensity for progress, of humankind's beginning command over nature. Prometheus's trickster spirit, his role in this ancient Greek origin myth, and his subversion of the existing power structure are each facets that inform a range of readings and interpretations about the creation of animate beings outside the medical framework of natural reproduction. Fast-forward several hundred years from classical Greece, to Enlightenment-era France. La Mettrie's provocative treatise *L'Homme machine* (*Machine Man*) provides commentary on the Cartesian approach to a hot-button philosophical issue of his day concerning the rational existence of a human soul, the least common denominator separating man from machine. In his elaboration, La Mettrie poses a delicate interconnection between the soul's immateriality made material via the neural network of the senses and the human body's organ-centered system of organization connected via a circulatory system of regenerative information, and he locates this interconnection in the human brain, center of both rational thought and imagination. La Mettrie's approach to a notion of machine-man is to view the human body as a complex, self-governing, and mechanical system of information, which is also informed by the soul's innate ability to sense and create knowledge from a variety of external inputs. Man is thus already a cybernetic organism with the added ability of imagined thought and reflection. In a certain sense, the separation of the mechanistic functions of the body and the sense-based perceptions of the soul speaks to a contemporary notion of distinguishing between information and knowledge, of those pieces of biological, chemical, physiological, etc. data required for automatic functions, and those pieces of emotive, sense-based, reflective creativity that inform knowledge and spur on thoughtful decision-making. Central to Aeschylus's interpretation, and the texts employed by Tanaka that come after, is the outfitting and/or embodiment of these newly animate beings with some type of transformative mechanical, supernatural, or cybernetic force or knowledge, which, through a process of making other, often lead to a common perception of these beings as monstrous, and thus transgressive to an existing social or political order. Both Goethe's 1773 poem and Shelley's 1818 novel pay a certain type of homage to the figure of Prometheus, with Goethe's poetic verse centering on Prometheus's role as a mischievous creator-god and Shelley's darker

Gothic text focusing on the male-centered alchemical creation of the other without the need of a mother. Where Goethe's poem celebrates the autonomous spirit of Prometheus and his creation and support of humankind in lieu of reverence for an omnipotent Zeus, Shelley's modern Prometheus prefigures the despair of a rationalized thought and scientific progress run amok in its attempts to harness the power of the natural realm beyond certain boundaries. Unlike Prometheus's creations, Shelley's chimeric progeny, who is forever reliant on his creator and forever vulnerable to his charnel house composition, is unable to move beyond, across, or within the dualistic boundaries set up by rationalized progress and the fear of the unknown that he embodies. Each of these four texts anticipate the work of feminist scholar Donna Haraway and her own philosophical musings on the figure of the cyborg as a foil for understanding the critical crossroads that feminist scholarship had situated itself in mid-1980s America.[16] While her goal in her essay "A Cyborg Manifesto" is to move away from the dualisms plaguing feminist discourse in order to open a fertile new terrain for discussions that engage with contemporary scientific and technical discourses and their crucial import for a feminist sociocritical practice, in her setting up of the cyborg as the site where these discussions would take place, Haraway also plumbs a history of a fictional, mythical, scientific, and philosophical engagement with this same figure. And she finds it imbued with the same sets of dualism she criticizes within feminist scholarship: too concerned with discovering origins, too tasked with achieving individuation, and too caught up with maintaining a myth of holistic community. Instead, her cyborg myth "is about transgressed boundaries, potent fusions and dangerous possibilities which progressive people might explore as one part of political work."[17] Haraway's cyborg combines the hybrid mechanistic imagination of La Mettrie's machine-man, celebrates the monstrous exterior of Shelley's Frankenstein and the rebelliousness of Prometheus in order to obviate, to move beyond the dualism of Western thought. It serves as a liminal space through which long-held traditions of progress based in hierarchical domination are being quietly supplanted by an informatics of domination, a system of networks of information flows, virtual exchanges, and clean rooms devoid of social and political ills. For Haraway, it is this liminal space of the cyborg, its innate duplicitousness to control, which must become the focal point of political action. Haraway's cyborg, Shelley's Frankenstein, La Mettrie's machine-man, Goethe's and Aeschylus's Prometheus figure and, by extension, Tanaka's *Kreatur* are the chimeric bodies along whose contours political and transgressive discussions about contemporary issues evoked by the multiple realms of techno-scientific developments must take shape; they are the free-flow matrix of an engaged and engaging oppositional consciousness.

Interface/Interactivity

The intertextual relationships exhibited by these five texts play a central role in the design and use functionality of the web installation's user interface. This interface area of *Wiretapping the Beast* consisted initially of a sign-in area, which appeared only for new visitors to the URL, or to return visitors who were entering the site from a different IP address than their first visit. Here one was prompted for name, email address, and SMS (short message service) contact information. Once this data was submitted, a second form interface was displayed, which allowed users of the site to contribute digital image and sound files to the growing database of image and sound materials, which themselves were used as raw material to feed the animated creature that formed the installation's main area. Providing contributions to the ongoing creation of this multimedia piece was far more involved than just browsing for .jpeg or .gif image files and .mp3 or .wav sound files and clicking a button to send them out into the data stream. In addition, the user interface in Tanaka's installation included a pull-down menu of keywords, a set of thirty-eight categories that users could choose from to associate with their submitted image or sound file. Ranging in scope from the broader keywords of representation, science fiction, realism, physiology, postmodernism, and humanism, to the more specialized categories of cyborg citizenship, evolutionary inertia, future shock, and informatics of domination, users of the site were again confronted with a moment of intellectual reflection, a moment that forced them to think about how the visual or aural piece of data they were about to submit to the project could or should be situated within the given taxonomy. As with the text excerpts, the keywords do not appear, at first glance, to be listed in any particular order — not alphabetical, not conceptual, nor in degree of specificity. Upon closer analysis the seemingly chaotic laundry list of terms does begin to acquire certain patterns of abstract meaning related to the same human–machine interaction commented on with the quoted passages from the five texts that structure and inform the piece. The points of this taxonomic constellation triangulate out to several overlapping spheres in which new technologies are affecting discussion and change. These broader areas include, from my reading, biomedical ethics, workplace transformation, community building, information control, surveillance, and intelligent machines.

Only after a period of trying to assemble the connections between the varying pieces that comprise the web installation would the average visitor to the site realize that the taxonomy is taken directly from Donna Haraway's "A Cyborg Manifesto" essay. In her essay Haraway refers to this tabular taxonomy as the "Informatics of Domination," a concept that stands in opposition to the "White Capitalist Patriarchy" and marks the transition she detects from "an organic, industrial society to a polymorphous information system — from all work to all play, a deadly game."[18] She conceives of this taxonomy of columnar concepts as demonstrating where a feminist political practice had been held in stasis, and where it should be focusing its attention. Tanaka's initiation of Haraway's taxonomy as a list of keywords for the *Wiretapping the Beast* installation breaks down the transitional balance that Haraway's table conveys, and confronts the user of the site with the need to navigate the nuanced distinctions that separate these keywords from each other. In this sense, users are asked to meaningfully choose from among the digital artefacts, the binary simulations of physical objects and sound objects that inhabit their personal dataspace, in order to collectively enhance and engage with the life of the creature taking shape on screen. The users' association of their image or sound file submissions with a particular keyword determines its place within the relational content database that powers the website, and that gives the online animated creature its visual and sonic form. Once this data creature has been nourished by the user, it acknowledges its caretaker by sending grateful and provocative emails

Is more needed, to prove that man is but an
animal, or a collection of springs which
wind each other up, without or being able
to tell at what point in this human circle,
nature has begun?

Representation
Optimization
Eugenics
Population control
Decadence
Obsolescence
Future shock
Stress management
Ergonomics
Cybernetics of labour
Functional specialization
Modular construction

Screen capture from *Wiretapping the Beast* of detail of the pull-down menu of keywords utilized by visitors to the site. www.frankensteins-netz.de. Copyright 2002 Atau Tanaka.

and text messages, while, by the same token, if it feels neglected it bombards the visitor with messages demanding to be fed. One example is from an email received from the creature dated May 8, 2002, with the subject line, "Why don't you come and see me?" and the message "Je suis ta créature" ("I am your creature.").[19] The web interface and the associated asynchronous communication aspects of the installation provide a level of interactivity unmatched by traditional ideas of radio. Not only are visitors to the website able to contribute actively to the growth and longevity of the web creature, but their actions or inactions on the site generate a dynamic line of communication that could be only cursorily achieved in radio's earlier and continued experiments with live audience and telephone integration.

Animation/Enlivening Sound

The main area of the *Wiretapping the Beast* installation is reserved for the growth, development, and movement of the creature. As I mentioned earlier, the creature appears as a pulsing, kaleidoscopic, noisy entity that feeds on binary data, incorporating the text, image and sound inputs into its nonrectangular, three-dimensional body. Here the excerpts from the literary and theoretical texts form the creature's skeletal framework, with the text scrolling through the bones, while the images input by visitors to the installation are stretched like skin over the spaces between these textual bones. In a similar vein, the contributed sound files provide a cacophonous atmosphere of random ambient noise for the creature's dance, which is powered by the creature's movements and erratic behavior. In an email interview I conducted with Tanaka in early 2003, he comments on the relationships the piece provokes among the visual and sound elements input by each visitor, and the dissonant creation that this interactivity engenders on screen:

> The noise of the network is mediated — this process becomes the critical issue of the piece.... Rather than go out to look for noise on the Internet, this piece instead incites people to come to the piece, to gather around the themes delineated by the texts, mood, and channel user participation. So people are asked to reflect upon the enigmatic questions posed on the web site, and to try to find images or sounds on their computers that might propose an appropriate answer.... The key was to create a balance between interactive satisfaction and frustration, hopefully creating a fascination that leads to the understanding that instant reaction is not the main interaction here, and that evolution of the creature, and of the piece, happens over longer periods of time.[20]

Incorporating Pierre Levy's notion of collective intelligence, Tanaka's role as artist and composer of this interactive, audiovisual work is to create a situation in which visitors to the web installation would feel compelled to participate as interactive players in the installation's composition through a reflective, and thought-provoking engagement with the web creature's hampered existence and continued growth.[21] A last element of interactivity is apparent here in the creature's movements, not only with the correlation between each visitor's level of input activity and the rate of movement, but also with the visitor's ability to interact haptically with the onscreen animation — the ability to use one's mouse to physically move points of the animation around the screen. This simulated physicality operates a bit under the radar screen, since it is not readily apparent that a visitor to the web installation can actually flip and turn the creature through movements of their mouse. However, these multimedial points of interactivity are always cast through the project's deference to radio:

> Throughout the compositional process, I was treating network and visual media, never forgetting that the project was ultimately a radio project. The use of text paid due respect to the medium of *hoerspiel*. At the same time, the multilingual and abstract settings build upon traditions of experimental radio art. Text readings were transformed through the process of network collaboration to create soundscapes guiding the radio listener through the dramatic trajectory. Linguistic abstraction creates dramatic tension and release of meaning dependent on the local language of the listener.[22]

Compositionally, then, Tanaka's creature is an enfolded mass of user-selected and user-engaged multimedia and specifically chosen text, tripping and skipping across the screen according to an underlying behavioral state, which is itself determined by the amount of data the creature is being fed. The web facet of the installation really brings together the aural, visual, and textual aspects of each media type (sound, image, text excerpt). In a sense these types of files can be described as the noise of the network — the trash that the new class of techno-worker has to contend with on a daily basis. Yet the mythos of the project (the excerpts from Shelley, Haraway, Aeschylus, Goethe, La Mettrie) provides the framework for understanding, for providing form to the network of binary data. The haptic element of the animation, the ability of users to move and flip corners of *The Kreatur* by using their mouse, adds a certain serendipity to the shape the data network actually takes. What we end up with is a highly interactive, visually and aurally stimulating and thought-provoking site, whose primary purpose is to create and arouse a web creature that is equipped with an array of visual, sonic, and corporeal elements that will be put into action during the live performance and set loose through the live radio broadcast.

Live Performance/Live Convergence

Tanaka pinpoints five stages (dormant, awakening, excited, out of control, and tamed) in the creature's development. The first three stages take shape during the preperformance phase of the project, as the creature grows and is nourished by site participants within the

web-based installation of the overall project. During the live performance the creature is allowed to relive these initial three stages, while
the nature of the live performance permits the creature to manifest
them in a new way. The fourth stage is added in the postperformance
phase of the project, where the creature continues to live on cy-
cling through all four of these stages. The final mix incorporates
the fifth stage of the creature's life and represents all five stages as
movements — no longer being nourished by participant interaction
or the spontaneity of live performance, the creature now exists in a
tamed state of stasis, a final mix that can be cast out, marketed, and
sold as a by-product of the creature's creation, lived experience, and
domestication.[23] It is in the transition from web installation to live
stage performance and concurrent broadcast that the role of the radio
device becomes more readily apparent.

The live performance occurred in Karlsruhe on March 23, 2002,
with simultaneous performances in Montreal, Canada, and Ogaki-
City, Japan. Joining Tanaka in his role as composer in Karlsruhe
were voice artist Reiko A. and audio artist i.d. in Japan, electronic
music composer Zack Settel in Canada, and the web creature as
a virtual fifth performer. The simultaneity of the performance was
made possible through the use of multiple client/server systems for
the transmission and reception of audio and images from each of
the three remote sites. This distributed network of data streams involved inputs of information from the three geographical locations
and from the web creature, which are then synthesized on the Karlsruhe stage by Tanaka in the form of a total mix and fed as live
sound to the on-site audiences in Germany, Japan, and Canada,
as broadcast to the radio audience and as streaming audio to the
Internet audience. The score of the final mix provides an intriguing
script cast in musical, spatial, temporal, and DJ scratch notation,
a choreographic rendition of the creature's movements from dor-
mancy to out of control and on to docility.[24] Reminiscent of Walter
Ruttmann's score for *Weekend*, Tanaka's score coordinates the variety of human- and machine-generated sounds sourced from his
companion physical performers in Japan and Canada and his virtual
performer in the network space of the project web space.[25] While the

score itself may suggest a level of compositional control over the outcome of the performance's final mix, any number of network-based or performance-based instances of unscriptable peculiarities suggest that the score serves more as a guide to the transgressive space of performance than an actual marked-off area indicating the limits of performance. Commenting on how this type of new interface between radio and digital networks are also producing new ways of listening, Sabine Breitsameter focuses on notions of receptivity and the politics of interaction:

> Listening is a concept that has to do with a very "receptive," settled mindset. One has to, so to speak, allow things to wash over them. We live in a time (and the Internet is an expression of this time) in which being active, accomplishing something is paramount. And this is an obstacle that those who desire to really hear, to listen, need to overcome. Namely to find the courage to sit back, to do nothing, to say "I'll wait for a moment, and listen to what is coming next. I'll take this time, and I won't intervene." I think this is a very important point. And I think that the mythology of interaction that is being circulated through [and about] the Internet is also a type of ideology, an ideology of interaction, which is not necessarily beneficial to the notion of listening or to this "receptive" mindset. In any case it is important to engage this issue, so that the notion of listening does not become lost to us.[26]

This is a crucial point, and it is one that calls attention to the specifically radiophonic elements that present themselves in Tanaka's web-based piece: engaged, relaxed, receptive listening, an approach to listening that is always related to the environment of the listener, what Breitsameter warns may be being replaced by this ideology of interaction. "These problematics show clearly," she writes, "That listening in the classic sense of the word must not and cannot be replaced by the interactive listening of the digital age. And broadcast media will be as important as ever, maybe even more important, as their role becomes illuminated by the networks, their possibilities and their limitations."[27] Her critique of a digitally networked aurality is based in this same notion of listening as participatory experience, that digital artists need to be mindful of balancing the interactive and the aural components, such that the levels of interactivity offered to the listener/user are not so complex that participation becomes an issue of being overstimulated and thus inattentive, or so simple that the buy-in needed for participation leads to a similar lack of interest. These are well-founded criticisms of an interactive digital art that incorporates elements of sound without regard for the uniquely aural receptivity that these elements produce, and it is here that Breitsameter locates the continued importance of broadcast media for maintaining the aspects of listening practice. It is in this vein that I read the relationships between the live web installation, the live performance, and the live broadcast of Tanaka's project. Each of his audiences is engaged in a very specific sensory encounter with the performance, depending on their spatiotemporal proximity to the geographical sites. Whereas any of the three live audiences are absorbed primarily in an aural and visual reception of the performance, the radio audience is limited to a purely aural experience of the work, while the Internet audience enjoyed a realm of possible receptions, limited only by their technical ability and the software they had on their machines. Unless, of course, members of the live audiences were carrying transistor radios tuned to the broadcast, or handheld devices synched in with the live streaming audio; or members of the radio audience were also logged in via Internet, or members of the Internet audience were tuned in via radio. Audience reception thus turns into various opportunities for audience interaction with the piece. The interchangeability or convergence of data between the three reception/broadcast devices occurs in the production of a "total mix," but the audience reception of this total mix becomes imbued with the transmission infrastructure and physical experience of each device. For example, a person attending the live performance in Karlsruhe will hear the total mix as it is being synthesized by Tanaka, while viewing both his physical stage performance, and the virtual performance of the creature projected on screen. A person listening to the radio broadcast, on the other hand, will not have this same visual experience of the total mix, but rather may visualize the performance from the various sound components found in the mix. Each will come away with a varying perception of what this multimedia art piece for Internet and radio is all about.

Wiretapping the Beast is not your mom and dad's radio, nor is it the radio we are lulled into believing is the only possibility for radio by virtue of NPR or Clear Channel programming, nor is it digital radio as it is perceived by radio engineers and the competing brands of XM and Sirius. Instead, *Wiretapping the Beast* represents a realm of artistic, critical, and scholarly possibilities. While the project casts its web into the artistic areas of music composition, narrative form, and photomontage, each of which provides a specific kind of orchestration for the on-screen design; it also engages several critical questions involved in our integration of technology into our workplace, into our systems of representation, into our sense of identity, and into our philosophies of self. This weave of artistic and critical relationships extends into regions of academic scholarship concerned not only with these same issues of human–machine interaction, but additionally with the historical and philosophical roots of various media and the devices that create those media, and ideas of data convergence and media differentiation. Atau Tanaka is careful to distinguish between the radio as broadcast device and the Internet as a network of computers and their very specific contributions to the creation of *Wiretapping the Beast*. Interestingly both technologies locate their technohistorical roots within the machinery of war, yet both embody certain interarticulations that challenge and rouse the other. Here the radio urges for moments of intellectual reflection and visualization, while the Internet draws out immediate interactive connections between the content it displays and the audience it reaches, achieving in one sense Bertolt Brecht's vision for the radio as both a device for listener reception and transmission.

In Tanaka's multimedia piece the Internet provides for that mode of audience participation and synchronous communication that the radio has always longed for, while the radio offers a moment of fixity to the Internet representation, a point where the intellectual work of the piece can take place without giving in to the immediacy that characterizes Internet-based information. Although encounters with sound are often described as fleeting and immaterial, the radio delivers a disembodied experience of sound. This is not sound taken out of its context; rather, this is an idea of sound that has been uncoupled from its descriptive connections to the visual, such that our encounters with it are unhindered by a desire to structure it visually. The fact that the web-based portion of the *Wiretapping the Beast* performance has been timed out, provides an interesting thread back out to the centrality of sound for this project. The impermanence of the visual, haptic, and interactive database facets of the project, their disappearance from the "Public" folder of the ZKM's hosting web server, brings to the afterlife of the project a sense of removal from the realm of commodified information and a return to the realm of reflective knowledge. The importance of these types of critical and scholarly overtures to the new work being done in the digital and information arts is reflected in Jackson Pollock's response to his interviewer's follow-up question to the statement about new artistic techniques that began my presentation. The interviewer, William Wright, asks, "Which would also mean that the layman and the critic would have to develop their ability to interpret the new techniques?" Pollock responded with a resounding "Yes."[28]

T W O

Between Military Innovation and Government Sanction

Early German Radio and the Experimental

Lyric and the Origins of Cultural Radio in Germany

The first broadcast of a German poem occurred in Berlin radiospace on November 3, 1923, just five days after the radio waves had been authorized for entertainment broadcasts by the still fledgling and volatile Weimar Republic government.[1] And so began the airwave collaboration between the world of literature and the medium of radio in Germany. The poem chosen for this honor was Heinrich Heine's "Seegespenst" (Sea Apparition) (1825/26), the tenth short poem in the first of a two-part cycle devoted to the North Sea.[2] From a twenty-first-century perspective the reading of a poem through a microphone hardly seems to scratch the surface of innovation or experimentation. Yet, as contemporary artistic experiments like Atau Tanaka's *Wiretapping the Beast* performance foreground, the importance of textual material within the interwoven design matrices of radio and web-based multimedia for providing additional layers of scripted movement, narrative structure, and intertextual threads enhances, in some fashion, listener engagement and interactivity with the broadcast piece.

But why this particular poem? When investigated more closely, the remediation of Heine's poetic text into broadcast sound holds profound significance for the beginnings of artistic practice with sound-based media. Beyond music broadcasts in the form of orchestral concerts, gramophone albums, and chamber music, the poem's role as broadcast in this early volatile year of the Weimar Republic carries with it important threads to its earlier role as poetic text.

When viewed next to the Weimar film industry's resurrection of romantic and medieval narratives and motifs for its films, Heine's blend of memory, imagination, folkloric myth, and romantic yearning for wholeness, provided excellent fodder for early radio's first broadcast blip in Weimar's entertainment media landscape. The relationship between the earlier textual form and the 1923 broadcast and this broadcast's subsequent influence on trends in early practices of German radio broadcasting raises some interesting questions. How does this poem serve as a type of metanarrative for the power of sound, in general, and for the new listening experience offered by the radio medium, in particular? What connections are there between the poem's role as a cultural product (i.e., its cultural currency), its impact on the German cultural imagination, and its contextualization of irrational seafaring mythologies with its reincarnation and adaptation to sound? And finally, how might the development of maritime communication technologies, absent but intimated in the poem, reflect the technical development of radio as a cultural entertainment medium?

Due in part to the fairly cursory mention of the poem's broadcast in the chronology provided in Alfred Braun's memoir and to the fact that no recording of the broadcast is available, it is not surprising that little critical writing exists on the relationship between Heine's poem and the development of entertainment radio in Weimar Germany. Written some sixty years before Heinrich Hertz's discovery of electromagnetic radio waves and almost a hundred years prior to its first performance on radio, the *North Sea* cycle of poems depicts the poet's romanticized encounters with the mythic realms connected with the landscapes and seascapes of the North Sea. Yet Alfred Braun's memoir does provide another, more veiled, clue that intimates the symbolic connection between the beginnings of broadcast entertainment radio and the poem's decidedly maritime content. The Heine broadcast is of special importance since it evokes the techno-historical origins of the radio in maritime communication, while still drawing on the ritual and myth production of the maritime culture. In this regard Braun recalls:

> Long before there even was a radio, a conference of German ship owners took place in Bremen with a presentation on the phenomenon of wireless telegraphy.

During the discussion the speaker countered the critical doubts and misgivings with the sentence: "Gentlemen, one day the time will come when none of your ships will leave the harbors without a transmitter and receiver, in order to call and listen into the solitude of the oceans."[3]

As Germany's first-ever lyric broadcast, the content of Heine's poem and its distribution over the airwaves draw together aspects of the political, cultural, economic, military, and technical implications of the radio in delivering a new information age to naval and merchant mariners alike. With radio technology the once solitary voyage across the vastness of the world's oceans is now accompanied by projected voices, which shorten the journey and dispel the world of myth through the currency of information. In the tenth poem of the *North Sea* cycle, "Sea Apparition," Heine merges folkloric myth, sensory perception, and the Romantic ideal of a sublime nature, and produces a complex audiovisual simulacrum based in ghostly imagery and diaphanous sound. The myth of Vineta, a medieval city purportedly engulfed by the sea in the twelfth century and a popular motif in German Romantic literature, provides the underpinnings for Heine's poem, which depicts a poetic narrator troubled by visual and acoustic memories of a former love. The poem begins with the lyric subject looking over the bow of a ship:

> I, however, lay at the rim of the ship,
> And gazed, with dreaming eye,
> Down into the mirror-clear water,
> And gazed deeper and deeper —
> Till deep, far down in the depth of the sea,
> At first like dawning mist,
> Yet gradually more distinctly coloured,
> Churches' domes and towers revealed themselves,
> And at last, clear as sunlight, a whole town,
> Antique, in the style of the Netherlands,
> And bustling with men.[4]

Here the poetic narrator's gaze from the ship's bow into the depths of the sea creates a hypnotic effect, producing at first only murky images, which slowly come into focus as the picture of a submerged city becomes apparent. The gradual move in visual acuity from indistinct forms to clear images reflects a sharpening of the lyric subject's dream-like memories to a virtual and hyperreal projection of them as mediated through the mirror-like surface of the sea. The depths of the sea echo and animate the depths of the poetic narrator's soul, as if providing a staging area or framework for deeply guarded thoughts and memories. This projection becomes more urgent and takes on a multimedial veneer with the addition and functionality of sound through Heine's description of cathedral bells and organ notes, and the onslaught of memory and grief they evoke in the poetic narrator:

> Aged women
> In brown, outmoded garments,
> Hymn-book and rosary in their hands,
> Hurry, with quick, short steps,
> Towards the great cathedral,
> Spurred by the chiming of the bells
> And the surging sound of the organ.
>
> Me, too, seizes the distant clangour's
> Mysterious dolour.
> Endless longing, deep-searching sorrow
> Steals into my heart,
> My scarcely healed heart; —
> To me it seems that its wounds were being
> Kissed open by dear lips
> And started again to bleed —
> Hot, red drops,
> That long and slowly fall
> On an old house, down there
> In the deep-sunk sea-town,
> On an old high-gabled house
> That is drearily empty of people,
> Only that there at the lower window
> A girl sits
> With her head at rest on her arm,
> Like a poor, forgotten child —
> And I know you, poor, forgotten child![5]

Like the aged women in the submerged city, the tolling of the cathedral bells and the murmuring of the organ music impels the poet, awakening in him a nostalgic feeling for a lost love. In a certain sense the sounds of the bells and the organ function as a sonar device, helping the poet determine the presence and location of the girl through their transmission of sound waves. Invented in 1906, the sonar system operates via transmitted and reflected underwater sound waves to locate submerged objects. As the first models functioned only as reception devices, with no capability of transmitting signals, they can be seen as having a reverse history of technical development when compared to the radio, which, prior to 1923, had not yet been regulated as a reception-only device. The physical pinpointing of this lost female figure, manifested in the drops of blood that fall down to the submerged city, causes such a yearning in the poet that he almost succumbs to the underwater visions and sounds. The entirety of the poem tracks a search, an inner journey of the poet's soul, for completion, for wholeness. This search is depicted as a move from the rational to the irrational, as a move from ocular to aural transmission of information, and as a move from the physical protection of the ship to the ethereal underwater space of myth and loss. The move back to rationality, to presence, and to security comes through the authority of the captain's voice and his grasp of the poet's foot: "But just in the nick of time / By the foot the captain caught me, / And pulled me back from the ship's rail, / And cried, angrily laughing: / 'Doctor, are you stark crazy?' "[6] The vocal and physical authority of the captain counteracts the visual and aural power of the mythic underwater city and provides a return to clear-headedness and rationality.

The intertextual play that Heine employs in the poem, the thematic blend of irrational myth and romantic yearning, and the subtle nod to the siren song of the bells and the lover's revived image capture moments of harmony between the poem's textual origins and its acoustic debut.[7] For example, Heine's references to works by such German Romantic writers as Ludwig Tieck and E. T. A. Hoffmann in the poem illustrate the importance of these folkloric and mythic motifs for an understanding of German cultural unity. The poem's radio broadcast echoes this importance, and recontextualizes this need for German cultural unity for an interwar audience. The airing of the poem via radio provides it with a level of cultural significance, simultaneously invoking the poem's own historical origins and associations with Heinrich Heine and imbuing it with the pioneering status of first broadcast. The adaptation of the poem for radio can also be read as a process of transmission and reception, as a type of textual broadcast that would evoke recognition and receptivity on the part of the listener, while also calling attention to the radio's entrance into the entertainment market already being saturated by film production. Although the German film industry would not fully incorporate sound as an integrated element in their movie-making technique until the late 1920s, the minds behind cultural and entertainment radio would have still needed to compete in some fashion with film for their audiences' attention, and one way to do this was to imitate film production's early focus on bringing clearly identifiable narratives from the worlds of German literature and folklore to the screen, by bringing them first to the headset and then to the loudspeaker.[8] The partnership created between poetic text and radio broadcast accentuates the power of Heine's poem by placing it within the networked airwaves of the radio, which, thus, enhances the synaesthetic relationships between the poem's visual and aural components through broadcast distribution on radio. In this respect, repositioning the site of the poem's performance from the literary and read textual culture of the mid-1820s to the spoken and heard radio culture of the mid-1920s aurally provokes and promotes the site specificity of the poem. The acoustic transformation of the poem for radio produces an acoustic transportation of the listener to the same bow of the ship upon which the poem's narrator experiences his own mysterious and acoustically driven imaginative wanderings.

In both its textual form and its remediation as aural broadcast this poem contextualizes many of the debates and discussions that were to play out in German radio circles throughout the period of the Weimar Republic. First, it calls attention to early radio debates about the purpose and goals of radio — whether the medium should merely reproduce or duplicate already extant art forms, or whether it should experiment and produce radio-specific art forms. Second, it marks the medium's transition from its early use in point-to-point communication scenarios to its use for entertainment broadcasts. The poem's broadcast as entertainment signals the development of broadcasting standards and state regulations governing transmission, while also maneuvering the technical design of the radio toward reception-only consumer products. And, finally, the poem's adaptation from written text to spoken word and its transmission over the airwaves, when coupled with its position in a cycle of interwoven short poems, point to the possibly unintended origins of experimentation with radio, sound, and multimedia. Whether or not the 1923 radio audience or the radio directors in charge of the poem's broadcast were able to draw these connections between the poem and its adaptation for radio must remain unanswered. But what we can say is that Heine's illustration of spiritual longing and unfulfilled desire within the frame of national myth make it an excellent choice for radio broadcast, when taken in light of other neoromantic adaptations for stage and screen so prevalent in these early years of the Weimar Republic. These and other aspects of early radio production and experimentation will be explored throughout the course of this chapter. Central to this chapter's investigation will be charting the parallel movements in the radio's early development as a medium for entertainment purposes and the elaboration of standards and regulations to guide this development. What this mapping will show is that as the radio continued to grow into a mass medium designed and regulated, as German radio's first director, Hans Bredow (1879–1959), writes, "to bring the German people motivation and pleasure into their lives," a separate conception of radio involving the creation of artistic forms specific to its technology and techniques also developed.[9]

Regulating the New Medium: The Social and Legal Backdrop of Early Experimentation

In this early period experimentation with the radio meant the continuous promotion and use of practices and techniques to expand and transcend the parameters approved and standardized for the medium's role in entertainment. Yet artistic experimentation in any form has always existed in a relationship of reciprocity based in action and reaction — a fleeting process in which avant-garde practices that are considered cutting edge one moment become mainstream and old hat the next. And in the new world of 1920s German radio entertainment and consumer product, it was in the best interest of the broadcast companies to maintain this fine balance between the need to establish and develop an idea of a programming structure on the one hand and the desire to support experimentation and the incorporation of innovative approaches into traditional programming on the other. It should however come as no surprise that this politics of program development in the fledgling radio landscape would also need to contend with and navigate the varying regulatory measures as set out by the ruling parties, the majority of which were established to safeguard the authority and survival of the government rather than to foster innovation with the new medium.

The short, but foundationally important history of radio regulation in the interwar years actually has its roots in April 1892 with the Gesetz über das Telegraphenwesen des Deutschen Reiches (Reich Telegraphy Act). This law instituted rules for the construction and use of telegraph and telephone systems, firmly establishing the sovereignty of the Reich in the early telecommunications landscape, stating that "the right to construct and operate telegraph facilities for the dissemination of news is exclusively entitled to the Reich."[10] These sovereign rights (Hoheitsrechte) are not peculiar to telecommunications law, but rather they span a variety of areas (e.g., financial autonomy, police powers, jurisdiction), in order to establish the internal and external authority (as well as the limits to these authorities) needed by governments to maintain order. This 1892 law required no real significant revision or revisiting until 1919, when it was expanded to include governmental control over systems of broadcasting and transmission.[11] The incident that prompted the expansion of this law in 1919, the ban on private reception of radio waves beginning in 1922, and the development of technical limitations for reception devices in 1923 was one that pitted the military's innovative use of radio networks during World War I against the democratizing forces of the new republic. Among the string of events that marked the end of World War I and the unsteady transition to the new republic was the takeover of the news agency Wolffsche Telegraphenbüro (WTB) (Wolff Telegraph Office) in Berlin by former members of the military signal corps on November 9, 1918. This takeover grew out of the revolutionary atmosphere and developing unrest as spurred on by the demobilized armed forces in the naval city of Kiel and in Berlin, which would quickly spread throughout the country and become tangentially aligned with the November Revolution and the system of soldiers' and workers' councils set up as alternative forms of government. Radio historian Winfried Lerg describes the occupation of the WTB as a method for wresting control of the official press and communications apparatus from the authorities and for instituting a level of autonomy for the workers' and soldiers' councils by way of establishing a Zentralfunkleitung (ZFL, Central Radio Committee):

> In fact, the units of radio operators played a particular role in the days [that unfolded] between war and peace, when communications had left the control of the primary war agency (War Ministry) but were not yet secured in the hands of the foremost peacetime regulator of communications — the Postal Affairs Ministry. The efforts for establishing autonomy were coordinated by an institution, which had been given the designation *Zentralfunkleitung*. This *Zentralfunkleitung* was formed on November 9, 1918, by members of the Technischen Abteilung für Funkgerät (Tafunk) (Technical Battalion for Radio Equipment) which reported to the Inspektion der Technischen Abteilung der Nachrichtentruppe (Itenach) (Inspectorate of the Technical Battalion of Signal Corps). By way of the broadcast station at Königswusterhausen the *Zentralfunkleitung* contacted each of the stations in the internal German radio network with the announcement that they, as the central soldiers' council, had assumed control of all facilities. With this, one intended nothing less than the design of a communication network independent from the administration of the postal service.[12]

This takeover of the WTB and its technologies of communication, the creation of the ZFL, and the subsequent receipt of a broadcasting license on November 25 handed the supporters of the November Revolution both a loudspeaker for their revolutionary parole and a medium by which to establish its broadcast authority. Yet from a far less political perspective, the takeover also meant the creation of jobs for these almost 190,000 demobilized and highly skilled soldiers of the signal corps. Lerg's detailed study of the development of radio in Germany also provides access to important eyewitness accounts, including this statement by Erich Kuttner, editor of the party newspaper *Vorwärts* of the Sozialdemokratische Partei

Deutschlands (SPD) (Social Democratic Party of Germany), from his testimony in the May/June 1919 trial of Georg Ledebour, leader of the independent faction of the SPD:[13]

> At that time I was of the opinion that it was probably good to send a dispatch through the Wolff'sche Telegraphenbureau. I arrived at these thoughts through my own experience, because I knew that in March 1917, when the reports about the victories in the Russian revolution were made known, that nothing had as much of an impact as the fact that the news was broadcast through the Petersburger Telegraphenbureau. [Petersburg Telegraph Bureau] . . . I also told myself: if one issued a dispatch about the victories of the [November] revolution through the Wolff'sche Telegraphenbureau, then it would be believed throughout the world.[14]

Kuttner's account underscores the role this takeover of the WTB played in establishing the voice of authority needed by supporters of the revolution while also lending it a level of global authenticity. It is this same set of beliefs about the functions of authority and authenticity provided through control of the radio that had members of the provisional government running in fear for their legislative pens. This event in German radio history is referred to by many media studies scholars as the *Funkerspuk,* a uniquely German word that teases out both the ethereal nature of the airwaves and the technical skill of the demobilized military radio operators and wraps them up in the governmental fear of an illicit radiospace incapable of being surveilled and controlled.[15] This "specter of the radio operator" would haunt the radio medium throughout its development in the Weimar Republic, its ideological shifts rendered by the National Socialists during the Third Reich, and its renovation and democratization in the post–World War II period. In each instance the specter of November 1918 informs the separate political reactions to the new medium and fear of its misuse by those either outside the sphere of power, or those with enough technical proficiency to somehow subvert the governments' sovereign powers, and, as I mentioned earlier, these reactions led to the expansion of existing regulatory laws and the creation of others to ensure that a similar incident would never happen again.

Between December 1918 and April 1919, on the heels of the events of the November Revolution, the young government had brought together members from the various offices that had participated in maintaining the government's sovereign rights over the wireless telegraphic networks (e.g., war ministry, foreign affairs ministry, postal affairs ministry, colonial affairs ministry, and treasury) to participate in a Reichsfunkkommission (RFK) (National Communications Commission) and included an invitation to the ZFL to participate in this forum to articulate the connections between official and public use of the telecommunications network. Where the ZFL had intended to build a parallel or alternative telecommunications structure to that administered by the postal service, and in the process secure jobs for those returning from the battlefields, it was now brought to the table to inform the commission on personnel and technical issues related to the telecommunications network. The commission had completed its work by April 9, 1919, the day chancellor Philipp Scheidemann signed two ordinances: one authorizing the postal affairs ministry to absorb the administrative duties of the Reich Broadcasting Administration (established earlier in February 1919) and the other declaring the postal affairs ministry as the central authority for the entire telecommunications network. Through this invitation and subsequent co-optation of the ZFL, the government was successful in reestablishing its sovereignty over the country's telecommunications systems and reaffirming the organizational structure of the postal service as the site for regulatory oversight. As Lerg puts it, "On this day [April 9, 1919], exactly five months since the formation of the Central Radio Committee (Zentralfunkleitung), all revolutionary traces had been eliminated from German broadcasting."[16]

Safeguarding the integrity and sanctity of the communications network from either unauthorized use or misuse would remain to be a central concern of the German government as broadcast communication technologies continued to develop from the telegraphic dissemination of encoded text into a public medium of broadcasted sound. It is in this context that the 1923 repeal of a declaration begun in 1922 banning radio reception by private citizens helped usher the radio medium into the cultural sphere. This ban on private reception clearly follows in this vein of protecting the medium from misuse, but it also points to the desire of the postal affairs ministry to develop the technologies of broadcasting for economic purposes. Although the ban seems to never have been codified into a law of its own with reproducible text, we can triangulate its reach and impact through a set of memoirs published by Hans Bredow in 1956, through documents reproduced from meetings of the RFK in 1922 and the certificates of approval required of all private radio listeners in 1924, and through descriptions of the early 1923 *Rückkopplungsverbot*, a ban on "backcoupling" or regenerative feedback, a technical process patented by several inventors prior to and during World War I to increase the sensitivity and selectivity of radio receivers through boosting signal amplification and allowing the receiver to oscillate (regenerate and sustain its own signals) via a controlled positive feedback coupling.[17] Each of these textual points demonstrates the complex of political, economic, legal, and technical issues that informed this uncertain evolution of the telecommunications landscape from a highly centralized one of state control to one in which the radio could become an economically viable service as an entertainment medium. It is also from within this mix of conversations about regulatory practices and standards for the radio's role in cultural entertainment that artistic experimentation with the medium in this early period would find fertile ground, as well as focal points for its content.

Hans Bredow, in addition to holding several governmental positions within the postal affairs ministry with respect to telecommunications media, worked early on in his career as an electrical engineer and is credited with the first experimental broadcasts of music to troops on the front in 1917. In his memoirs Bredow situates the ban on private reception in the context of national defense rhetoric inherited from World War I, and in terms of political support for the new parliamentary democracy, both of which, to a certain extent, operated per their relationship to the 1892 telegraphy law and to the directives applied by the Versailles agreement ending the war:

> During the war the use of a transmitter or receiver by private citizens was banned in the warring nations with regards to national defense.... In Germany the radio ban was reinforced by its connection to the telegraphy law, and exceptions to the ban were made only to franchised and state-monitored, private sector telegraph companies in maritime and international communications, as well as for purposes of industry and research. On the surface the

perpetuation of this constraint after the war was justified solely on the necessity for secrecy of public radio communications, but in reality political reasons were the decisive factor.[18]

While keeping the political stability of the government as its central denominator, the ministry and Hans Bredow sought to develop various wireless broadcasting services in the realms of journalism and commerce that would be financially lucrative and would move the ministry closer, at least technically, to offering radio broadcasts for the entire public. If these services were to be successful, there would need to be reception stations located at the various individual businesses that would be capable of receiving transmissions from a centrally located broadcasting station. These experiments remained telegraphic-based until autumn 1922, when the only real commercially successful venture — the Eildienst GmbH (a commercial news broadcasting service) — was able to take advantage of technical advances that had made possible the transmission and reception of sound. However, in addition to a general lack of trust in the technology on the part of industry leaders, the primary sticking point to these experimental uses for broadcasting continued to be the underlying fear of manipulation by the many people disloyal to the government. To create a media landscape of radio reception devices, even at a more easily monitored level such as this, sent up red flags and resulted in the continued ban on reception by private citizens as an attempt to respond to government fears of unsanctioned evesdropping by *Zaungäste*, or lurkers illegally tuning in to the airwaves with their own homemade transmission and reception devices.

The primary focus of the RFK's June 1922 report was on innovative methods for circulating the news that were being implemented in other countries like England and the United States. This dissemination is described as "an anomaly of wireless telephony," which demonstrates a certain amount of unease regarding these new methods and leads to the conclusion that "the concerned parties must henceforth take a position on the question of whether and under what precautionary measures this type of wireless reception device should be handed over to every prospective consumer."[19] The issues underscoring this report are ones of control and access. In terms of content surveillance (control over what is being transmitted) and in terms of restraints on reception (control over who is allowed to listen), the report falls squarely within the realm of regulation of rather than innovation with the radio medium. Balking at what they determined to be detrimental to an idea of political and economic inviolability, the RFK, while not rejecting the possibilities of these new dissemination techniques out of hand, sought instead to guide the medium away from "chaotic conditions" and toward "legal regulations," away from the lurkers and toward "paying subscribers."[20] Although the report does not mention radio amateurs specifically, the phrase "paying subscribers" should be a clear indication of the postal affairs ministry's discomfort with this highly active group of amateur radio operators, not only for their position as nonpaying eavesdroppers on the radio network, but also for their technical ability in building devices with circuits that could transmit and receive at various frequencies along the electromagnetic spectrum. The existence of these radio amateurs outside the viable structures of governmental control and external to the framework of economic practices of attracting and categorizing consumers was abhorrent to the hierarchically organized vision adopted by the new state and its postal affairs ministry — a vision meant to protect the state rather than to encourage experimentation and innovation with the medium. But even Bredow, in his memoirs, sounds fairly unconcerned that these groups of amateurs and hobbyists posed any real threat to military or national security, and even goes so far as to dismiss the architects of the *Funkerspuk* as unimportant:

> We [the postal affairs ministry and the military] were in agreement that the continuation of the ban on reception could not actually prevent the emergence of countless unauthorized reception sites. First of all the military radio operators had practiced the wiretapping of news from out of the ether as sport. Eventually a hobbyist movement like that in the United States would also have fascinated the younger generation interested in the technical aspects of the medium. One knew that there were already thousands of illegal reception sites without there ever being the possibility of serious retribution against them.[21]

The October decision to extend the airwaves to entertainment created what art historian and media theorist Dieter Daniels refers to as a "growing frequency jungle," which inevitably required the plotting of frequencies for specific types or genres of transmission (i.e., military-industrial, entertainment).[22] While there were a number of German amateur radio enthusiasts and hobbyists prior to October 1923 (and even before World War I) who put together their own talk and music broadcasts for this arguably small community of listener-practitioners, German radio transmissions up to this point were utilized primarily for industrial and military point-to-point communications. Daniels describes this culture of amateur radio enthusiasts as a group of loosely affiliated tinkerers content to build and produce experimental broadcasts with their radio sets using at first Morse code and then later sound. He writes:

> Before World War I, there were already approximately 100,000 such wireless enthusiasts. They formed a communication structure outside of government or commercial control—a kind of rhizomatic collective of initiates. With Morse code, they developed their own language style and collective ideals. A few expanded their transmissions to include talk and music and produced small but periodic "broadcasts" for their colleagues.[23]

Although somewhat sanguine in its phrasing, Daniels's description of this group as a "rhizomatic collective of initiates" with a "communication structure outside of government or commercial control" locates a space of experimental possibility within the early 1920s media landscape and suggests that these radio enthusiasts were participating not merely on the level of lurking or playing the role of the passive listener, but rather were actively seeking out and interacting with the varied bits of information being broadcast. Daniels distinguishes this active radio user from the more politically biased *Zaungast,* and what he refers to as the "ether-flâneur," which he equates with our contemporary notion of the web surfer — more of an explorer of information than an engaged user-practitioner of information. Yet neither the term *Zaungast*/lurker with its negative associations with suspicious activity and criminality, nor the concept of the ether-flâneur with its sense of indifference stemming from the combined spatial detachment of the ethereal and the aimless mobility of the flâneur, are suitable signifiers to describe the types of interactivity that Daniels is suggesting. While both of these descriptions situate this elusive radio user as a listener or decoder (in the case of Morse code) to a broadcast that has been produced either by another user in this rhizomatic collective, or by an official governmental agency, in the years prior to entertainment radio the passivity we associate with radio listening had not yet been circumscribed by the radio's transition to a consumer device. Perhaps, as Daniels suggests, the judgments passed on users of radio in terms of criminal activity (lurker) or consumer passivity (ether-flâneur) are a direct consequence of the transition from transmission of Morse code, with its more actively engaged processes of decoding/encoding and haptic movements, to that of broadcast sound, with its tendency to become folded in to the other background or ambient sounds surrounding the context of listening.

What is also of interest here is that both terms ("lurker" and "ether-flâneur") contain within them varying degrees of operability. Depending on the use-value of the information being gathered, either type of radio user engages in a range of active or passive listening practices. In this framing of early telecommunications practice, information is still conceptualized as being alive, as not having yet been transformed into a product available for listener consumption. It continues to exist as raw data to be recycled by this group of wireless enthusiasts regardless of political, artistic, entertainment, or any other content. It is this very core functionality of interactivity that leads Daniels in his essay to question leading media theorist Friedrich Kittler's assertion that broadcast radio as we know it today had its roots in the military innovations of World War I, and to suggest instead that radio would have come into its own by way of these amateur transmissions had the war not erupted.[24] Although these types of "what if" claims rarely produce enough unretractable evidence to disturb hypotheses like that of Kittler's, Daniels's argument does point to the economics of broadcast interactivity (technical ingenuity and invention, formation of a practitioner network, creation of programming segments, etc.) as areas where broadcast radio would have flourished and come into its own regardless of the radio's technical development in the context of the war. Yet Daniels's optimistic tenor does require some tempering, since these amateur transmissions would have run into the same or similar regulatory quandaries as that encountered by Hans Bredow's movement of the radio into the cultural sphere, regardless of the technology's use in the war or the

impact of the *Funkerspuk* event from 1919. Nevertheless, the power
of the radio amateurs and their interactive practices would still find
resonance in the later radio theories (1927–32) of Bertolt Brecht, and
would continue to guide an idea of what radio could become outside these myriad attempts and successes to legislate standards and
regulate practices for radio transmission and reception.

The fear of interactivity and actual engagement on the part of the
listener practitioner — the idea that the lurker or ether-flâneur could
record, analyze, and interpret the information they heard or decoded
and subsequently create a second broadcast with it, or transmit it
in some other form — aroused much concern and attention from
the state. In October 1923 this fear translated into what Ingo Fessmann refers to as the Verfügung Nr. 815 (Ordinance No. 815).[25]
Put to paper just five days prior to the first entertainment broadcast
on October 29, 1923, this ordinance was obviously a type of stop-
gap measure to placate government officials mindful of the power of
broadcast, until more official laws regulating content and the relationship between the radio transmission stations and the government
could be developed. The nuances of this relationship would be addressed in an ensuing ordinance from March 1924, the Verordnung
zum Schutze des Funkverkehrs (Provision for the Protection of Radio
Communication). They would be developed further at the end of
1926 in the Richtlinien für die Regelung des Rundfunks (Directives
for the Regulation of the Radio) with a series of provisions establishing the radio industry's autonomy from all political parties and
outlining the specifics of the separate supervisory panels to oversee
political and cultural content being produced for the airwaves. These
provisions would be changed once again with the implementation of
the Richtlinien für die Neuordnung des Rundfunks (Directives for the
Reorganization of the Radio) in November 1932, which opted for a
less stringent supervision of content by prohibiting private investment
in any of the nine regional stations and establishing ownership as a
"partnership" between the government (51 percent) and the National
Radio Company (Reichsrundfunkgesellschaft) (49 percent). As part
of this effort the directives provided a reorganized set of objectives
and guiding principles with which to operate, that spoke to the great

moral and ethical responsibilities carried by all producers of content for radio broadcast.[26]

The earlier ordinances from 1923 and 1924 identify the procedural and legalistic language necessary to meet the challenges of opening the radio waves up to entertainment. They range in scope from providing a set of requirements governing the construction of radio reception facilities, restrictions on which firms could produce approved devices and antennas, guidelines for obtaining the appropriate permissions and official stamps needed to even acquire a radio for personal use, to outlining procedures for punishable offenses for disobeying these regulations. The former defines the procedural steps for obtaining permission to own a radio receiver and the legal boundaries demarcating transgressive behavior, while the second expands the legal language of the 1892 telegraphy law establishing the sovereignty of the state over all transmission and reception of "news, signals, images or sounds, either through means of electric wireless devices or by means of the conducting of electric waves along a conductor."[27] The October 1923 ordinance even goes so far as to delineate a set of conditions to control the proper use of the radio receiver once the privilege of having one had been granted. Two of the most interesting of these center on improper technical modifications to the device, and on misuse of the device and/or information received through the device:

> 3. Changes to the device and its accessories, cracking of any lead seals, connection of any parts to change the calibration of reception waves are prohibited....

> 6. The reception of news from other radio stations is not allowed. Overheard radio communications from an unauthorized source may not be written down, disclosed, nor reused in any fashion. The holder of an approval certificate must supervise the use of his radio receiver by others, and must prevent its operation by unauthorized users.[28]

Both of these points illustrate clearly the desire to legislate the ways in which radio would be listened to and operated and show the beginnings of moving the radio away from being a device of interactivity and toward becoming a medium for passive consumption of enjoyable and safe content. Again, this regulation of listening and communication practices sought to safeguard the sanctity and sovereignty of the government and was a clear reaction to the earlier takeover of the Berlin telegraph offices in 1919 by decommissioned officers from the signal corps, and to that rhizomatic collective of radio enthusiasts and hobbyists described by Dieter Daniels as operating outside the governmental structure.

The level of interactive engagement prompting these types of regulations required technical devices that would allow these early radio practitioners to receive information from their cohorts and transmit their responses or reactions to it, first in Morse code and later as sound-based broadcasts. These early transceivers combined both reception and transmission capabilities in a single device, and allowed for the ability of two-way communication. Unlike our contemporary consumer notion of radio being purely a passive reception device, up until 1923 the equipment used by both amateur and military radio operators alike was capable of receiving and transmitting signals. It is here in this area of technical design and capability that the last set of restrictions were to be carried out, in order for radio to transition into the realm of entertainment. Again in his memoirs from 1956, Bredow comments on the compromise that was reached with the military regarding the type of technical modifications that would need to be made to the receivers put on the market, so that the safety of military frequencies could be assured without the possibility of unauthorized eavesdropping:

> The military was prepared to shelve its opposition if its interests were protected. One consideration was that any request for a receiver should be accompanied by the issuance of a reception license, but that to protect radio communications certain technical constraints also had to be imposed on listeners and the radio equipment industry. The licensed receivers should be designed in such a way that reception of military and postal radio signals could not be disrupted by the transmission of regenerative feedback or back-coupling waves [*Rückkopplungsschwingungen*]. Additionally, the wiretapping of military radio transmissions was to be made technically impossible through the institution of a wave frequency range reserved for military communications.[29]

The technique of back coupling, or using regenerative feedback to boost or amplify signal coverage and to improve the quality of output signals, held a direct correlation to improving the quality of radio reception. However, the use of this regenerative feedback could often generate distortions along the electromagnetic spectrum, resulting in the transmission of interference along other frequencies. Heide Riedel, a researcher at the Deutsches Rundfunk-Museum (German Radio Museum) in Berlin, elaborates on these constraints in her book *60 Jahre Radio:*

> In July 1923 a compromise was reached: The [radio] industry was given the constraint to only produce radio receivers which could capture nothing beyond the wave range of 250 to 700 m (mediumwave), and additionally should not be capable of producing or emitting radio waves themselves (ban on regenerative feedback).[30]

A solution to the "growing frequency jungle," as termed by Dieter Daniels, required the separation of types of broadcast into amplitude ranges among the available wavelengths of the electromagnetic spectrum, thereby earmarking a place for entertainment radio to reside within radiospace next to both military and commercial communications. However, in order to control the porous borders of ethereal radiospace even more, companies building radio sets for consumer purchase were obliged to take a step backward by making it technically impossible to amplify an output signal through back-coupling or regenerative feedback, thus preventing the possibility of interference into other bandwidths. In an early advertisement from 1923 for a radio experiment kit supplied by the company Radiokosmos Stuttgart, sold primarily to devoted radio amateurs, the impact of the July 1923 technical restrictions and the October 1923 ordinance can readily be seen: "As long as the October 1923 legal ordinances regarding radio communications by enthusiasts are in effect we can only deliver complete instructional and experimental kits or individual parts to foreign customers. — Domestic schools that require equipment for experimental purposes should contact the proper postal authority for an acquisitions license."[31] Later in 1956, with the added benefit of hindsight, Hans Bredow goes so far as to dismiss the importance of these underlying issues related to radio reception for the actual approval of entertainment radio:

> Incidentally, the risk of eavesdropping was not taken into account all that much due to the encryption of military communications. Espionage could not be prevented via bans anyway. In contrast, the military rejected the deregulation of general transmission capabilities for private stations requested by

many in the business sector, since circumstances could arise, which would make controlled military radio communications impossible.[32]

The July 1923 compromise represented a decision of technical regression, since it prohibited the sale of radio receivers with the state-of-the-art in reception technologies, with sole regard being given to the protection of postal and military telecommunications. The consent to release the 1922 ban on private reception of radio signals, and the almost simultaneous restrictions placed on the technical capacity of the receivers being built for the consumer market indicate that the military was concerned about the sensitive nature of the information being transmitted, and that this was given precedence over sensitivity in signal reception. Yet Bredow's later comments clearly indicate that the compromise was really of no consequence, and what did matter was the continued refusal to allow a market for private transmission technologies, which made the possibility of collaborative multiorigin broadcasts like those performed by the group of early radio amateurs unlikely.

The advent of the radio in Germany as a mechanism for entertainment in 1923 carried with it the delicately nuanced beginnings of telecommunications law — a legal structure which grew out of concerns about governmental sovereignty, military innovation, and economic viability, rather than from any deeper sense of how this new communications medium provided any inherent epistemological structures of its own. Dieter Daniels's optimistic description of early radio amateurs operating as a rhizomatic collective outside of governmental hierarchies provides one possible way that the advent of radio could have played out differently. While I am supportive of the type of extra-legislative organization Daniels discusses in his short investigation, the resonances of the 1892 Reich Telegraphy Act outlining governmental control of the early media landscape would have still impacted radio regulation even if military applications for the medium had not been developed. As in the case of Heine's ship-bound poet being pulled back to rationality from his sonorous underwater visions by the authoritative voice of the ship's captain, the technical transformation of the early radio device and its role in experimental broadcasts by a sporadic group of radio enthusiasts is controlled by a rationalized regulatory apparatus based in the sanctity of information and the networks it travels. In both instances, the uncharted depths below the ocean's surface and the, as yet, unmapped ethereal regions of radiospace provided fodder for exploration and fuel for legislative abandon. As we have seen, the radio's move into entertainment broadcasting brought with it numerous laws, ordinances, and directives meant to monitor its development, regulate its reach, and standardize its programming. But this move of the radio into the public sphere also carried with it the unique possibilities bound up with the technologies of sound transmission and sound reception, and opened it up to a broader audience of artists, filmmakers, authors, and musicians, each with their own ideas on how best to work with and through this new medium of communication.

The next section of this chapter explores several crucial early examples of experimental artistic practice with the radio as a medium and the radio as a technical device. It builds upon the discussions of Walter Ruttmann's early radio work undertaken in chapter 1 by closely investigating radio pieces by three additional key figures in early German radio experimentation, namely, Hans Flesch (1896–1945), Friedrich Bischoff (1896–1976), and Friedrich Wolf (1888–1953), who each, in some fashion, engage with and/or combine the varying technical, programming, and imaginative facets of the young medium in their own productions for radio.[33] I have chosen to focus this chapter on the work of these three individuals for the types of innovative structures and practices they implement in their respective pieces for radio, for the connecting threads I detect in their work between the novelty of early experiments with radio and contemporary radio's uncertain position in a saturated intermedia landscape, and for purely pragmatic reasons — recordings of many of the earliest artistic sound broadcasts simply do not exist and so analysis of early radio must focus on these choice examples. What is patently missing from this chapter's investigation of early experiments with and for the radio is a discussion of Bertolt Brecht's theoretical musings about and practical work with the radio medium. Even though Brecht's radio writings and radio productions fall squarely within the timeframe contextualized by this chapter, I have chosen instead to include my discussion of Brecht's work in the next chapter, because it is in the years following the Weimar period and the end of World War II that his theories concerning the radio assume a larger significance with regard to their insights and opinions about the interactive possibilities that radio could play culturally, socially, and politically. This decision is also guided by a desire to foreground the work of Flesch, Wolf, and Bischoff, as well as that of Ruttmann, not in an attempt to downplay Brecht's contributions to radio studies, but rather to broaden our understanding of experimental artistic practices with radio in this early period, and to negotiate these practices within the larger legislative scheme hashed out in the years leading up to the radio's public debut, and within the subsequent modifications to this scheme in the years following its arrival.

Where Hans Flesch's 1924 radio drama *Zauberei auf dem Sender: Versuch einer Rundfunkgroteske* (Radio Magic or Wizardry on the Air: Attempt at a Radio-Grotesque) plays with imprecise notions of spatiotemporality, feedback distortion, physical presence, and ethereality within the bounded and technically driven space of a broadcast sound studio, Friedrich Wolf's 1929 drama *S.O.S. . . . rao rao . . . Foyn. "Krassin" rettet "Italia"* (S.O.S. . . . rao rao . . . Foyn. "Krassin" Rescues "Italia") relies on the accuracy and immediacy of actual radio transmissions related to the international rescue operation of a downed Italian airship in the North Pole to compel its audience. In contrast, Friedrich Bischoff's 1928 radio play *Hallo! Hier Welle Erdball! Eine Hörsymphonie* (Hello! Here Frequency Earth! An Aural Symphony) takes up these same ideas being explored by Flesch and Wolf and produces a more critical sound piece, which examines the modern day-to-day experience of time and calls attention to the modernist obsession with catastrophe and sensationalism, both facets the early radio medium was contending with thematically and programmatically. What each of these pioneers demonstrate through their work, is that as the radio developed as a journalistic tool for the dissemination of information, as an echo device for the rebroadcast of music and other light entertainment, and as a framing mechanism for the continued elaboration of telecommunications policies, there was also room to scrutinize, expose, promote, and theorize about the intrinsically artistic nature of the medium itself.

Hans Flesch and the Imprecision
of Early Broadcast

The radio's development from the workshops of amateur hobbyists and survival from the trenches of World War I and its eventual resurrection as an entertainment device in 1923 under the regulatory umbrella of the country's postal affairs ministry was seen by many as a type of panacea for Weimar Germany's socioeconomic and political ills. Hans Bredow's comments introducing the cultural program of German radio at its outset in 1923 echo these sentiments:

> In a time of difficult economic hardship and political adversity the radio has been deregulated for the general public. No longer will it serve only economic purposes, but rather an attempt will be made to use this cultural advance to bring the German people some encouragement and joy to their lives.... The German people are economically impoverished, and it cannot be disputed, that even spiritual and intellectual depletion is advancing. Who can today afford to buy books and magazines, who can indulge in the joy of good music and entertaining and educational lectures? Recreation, entertainment, and variety distract the spirit from the difficult worries of everyday life and refresh and increase the enjoyment of work. But a joyless population is a population that is reluctant to work.[34]

Linking the development of cultural radio broadcasting to economic and social stability, Bredow's comments point to the overarching principles behind entertainment radio, praising it for its abilities to distract rather than engage its listeners, its ability to promote productivity rather than dwell on economic troubles during this historical period of hyperinflation. Bredow's comments also point to the radio's early role in remediating content from print and other media (books, magazines, concerts and lectures, phonograph albums) via aural transmission of broadcast to enhance access to these increasingly more expensive media. Yet while the issue of access to content is an important factor in strengthening the radio's position in Germany's media landscape, the statements Bredow makes here also locate the prevailing use value for radio in these early years in the realm of duplication of content. Experimental artistic practice with the radio medium had to negotiate the inherent divide of cultural broadcasting set up by these very histories of technical experimentation and regulatory positioning which led to its development, and for radio to survive as a cultural medium, it had to embrace both histories. It had to draw on the intrinsic culture of possibility represented by the amateur radio movement and it had to engage with the culture of fear bound up in the legislative policies set forth by the state and embodied by the vision for radio as being purely a device for the reception of sound produced for other media.

Enter Hans Flesch, whose approach to radio was grounded in the economy of possibility based in the technical materiality of the device, rather than in endorsing a pattern of remediation as evidenced in Bredow's economy for entertainment broadcast, which sought to replace expensive venue- and product-based entertainment with the more economical processes of broadcast. Initially trained as a radiologist, Flesch moved early on into the burgeoning field of broadcasting, serving first as the artistic director for the Radio Frankfurt (officially known as the Südwestdeutsche Rundfunkdienst AG) from 1924 to 1929, and then as the head of the Berlin-based *Funk-Stunde* (Radio Hour). He later became one of the first directors of the newly built Haus des Rundfunks until 1932, when he was forced from office, endured two subsequent trials before Nazi courts with other defendants from the upper echelon of Weimar radio in 1933 and 1934, and was imprisoned until 1935, with part of that time spent in Oranienburg concentration camp.[35] Not much is known about the life or death of Hans Flesch. What print and electronic sources do exist appear to repeat the primary facts of his life: they mention his training in radiology; his eight career years with the broadcasting stations in Frankfurt and Berlin; his marriage to Gabriele Rottenberg, the elder sister of composer Paul Hindemith's wife, Gertrud, his ill-treatment by the Nazis soon after they took power in January 1933, which resulted in the aforementioned trials and imprisonment in Oranienburg; and finally his vanishing without a trace in the outskirts of Berlin in spring 1945.[36]

In the face of these lasting uncertainties about Hans Flesch's untimely disappearance at the end of World War II, it is perhaps even more important to revisit both his hands-on work with early Weimar cultural radio production and his theoretical work in developing the radio medium beyond its role in remediation. As I mentioned earlier, Flesch approached his new job as artistic director of Radio Frankfurt

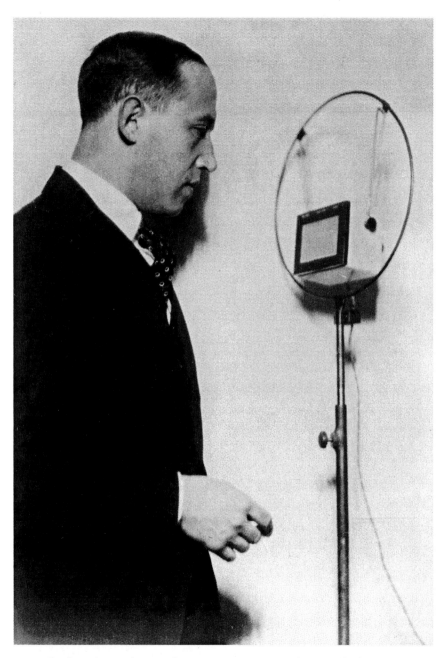

Hans Flesch in front of microphone. From *Der Deutsche Rundfunk* 7 (1929): 581. Copyright 1929 Deutsche-Presse-Photo-Zentrale. Courtesy of Deutsches Rundfunkarchiv, Frankfurt am Main.

with rigorous and dynamic plans, gaining a reputation, depicted by Marianne Weil, as:

> One of an imaginative and enthusiastically experimental program designer, who awakened an interest in the new medium among contemporary musicians like Paul Hindemith [his friend and brother-in-law] and Kurt Weill through specially commissioned compositions, who sought out new radio-specific forms in the emerging genre of the radio play [*Hörspiel*], and who approached the delicate area of politics with the opinion that the radio had to engage with the relevant questions of the time period and should not fearfully avoid everything controversial.[37]

Weil's description points to the three areas of radio production (music, *Hörspiel,* and political discussion/reportage) which Flesch considered important for innovative development, both in terms of their originality and modern outlook, and in terms of pushing the envelope beyond what was considered either economically advantageous for the young medium or legislatively mandated to ensure governmental sovereignty over the airwaves. In an account of a lecture delivered by Flesch, as well as in a series of four short articles written by him during the radio's formative years (1924–25), the problems associated with developing an entertaining program for a wide range of listening audiences are explored.[38] The general tone of these five radio journal pieces speaks to the programmatic issues of balance between production and consumer expenditure: how to avoid fixing the medium to one particular type of broadcast and ossifying in the minds of the listener that the radio was only valuable for listening to concert music or other types of remediated content; how to navigate the need to advertise broadcasting schedules and support the fledgling market in radio-specific print journals while still allowing for the possibility of spontaneity in bringing an evening of programming together; how to negotiate between the medium's required function to broadcast a bit of everything to satisfy all listening publics and its desired function to produce radio-specific art forms. These five pieces also form Flesch's earliest theoretical examination of the new medium, with issues spanning sound fidelity, the spatial relationship between the material at the point of transmission and the material at the point of reception, to the interactive role of the radio listening process in that relationship.

The first is an account of a talk delivered by Flesch in late March 1924, presumably as part of the opening phases of the station in Frankfurt, which began broadcasting on March 30, 1924. Appearing in the column "Mitteilungen des Frankfurter Rundfunks" (Notes from Radio Frankfurt) in the weekly trade journal *Radio-Umschau*, the account summarizes the primary threads of Flesch's presentation: to placate the early listening audience (however small, however skilled) regarding the difficulties of putting together a program design to satisfy all constituencies and their entertainment wishes, and to highlight two experiments — one involving the broadcast of music, the other the broadcast of dialect. The reporter details these latter experiments in terms of sound fidelity and sound clarity, respectively:

> The speaker [Flesch] continued by addressing more closely the acoustic changes of sound transmission via radio and substantiated his remarks through comparative reproduction of music. A violinist and a trombonist performed a few pieces in a concert hall; then they were sent to the broadcasting studio in the postal check office by car and played the same works. It was interesting now to see how the reproduction via radio (sound amplifier) altered the tone of the instruments, especially the violin, and during other performances it could be heard how particularly the piano loses its tonal traits, while the cello was barely altered at all.... With its nasal and inarticulate diphthongs the Frankfurt dialect is not suited for reproduction via radio. On the other hand, a person from Berlin with his clear, sharp articulation is an especially good broadcaster.[39]

These were two experiments that were meant to test the limits and possibilities of broadcast sound in both technical and programmatic terms. Since they focus on detecting the diverse acoustic variations precipitated by radio that affect sound transmission and reception, they are clearly concerned with sound quality as measured in notions of fidelity and clarity. Overlooking for a moment the problematics of the second example with its obvious traces of linguistic discrimination, these two experiments highlight for Flesch that both the devices and practices of radio broadcasting and reception were not yet technically capable of assuring the fidelity and clarity of the transmitted content to the listeners' headsets or loudspeakers. Flesch's experiments were not carried out purely to improve the technological means of broadcast, but were completed for economic reasons as well. If the gold standard measuring early successes with the radio medium consisted in the seamless remediation of performance captured in a live venue, or simulated in the broadcast studio, then the ability to trick the radio audience into believing they were experiencing a live broadcast was an extremely important factor to pursue technically. Both experiments demonstrate a move toward the professionalization of the medium by standardizing broadcast speech and pronunciation, and by increasing the level of perceived authenticity between the source sound taken up by the microphone and the transmitted sound arriving via the receiver in the family living room. These experiments anticipate, then, what Canadian sound theorist R. Murray Schafer would come to term "schizophonia," a strangely acoustic term reminiscent of Walter Benjamin's theoretical musings on the new position of art in the age of its technical reproducibility. Schafer's concept not only describes the split that occurs between an original source sound and its contexts of production and an electroacoustic representation of that original and the contexts of its reproduction, but also captures the specifically modern nervosity evoked by this split.[40] Although Flesch's conclusions regarding the transmission of particular instruments clearly indicate that there is a wide range of tonal discrepancy between the sound of the instruments in the live performance and their same sound in the broadcast performance, the second example involving the transmission of regional dialect raises questions about the practices of sanitizing the airwaves of regional vernacular in favor of a more readily comprehensible speech. Comparatively, the actual range of decipherability of either the Frankfurt or Berlin dialects is dependent on each individual listener's familiarity with the dialect region. The description of the Frankfurt dialect as nasal and inarticulate, while that of Berlin as clear and sharp, imposes a value-judgment linking coherence with authoritative voice and reliable speech. So, in the move to professionalize and standardize the new medium along lines of sound quality and technical reliability, there were also the initial stirrings to nationalize it by envisioning and promoting a national, rather than regional, acoustics.[41]

The issues of sound fidelity and sound clarity pinpointed by the two experiments described in this account demonstrate that Flesch's work with the radio was equal parts technical and programmatic experimentation. Later, in a 1926 retrospective piece "Die kulturellen

Aufgaben des Rundfunks" (The Cultural Duties of the Radio), Flesch explains this need for experimentation to help broaden both the radio practitioners' employment of the device and the listeners' expectations for the medium:

> If one examines retrospectively the development experienced by radio programming since its inception, then one can make out very distinct periods. In the initial period, if the word "trend" is appropriate here, an instrumental or experimental trend is often spoken about. A completely new device was given freely to the director, [yet] nobody knew anything about it beyond its physics and its purely realistic effects. For the audience this was actually quite sufficient. The listener was appreciative for every sound and for every word that he was able to hear, regardless of how he heard it, as long as he had reception.[42]

Here Jonathan Sterne's 2003 study, *The Audible Past: Cultural Origins of Sound Reproduction,* sheds some interesting light on this desire for fidelity and clarity, especially at a time when technologies for measuring such attributes of sound were not yet widely available: "Sound fidelity is much more about faith in the social function and organization of machines than it is about the relation of a sound to its 'source.'...From the very beginning, sound reproduction was a studio art, and, therefore, the source was as bound up in the social relations of reproducibility as any copy was."[43] Sterne's comments remind us that Flesch's early tonal experiments were less about actual fidelity between an original source sound and its copy, and more about training its consumer base to expect higher levels of reliability in sound production and sound reproduction from their station broadcasters and at-home receivers, as well as about establishing an equally reliable track record for the industry. In demonstrating a concern for sound quality at these indeterminate levels, following Sterne's argument, then faith in the new technical device and the new artistic medium would increase the at-home listeners' satisfaction beyond just being able to hear something from their receivers to expecting higher quality sound reproduction and consequently higher degrees of programming.

From Hans Flesch's perspective, improving radio programming also meant increasing the number of households with radio receivers, since revenue streams for improvements to both broadcast technologies and to programming were intimately connected to the monthly license fees required of all radio receiver owners. According to the Gebühreneinzugszentrale (GEZ) (Central License-Fee Collection Office) in their online chronology of German broadcasting history, prior to the stabilization of the currency, "in 1923, the year of inflation, the yearly fee added up to 350 billion Papiermark (1 loaf of bread cost 2 billion Papiermark)."[44] In his own short chronology of radio history, Alfred Braun lists the number of radio subscribers in January 1924 at 1580, with a yearly fee of 60 Reichsmark, which was reduced to 2 Reichsmark per month in early March 1924. Although the stabilization of the German currency in 1924 led to the reduction of the license fee, this did not immediately translate into more Germans purchasing radio sets. The jump in number of radio owners between January and May 1924 of only plus/minus 15,000 (16,467 licensed subscribers) is an excellent indication of this. The larger increase to 100,000 subscribers in July 1924 is most likely linked to the addition of new broadcast stations in May and June 1924, and the very large growth by year's end to 548,749 subscribers is likely the result of the high-profile public radio exhibition held in Berlin in December 1924, and the increased variety in programming between September and November 1924.[45] Flesch's two experiments seem to signify that without greater degrees of sound fidelity and sound clarity and a simultaneous increase in the variety of programming, then the number of new households acquiring radio receivers would slowly languish, thus upsetting the delicately balanced equation that tied programming innovation to assets from these mandatory monthly fees. However, this was not the only balancing act that Flesch was able to discern and implement into his own economy for radio programming. He also understood that programming had to balance between the entertainment of distraction proposed by Hans Bredow in his 1923 address and a more engaging style of broadcast to galvanize and enlighten the listening audience.

Flesch's additional programmatic essays from this early period of radio development emphasize this precise role for radio in mediating between intellectually stimulating content on the one hand, and content meant to lull its audience away from the social and economic stresses of their daily lives on the other. Central to Flesch's conclusions that radio would and should perform in both of these capacities is the interactive role he affords to participants on both the transmission and reception ends of the radio dial — the artists and technicians on the broadcast side, and the listening public on the signal reception side. The September/October 1924 essay "Zur Ausgestaltung des Programms im Rundfunk" (On Radio Program Design), the January 1925 article "Wie kommt ein Rundfunkprogramm zustande?" (How Does a Radio Program Come About?), the April 1925 retrospective lecture "Ein Jahr Frankfurter Programm" (A Year of Programming in Frankfurt) and the 1925 short essay "Mein Bekenntnis zum Rundfunk" (My Commitment to Radio) each further iterate the position of radio within a larger, already existent, landscape of cultural media, debating particularly the idea that radio could only serve as a substitute for the concert hall, rather than produce its own artistic forms, and delineating radio listening as an interactive practice that would make these radio-specific forms more successful.

In the first of these essays, "On Radio Program Design," Flesch invokes comparisons to the media of film and gramophone to help theorize about the unique artistic character of radio broadcast, suggesting that it is in the permutations arising from the varied functions of these other two media in information delivery, mediation, and archivization that the radio should locate and foster its artistic capacities. In his discussion of the cinema, Hans Flesch expands beyond earlier debates concerned primarily with the medium of film replacing theatrical stage performance and touches instead on the cinema's ability to place the machinery of its production at center stage:

> The cinema grew into a substitute [medium] when it began to want to replace theater, and under no circumstances can a substitute be considered art. When it again later aspired to be its own unique form and consciously broke away from the theatrical form . . . and positioned itself in those areas where the theater was exhausted in its possibilities with the use of trapdoors and wind machines, there the cinema began to interest us once again. The role of substitution was no longer apparent, because these techniques were not permitted to be transferred back to the theater or improved upon on stage. Here the machine was not prudishly veiled as the agent of all cinematographic being, but boldly accepted as such, even pitted against the techniques of the theater itself. The machine was not concealed but was instead proclaimed, and we believe that artistic works can emerge from the machine — but only when it originates autonomously, never if it is hidden: Every unique form can create artistic value.[46]

In his search for a peculiarly radiophonic form to separate the medium from its assigned role in repetitive regurgitation of content, Flesch rests upon the ability of the cinema to acknowledge and embrace its machine-centeredness, its technically driven narrative structure, and its mechanically produced and reproduced images, as central to what constitutes its unique artistic form. Relating this to radio, Flesch warns: "even with radio the machine acts as an intermediary between presentation and ear and not as a moderator to be overlooked. Therefore nothing of artistic value will come from a radio concert, if the radio sees its task merely to transmit good concerts. It then just ossifies as an inartistic substitute for concerts."[47] In his discussion of the cinematic, Flesch nostalgically recalls that some of the earliest films were quaint in their subject matter, but primitive in their technical abilities, and only too aware of what lie in the realm of possibility for advances in the medium.

The same holds true for Flesch's insights into the gramophone, which provides the radio with an example of archival possibility, and hence, with an example of studied distance or reflection.[48] Again, Flesch's comments concerning the gramophone contain a certain amount of nostalgia for a device and a medium still experiencing its own awkward puberty. Flesch situates the points of convergence between the gramophone and radio not only in terms of their proximal sound fidelity to an original concert performance, but also in terms of their ability to either enhance or anticipate a live concert experience:

> Here we want to think about the gramophone as a teacher. In the concert hall we are not left with the sense that musical compositions can be studied. The gramophone offers the best opportunity to grasp the art of a great singer, in all nuances, at home. A good Caruso album can reproduce for us the nuances of this imaginative singer in such detail that we can become unsettled through the memory of what has already been heard, or, if we have not heard it yet, through the thought of it, that something such as this exists.[49]

As with his comments about cinema, Flesch focuses on the gramophone's mediacy — its ability to record and play back reproduced sound and provide something new not found with the concert-going experience — and craves this same level of functionality and reflective distancing for the radio. In our age of iPods and digital music downloads, we tend to forget (if we knew at all) that the early phonograph, invented in late 1877 by Thomas Edison, was both a sound reproduction device and a sound/voice recording device. Although the wax phonograph cylinders utilized to record short durations of sound (up to four minutes of playing time) would, by 1929, be supplanted by the more durable disc records produced by Emile Berliner for his gramophone, replacing the cylinders' recording feature would not be possible as a viable and simple recording and playback technique outside the studio until the development of electromagnetic recording technologies revolutionized the worlds of radio and film late in 1929 and early in 1930. In his survey piece "Audio Art" for the online curated multimedia project "Medien Kunst Netz" Golo Föllmer correctly points out that technologies of sound recording, like the gramophone, successfully uncoupled the production and reception aspects so closely associated in live music performance:

> The storage of sound through the phonograph and the gramophone enabled the unlimited reproduction of music.... Like transmission, sound recording also changed production and reception as the two areas were now separated in terms of both time and space. Because listeners were no longer dependent on musicians, for the first time they were able to integrate music into their daily lives. Music had, so to speak, become a ubiquitous source of nourishment.[50]

Even without the innovation and quality of recorded playback, Flesch's comments from 1924 position the gramophone, and by extension the radio, directly in the midst of an enhanced listening experience, one that expands on the immediate and performative contexts of the live concert through extending this performance into the domestic space of the family living room.

The gramophone's reliance on recorded discs and its location in the domestic sphere creates a spatiotemporal distance to the live performance, which transforms this more emotion-driven experience of *unmittelbares Hören* into one based in intellectual/studied reflection through routes of anticipation and remembrance. Flesch characterizes the live concert performance as a moment of immediate or proximate listening, through which the listener "experiences in the concert hall each of those effects of the music, which one finds described in a thousand poems: better emotions are inspired, joyful moods are produced, heroic sentiments, painful mourning, in short the person is gripped at his most internal space and 'lifted into higher spheres.' "[51] Like Heinrich Heine's poetic subject in the "Seegespenst" poem, Flesch's concertgoer is transported to a higher plane or sphere of emotional connection with the music being heard as a result of his or her spatio-temporal proximity to the origin of the sound. In speaking to the immediacy of live sound events, Flesch opens a discussion exploring the radio's function as a device that always mediates, filters access to, and structures the experience of any particular broadcast. He continues this discussion by elaborating on the inability of machine-based sound production or reproduction (e.g., gramophone or radio) in achieving this same level and effect of interiorized emotion offered by the immediacy of a live event: "To produce this same effect can never and may never be achieved by way of the radio, and if it appears to have been realized, then it must be a false and sentimental attempt, since only *Unmittelbarkeit* (immediacy) and not a machine lifts us into higher spheres!"[52] This term *Unmittelbarkeit,* while denoting both spatial and/or temporal proximity to a place/object or an event/occurrence, also conveys a sense of unmediated experience, an understanding of the world in which objects and events are experienced intuitively, rather than through the filter of an objective, rational, and mediated distance.

As a blending of both immediacy and unmediated experience, Flesch's understanding of *Unmittelbarkeit* in the context of a listening experience draws on Immanuel Kant's ideas about human understanding of reality, which operates through the interrelationship between the abstract realm of the noumenal, a field of indeterminate and thus, unknowable, entities, and the material realm of the phenomenal, the range of perceptible, quantifiable, and quality-laden objects that populate our field of sensory perception. In short, Kant posits that our experience of the world around us is based on the encounters we have with both of these realms, i.e., by way of the objects or phenomena that we encounter on a daily basis vis-à-vis sense perception (sight, sound, taste, smell, touch) and by way of an intellectual understanding of things that exist outside or beyond the senses (noumena) vis-à-vis an abstract or metaphysical questioning or challenging of these same phenomena (i.e., what makes this thing the object we perceive it to be? etc.). Both realms of understanding work in concert to help us make sense of raw unstructured experience, although in a media-saturated world these types of raw, unfiltered experiences are rare, if they were even possible outside of philosophical discourse at all. Nevertheless, Hans Flesch's description of an emotion-laden live concert performance with its intensely transformative capacity provides a glimpse at how these Kantian notions of the phenomenal and the noumenal are brought together within the concert-goer through the tangible, observable reality of the phenomenal and the immateriality of the noumenal. Here the visual cues from the performers and their movements on stage, the aural resonances and tones filling the acoustic space of the concert hall, and the physical reverberations of the music resounding through the seats and floor of the venue could be seen to trigger the intellectual, abstract meanderings of the noumenal mind, propelling the concert-goer into these higher spheres that Flesch seems to regard with some special significance. The spatial and temporal immediacy he associates with this live event would seemingly belie its very structured, very filtered, and very devised sense of mediacy — that the experience of the event is guided and framed by the structure of the venue and the arrangement of the program. Yet there is something in the course of the performance that provides for this transcendent moment, something that relies on the communality of the listening experience, the spontaneity of the performers, and the talent of the conductor that cannot be reproduced via radio broadcast.

Instead, Flesch maintains that the radio can never fill this role of unmediated listening provided by the live concert and can only produce a range of varying points for intellectual reflection. He writes:

> Through the idea of it: This concerns a purely mental, an intellectual process, which is mediated for us by the machinery of the gramophone. On the detour through the purely intellectual we can become emotionally unsettled. We must however be constantly aware of this detour both with respect to the gramophone and with the radio. It would be wrong to prepare a program based on the same sets of criteria that a program is normally produced for the concert hall. The notional components must be placed in the foreground.[53]

For Hans Flesch, the issue comes down to broadcast programming, and the radio establishes its unique identity in this early media landscape of cinema and gramophone through its ability to hook into these notional components, to establish for its listening audience a range of entry points for thinking about the broadcast. Unlike the users of the gramophone, purchasers of radio receivers remained caught at the whim of a broadcast's producers both for their programming and for establishing the ideational context in which it would be heard. Flesch's reference to the gramophone's teacherly capacity, mentioned earlier, as well as to the sense of archival possibility that it affords vis-à-vis its ability as a storage medium for sound and sound-based performance, identify the gramophone as facilitating a new type of media event centered in the performance, recording, transmission, and consumption of sound, a media event that he desires to implement within the structures of radio production, broadcast, and reception.

Beyond their similar function as storage media for visual and aural data, respectively, the cinema and gramophone couch the consumer experience of purchasing content for their particular technologies in a space outside the household, while the radio depended on monthly licensing fees for financing content production costs. The gramophone and the radio initially followed the example of the cinema in locating the listening experience in public listening venues, due in part to the cost of the equipment, but possibly also in an effort to regulate or surveil the aural field. Yet they both eventually found their way into Germany's living rooms and parlors, most likely as a result of heightened marketing on the part of their manufacturers, and most assuredly as the devices became more affordable.[54] Kate Lacey, in her 2005 provisional study on public listening practices in Weimar Germany, specifically in the social context of workers' radio groups, points out that this relocation of the radio into the household created a type of domesticated listenership, which has often been interpreted as a feminization and, thus, emasculation of listening practice. She describes it as:

> beginning with the early intoxicating days in which young men withdrew into the attics from the monotony of daily life, in order to build and improve their own transmitters and to communicate with exotic foreigners via the magical ether; and extending to the feared years of passive, isolated inertia in the domesticated and therefore feminized mass culture. Incidentally, this version of the historical account offers a possible explanation for the glorification of "interactivity," which has surrounded the fervent adoption of new computer technologies through a new generation of predominately male enthusiasts.[55]

According to Lacey, this gendered interpretation suggests the move from the predominately male world of the early radio amateur, where listening privacy was guaranteed by the headset, to the predominately female space of the household, where the radio's loudspeaker rescinded the possibility of complete listening privacy and transformed the listening experience into one of conviviality. Lacey argues that this approach essentially recasts the listening experience in terms of a binary opposition between activity and passivity, since the earlier forms of broadcast interactivity enjoyed by radio amateurs continue to be carried through in successive iterations of the radio apparatus, regardless of whether interactivity in the realm of broadcast was actually possible. Instead she proposes that this focus on interactivity overlooks the existence of other, alternative listening publics, which locate the experience of listening as a community practice and understood themselves to be the point of collective, and oftentimes political, activity.[56] Lacey's focus for her research into early public listening practice centers on the workers' radio clubs, which developed early on in 1924 as products of both the social democratic and communist political parties, and their tactics in promoting a proletarian-based radio practice. These included demonstrating how to build broadcast and reception devices, how to agitate for a workers' radio, and, in one case from 1931, how to disrupt signals from bourgeois broadcast stations. Yet aside from these rather hands-on tactics, Lacey argues that it was in the advance of a collective listening practice in order to develop a critical ear vis-à-vis bourgeois radio broadcasts that this idea of community listening demonstrates its strengths. I would argue, however, that this type of community listening is as much an interactive practice as the types of tinkering and fiddling she associates with the early male amateur radio enthusiasts. Although community listening practice is based more in a reflective and dialogic exchange, the types of tactics Lacey describes certainly reflect a type of interactive practice. In addition, even with the mutation of the radio device away from broadcast and reception to reception-only capabilities, the desire to reclaim a position of power in broadcast still accompanied, if not the practical then the theoretical idea and ideals of what radio was and could be again. The interface with digital technologies in the face of Internet-based communications has thus been embraced as one way of reclaiming the interactivity formerly associated with broadcast.

Kate Lacey's research engages several key points in our discussion of Hans Flesch's comparison of radio with the other early media of cinema and gramophone. The myriad relationships set up among active/passive, male/female, public/private, and interactive/convivial listening practices in Lacey's preliminary investigation of public listening illustrate that the domestication of the radio did not necessarily rule out the possibility of engaged, even politicized, listening. Rather, many of the practices associated with earlier encounters with the radio (the hands-on activity of the radio amateur, the community atmosphere of public venues) continued to survive in the form of trace, as the radio apparatus and the venue for its integration into daily life adapted to changing regulatory policies and broadcast standards. Hans Flesch's focus on the notional aspects of broadcast programming in this essay from September/October 1924 provides a nodal point for thinking about and responding to the quick pace of change prompted by the deregulation of radio reception and the subsequent emergence of new listening practices both inside and outside the family home. Flesch, in setting up and justifying the radio as a medium for music, writes about the intellectual capacity of radio programming, which associates it with the gramophone and differentiates it from the concert hall:

> The emotive must remain a secondary thread, an indirect outcome, in the radio. It must depend on mental work, and so, radio concert programming is at its most intrinsic an intellectual undertaking.[57]

This significant demarcation creates in the art of radio broadcast cognitive links to the earlier interactive practices of the radio amateurs and to contemporaneous ideas about the power of listening. That this move occurred via a transitional phase of public group listening that paradoxically sought to control the use of the device but could not control the possibility of a collective listening experience, demonstrates that this was done as much to create a listening spectacle as it was to protect against the auscultation of sensitive data. Spurred on by the earlier fear that governmental sovereignty over the airwaves was in jeopardy, this retooling of the radio from communications apparatus to consumer listening device prompted its move from these public listening venues back into the semi-privacy of the domestic sphere where it had begun with the earlier amateur radio enthusiasts, albeit with little or no power for consumer-based production.

Within the context of these early listening publics — from the engaged groups of innovative radio amateurs and the watchful eyes and attentive ears of postal regulators to the fledgling members that formed both the public and at-home listening audiences — Flesch considers some of the problems facing the radio program director in developing a radio program that would hold the diverse interests of these varying audiences, while also following the guidelines set out to safeguard governmental sovereignty over particular kinds of information deemed sacrosanct to the viability of the government — a remnant from the *Funkerspuk* scare of 1919. While being able to negotiate this type of balance is difficult enough, also trying to provide wide-ranging content to appease the more devoted radio amateurs, continuing to introduce the medium to novice listeners without stagnating in the realm of novelty, and staying informed of technical innovations in the worlds of sound transmission and reception was no small task. In a second programmatic essay strangely evocative of one Bertolt Brecht would publish two years later in 1927, Flesch tackles these issues by intimating a case for professionalizing the program director's position.[58] In his January 1925 article "How Does a Radio Program Come About?" he dismisses the need for the program director to be a jack-of-all-trades, cognizant of new developments in technology, aware of new trends in music, and able to field new approaches to advertising revenue. In the earliest days of broadcast radio these types of responsibilities were most likely an asset, but, as Flesch suggests in this essay, they distract the director from the more instinctual aspects of his job:

> Arranging musical composition on musical composition does not produce a program. Clusters of products by the greatest musical geniuses can assume a form or rather an unshapely mish-mash, entrancing crude people into using the ugly expression "goulash." Here we become acquainted with the idea of the will to form as an influential tool in program design as the second point [in understanding program design]. If we add an instinct for radio, something absolutely essential for the director to possess, then we can already visualize that a program comes about. To this point everything would be fine and good.[59]

Beyond a rote compilation of musical compositions ("Tradition, taste, and a music encyclopedia advise on what is good and bad, and, well-equipped with these three things, especially the lexicon, the radio director cheerfully ladles from the aforementioned fount [of music]"[60]), which elides the sheer magnitude of music ever produced in favor of those pieces that are conveniently described in a lexicon or that passed the popularity test of the early culture industry, Flesch clearly believes that the creation of a successful radio program requires an innate aptitude on the part of the radio director to detect what he refers to as the "will to form" (*Formwille*) and foster this through the "creative power" (*Gestaltungsvermögen*) of the practicing artist. Both of these terms relate back to our previous discussion of the notional aspects of radio broadcast, which Flesch offers as a uniquely radiocentric characteristic that helps set it apart from the media of cinema and gramophone. Both the *Formwille* of the radio director and *Gestaltungsvermögen* of the practicing artist occur prior to any mediation of the broadcast via the radio transmitter or the radio receiver. And each occurs on a notional level, irrespective of the other, until the collaborative moment takes place. In some sense this would provide an example of Flesch's desire to furnish the radio medium a similar type of unmediated experience that he attributes to live performance. Obviously the radio director's instinctive nature concerning programming also accounts for a level of mediation with regard to the artistic practice of the musician or author providing content for broadcast. Yet I think what Flesch wants to make clear is that the collaboration between director and artist in shaping an adaptation specific to the radio medium clearly provides for another type of notional moment that brings together the original ideas of the artist and the director's knowledge of programming and the medium. Here Flesch casts his critical gaze at the numerous radio journals that appeared during these early years and points to their need to print program guides for their readership as the place where the finely tuned relationship between artist and radio director begins to fall apart. While structurally important for keeping listeners and potential listeners apprised of when to tune in to hear a certain program and economically important for the types of advertising revenue the journals could produce for both themselves and the broadcasting stations, these program guides effectively dismantle the noumenal conduits set up between the artist and the radio director by squashing the sense of spontaneity of the relationship. Flesch says of the journals' publishers:

> Actually he is pitiable. He suffers from an *idée fixe*. He has it stuck in his publisher's mind: (a) that a program always has to be printed for an entire week (read, an entire week!) (b) that the aforementioned weekly program has to be in his hands 10 days before the beginning of the week specified. Those who have ever heard of "will to form" and "creative power" know how difficult it is to bring together a union between these two important but demanding people [the artist and the director] under such circumstances.[61]

In addition to the notional/noumenal disruption between the artist and the radio director caused by the publisher's need for timely programs, is the equal interruption in the intellectual process that scheduling produces for the listener. Flesch himself fails to take the position of the listener into consideration in his critique of the journal process and its effect on the development of the radio program. This is an omission that was not necessarily done out of malice toward the listener, but more likely out of a lack of significance attributed to the listener, who at this early stage in the radio media landscape assumed a more passive role in the economy of broadcast. The role of the listener in the program development equation devised by Flesch in this essay was simply not a priority for the fourteen-month old medium. Since audience reception studies specific to radio and other mass media would not begin to appear until the 1930s through the work of the Frankfurt School, investigations exploring the effectiveness of certain modes or genres of broadcast and the listening audiences' ability to engage intellectually with the broadcasts shaped and brought together by the artist and the radio director lagged behind the more pragmatic and programmatic issues encountered in other areas of the media landscape and culture industry brought into existence by the fledgling radio medium.[62] Flesch's focus on the problems that arise when the publishers of radio journals enter the equation may speak tacitly to the place of the listener in the notional/noumenal development of a radio program out of the techniques of "will to form" and "creative power" brought into dialogue by the radio director and the artist. The numerous points of reception with the listening audience would then add additional layers of notional/noumenal interaction respective to the listening context of each individual listener — whether the listening moment occurs publicly or privately, or whether the listener is a novice or an experienced enthusiast.

The position of the listener takes on more of a role in Flesch's consideration of the first year of broadcast programming at Radio Frankfurt, which is the topic of two essays from 1925. The first, a lecture and subsequent publication called "A Year of Programming in Frankfurt," provides an accounting of technical, programming, administrative, and other studio developments to the listeners of the now one-year-old broadcasting station, while the second, the short essay "My Commitment to Radio," treats an actual economy of listening with respect to the type of radio genres being broadcast. Even with the relatively small listener base attracted by the Frankfurt broadcasting station, or, for that matter, by the medium, both essays acknowledge the importance of the listener for justifying the paths chosen by all of the fledgling studios in their first year of existence. Referring to these early listeners as the *Paten des Kindes* (godparents of the child),[63] Flesch's retrospective essays place the new technical and programming developments in the context of the uncertain socioeconomic fabric produced and experienced by the new medium (e.g., monthly subscription fees and cost of expensive receivers meant a healthy buy-in on the part of the listening consumer). Yet they also reiterate his view concerning the role and function of the radio as a medium for educational rather than entertainment programming, and as a medium to access but not replace artistic content given its machinic role in mediation. Both essays reassert Flesch's ideas related to the notion of immediacy, and the radio's assistant capacity in providing both aural and intellectual access to concert performances and new music, but they also revise these ideas somewhat to position the radio as a possible artistic medium in its own right:

> In previous lectures I have frequently alluded to why the radio needs to develop along the paths of education and not entertainment; . . . because the radio can hardly be considered art in and of itself. — The absence of a direct immediacy, the insertion of the machine in the mediation process, will always position

the radio as an agent, and never as a thing-in-itself [*Ding an sich*]. When one articulates this, then one does not hinder notions about radio; rather one raises them by placing radio on its own pedestal. The radio as a replacement for art will always find rejection, and rightly so; the radio as its own artistic genre exists in the realm of possibility, but seems to only have a limited scope. The radio as agent, as a guide to art, as a guide to the fine and good objects of science, of education, with a word, the radio as an intellectual aide, will always play an excellent role.[64]

In a clearly Kantian fashion, Flesch acknowledges and celebrates the radio's role in providing intellectual access to educational and artistic content, but also wants to create a space for radio-specific artistic production beyond the limitations set up for it as an entertainment device. His mantra throughout this essayistic excursion has consistently been one that places the radio alongside the cinema and gramophone as a device to enhance, not replace, the cultural experience of the "true" art forms of theater, opera, and concert. In this respect, his thoughts about radio align themselves with and anticipate much critical debate at the time concerning the position and function of art with the advent of new technologies of artistic reproduction. In the midst of the mass of criticism these new media received for their transmutation of art, Flesch instead focuses on the ways in which the cinematic, the gramophonic, and the radiophonic provide for moments of intellectual reflection vis-à-vis their respective visual and acoustic modes. The art of listening and the discomfort of the listener are key elements in facilitating this intellectual reflection:

> Radio listening is the same type of thing as reading a score, i.e., it communicates to the layman the same kind of knowledge — naturally not in the same amount and in completely different ways! — that the musician acquires through the reading of a score. Thus, I am against the widely propagated perspective of celebrating the radio as a device of convenience: the view which brings everything quaintly into the house, into the soft lounge chair, so that one only needs to reach for it and spares them the inconveniences of a visit to the theater or concert. No, the radio is there to provoke such a visit from the comfortable and the undecided![65]

The analogy of a musician reading a musical score provides to the act of radio listening a level of interpretive skill. But where the musician interprets a written musical composition or score into sound, a radio listener interprets a range of already produced sound by folding it into an existing array of experience and knowledge. Both are individual acts that operate in or through the realm of imagination, with the musician transforming an imagined auscultation of the score into produced sound, and the radio listener actively parsing the sounds of a broadcast into points for reflective thought. Yet while the musician is able to weave his individual interpretation of the score into an arrangement of other instruments through the public space of performance, Flesch disturbs the radio listener from his isolated and distanced position in the relative comfort of his home and easy access to the radio dial in a bid to engage the listener in this same public space of performance. Since theater and concert performance are so closely bound up with our contemporary notion of entertainment, it is easy to understand how some could argue that Flesch's relocation of the at-home radio listener into the public sphere ultimately recasts the radio listener into the perpetual role of passive listening. But the distinction that Flesch draws between the radio's value as entertainment, seen in its leisure-producing mentality, and its value as cultural experience, apparent through its intellectual engagement of the listener, clearly indicates that he wishes to promote a direction for the radio medium that embraces experimentation and serves as an initiation point for engaged listening practices. When he positions the listeners as the "godparents" of the medium, discusses the improved sound clarity achieved by a new type of microphone, waxes poetic on the virtues of increased voltage of transmitter tubes to avoid transmission disruptions, or alludes to putting radio on *sein eigenes Postament* (its own pedestal), he is doing nothing less than demonstrating the importance of sound in all of its receptive and transmissive aspects for the creation of a specifically radiophonic space of artistic production. Formed from the technologies, practices, and economies of sound production, sound reproduction, and sound reception, Flesch's radiophonic space resigns itself to the entertainment model of unidirectional transmission and reception of a broadcast, but at the same time makes a case for a more nuanced approach to listening and pushes the radio to experiment beyond the mediocrity of duplication, and beneath or around the range of standards and policies seeking to legislate its use.

Examples of Early Radio Experimentation in Weimar

Hans Flesch: *Zauberei auf dem Sender* (1924)

In a 1954 essay honoring Hans Flesch and his contributions to German radio, Kurt Magnus, the co-founder with Hans Bredow of the National Radio Company (RRG) overseeing the nine regionally based radio companies that were organized between October 1923 and October 1924, describes Flesch's avant-garde approach as "modern to the core, open to everything new and not trapped by any one type of special form."[66] Where Magnus's description of Flesch would seem to celebrate the sense of cultural engagement proffered by the new medium — the idea that the radio should both convey and be permeated by the exhilarating cultural atmosphere in which it was born, Wolfgang Schivelbusch, in his study of Frankfurt's intellectual life in the 1920s, lights upon Magnus's comments to showcase Flesch as a perceptive designer of programming, mediator of talent, and media critic, rather than as a successful practitioner of the medium. He writes:

> What he himself created as an author was not especially exciting or impressive, like, for example, the 1924 revue farce "Zauberei auf dem Rundfunk," which demonstrated all the technical and dramaturgical tricks of the medium. His actual achievement resided in his choice of collaborators and the opportunities he gave them. Here Flesch really showed a "modern to the core" flair for talent and innovation. The collaborators and authors, who made Radio Frankfurt into a center of innovation for the radio genres of *reportage, new music*, the *radio play*, and *open debate* in the 1920s, could freely develop there because the organizational structure of the enterprise was fashioned in the same way.[67]

In addition to highlighting Flesch's cutting-edge programmatic designs for the medium, Schivelbusch focuses on his organizational abilities, his innate collaborative demeanor and ability to draw out and capitalize on the talents of those he urged to contribute to the new medium. As we have seen from Flesch's range of radio essays, this success and "modern to the core" flair and innovation were as much about the organizational structure apparent on the broadcast side of the medium, as they were about his attendance to issues on the reception side. It was the combination of the two that propelled Flesch as an innovator in the field of cultural radio production and allowed for the experimental success of the new radio genres mentioned by Schivelbusch. In fact, it was Flesch's ability to intimately weave together innovative approaches to broadcast programming and interactive ideas about the listening experience that most likely catapulted his career move from Radio Frankfurt to become artistic director of the *Funk-Stunde* in Berlin in 1929 and that laid a theoretical foundation for ensuing radio artists to experiment with in their creation of pieces for the medium.

The aura and excitement of these innovative approaches is captured in a 1931 caricature depicting Flesch hard at work in a laboratory surrounded by flasks, test tubes, books, and chemicals. In his right hand he holds a flask labeled "Dramaturgie" from which he is delicately pouring a single drop into a test tube in his left hand, which is labeled "H_2O." The surrounding tubes are tagged with the rubrics "Interview," "Neue Musik," and "Studio," while the two flasks contain elements of "Reportage," steaming away on the Bunsen burner to create an unknown distillate in an unlabeled flask nearby, and "Wein-Zeit-Geist," sitting atop a thick tome, presumably combining the amorphous spirits of the flask with the bounded textual knowledge of the book through the process of osmosis. One possible reading of this image stems from an understanding of the range of radio theoretical writing that Flesch engaged in, and that we have been discussing at length. Here the cartoon illustrates the work of a radio program director as being part chemist, part organizational maestro in mixing together the various elements and techniques of dramaturgy, reportage, and a spirit-infused zeitgeist to create original program designs, while keeping a watchful eye on all aspects of programming. Although we cannot know what the caricatured Flesch is currently in the process of mixing since the test tube is labeled only "H_2O," we can make a fair assumption that he is in the midst of adding one more innovative radio-based genre to the collection already available in the test tube rack — interview, new music, and studio-based — and the clue of dramaturgy hints that the new tube will hold the *Hörspiel.* Another way to interpret this image involves seeing it only in this context of the *Hörspiel,* a radio-specific genre that Hans Flesch cultivated from his very first days at Radio Frankfurt. The clear intent of the drawing's original caption *Der Hörspielmixer* (the mixer of radio plays) points to this,

Hans Flesch caricatured as "Mixer of Radio Plays." From *Der Deutsche Rundfunk* 20 (1931): 4. Copyright 1931. Artist and image rights unknown. Courtesy of Deutsches Rundfunkarchiv, Frankfurt am Main.

as does the thematic focus of the issue of *Der Deutsche Rundfunk* in which it appears, which contains a lead article by editor Hans S. von Heister titled "Das Hörspiel — Heute" (The Radio Play — Today). In this regard the caricature suggests that the radio play Flesch is in the process of mixing takes its substance from all aspects of radio broadcast as it then currently existed, and thus would be a permutation of any of the elements of dramaturgy, reportage, interview, new music, zeitgeist, and the site-specific functionality of the broadcast studio. The *Hörspiel,* as conceived and actuated by Flesch, is in one sense a self-referential genre, one that explores its very connections to the medium that produces it, and in another sense, it is a form that delights in its own intermediality by drawing on the dramaturgical techniques of stage drama, the journalistic techniques of reportage and interview, and the compositional techniques of new music, while being aurally bound to the technologies of the broadcast studio.

When seen from this perspective, the 1931 caricature harkens back to Flesch's only creative production for the radio medium, the October 1924 radio play *Zauberei auf dem Sender.*[68] Broadcast exactly one year following the beginnings of entertainment radio in Germany the play is significant not only for being the first of its kind ever to be broadcast over the German airwaves, but also for its playfulness in challenging the medium to experiment beyond accepted standards and for calling attention to the possibilities of a radio-centered program format. For his own part, Hans Flesch would have probably agreed with Wolfgang Schivelbusch's criticism (not especially exciting or impressive) of this particular radio play, which he regarded as a theoretical experiment:

> At one point I undertook an experiment to create a characteristically radiophonic *Hörspiel,* wrote the play *Zauberei auf dem Sender,* — not as an author, as a theorist, actually — in order to put forward an artistic genre peculiar to the radio through the harmony of noises; this grotesque would never be transferable to the stage or concert hall, and this is the decisive point.[69]

The fact that Flesch envisioned this particular radio play production as a theoretical engagement with the artistic possibilities of the radio medium is crucial for understanding the constant struggle he faced in these early years of radio between falling into the monotony of entertainment and creating thought-provoking radio broadcasts. In one sense, both Schivelbusch's qualitative criticism and Flesch's own misgivings about the piece's creative success underscore the importance of broadcasting radio shows that maintained a delicate, perhaps invisible, balance between fulfilling an audiences' listening pleasure and engaging their critical faculties. In another sense, this criticism demonstrates that artistic experimentation with the radio medium could garner no real cultural currency given the regulatory structures governing its use, the economic framework making it viable, and the programming standards already beginning to ossify in the minds of listeners and practitioners alike. The nature of artistic experimentation requires it to always stay one step ahead of the processes that seek to subsume it into the structures and patterns of the larger culture industry of entertainment economy. Rather than celebrating the experimental as an operative mode in the context of its transitoriness, and permitting it to remain elusive, it was instead often utilized to develop new formats, whose success was gauged by virtue of their potential to entertain an audience and thus ensure continued revenue, and not on the basis of the questions they raised about the medium itself. It is in this sense that Wolfgang Schivelbusch's verdict concerning Flesch's *Zauberei auf dem Sender* begins to fall short, and where Flesch's own qualification of the piece, (e.g., that he wrote it "not as an author, [but] as a theorist"), begins to sabotage its importance for both reconceptualizing already old-fashioned broadcast formats and for triggering a rash of experimental sound plays like that of Ruttmann discussed in the first chapter, and those of Wolf and Bischoff, which will also be explored more closely in this chapter. Each of these points warrants giving Hans Flesch's radio play a closer listen.

On October 24, 1924, at 8:30 p.m. listeners in broadcast range of Radio Frankfurt, who tuned their receivers to frequency 467 expecting to hear the nightly concert were instead confronted with what sounded like a major programming fiasco occurring before their ears at the studio. What should have been a lulling evening of relaxing concert music emanating from their headsets or speakers, for those who could afford them, was instead a cacophony of arguing voices, urgent whisperings, and commanding shouts, which quickly devolved into a range of odd noises, ghostly sounds, out of synch instruments, and unsourced music. Rather than tuning in to their accustomed evening of well-rehearsed and well-organized concert music, radio listeners instead were made witness to a malfunctioning of the neatly packaged programming standards that the fledgling medium had already grown into in the minds of many listeners. A review that appeared one week later in the trade magazine *Radio-Umschau* provides an excellent synopsis of the drama and also highlights how it was critically received at the time, at least by one critic:

> At exactly 8:30 it begins. With an "infernal" Fra Diavolo overture. Every radio subscriber jumps from their seats appalled. But what is this supposed to be? Dr. Flesch, the ruler of the broadcast kingdom, is being interrupted during his program. Actually interrupted. By the storyteller. Who also once wants to be able to tell fairytales in the evening. And while things are being negotiated nicely with her, numbers echo forth, nothing but numbers. No: already there are the audible sounds of a soprano, already the orchestra is beginning to play, already philosophical problems are being discussed. Simultaneously. Everything simultaneously. The broadcast station is crazy! Chaos, a confusion of voices, an assault on the eardrums. Until a deep voice emerges, powerful, suggestive, the voice of a magician, who praises his own work for the destruction and confusion. In vain Dr. Flesch asks his orchestra to play the Danube waltz. A funeral march is the result. Disorder appears to have overtaken order. Until Dr. Flesch, with a warning cry to the will of the people, becomes master over the magic. The waltz flows free and clear. Serious desires subdued the spook.[70]

While this may all sound fairly innocuous and somewhat perfunctory for a contemporary audience, for a 1924 audience settled in their ideas about what types of programming the radio would deliver, this twenty-two minutes would also have been taken as a disturbance, as another type of interference in their paid-for expectations of sound clarity and an entertaining evening.

Unlike the notorious interruption of radio programming engineered by Orson Welles in his debut of *War of the Worlds,* which duped its listeners through the serious tones of a mock news broadcast, Flesch's radio drama takes the radio medium itself as its subject matter. It confronts its listeners with the actual staff of the studio (artistic director — Hans Flesch, his assistant, the announcer, business director, technician, violinist from the radio orchestra, and the typist), who themselves become the central characters of the drama. Except for the announcer these are all people who normally kept themselves behind the scenes, whose voices rarely, if ever, were transmitted across the radio waves, and whose primary tasks were devoted to keeping the broadcast station technically, financially, administratively, and artistically operational. The appearances of both the *Märchentante* (the teller of fairy tales) at the very beginning of the disruption and a *Zauberer* (magician) later on in the piece add a touch of the otherworldly and provide the needed jumping-off points for the unexplained array of sounds that begin to resonate from various material and immaterial sources in the broadcast studio. What each of these additional characters signals for the 1924 listener is a set of spatial and temporal improbabilities. The presence of the *Märchentante* in the evening hours would seem peculiar, as she normally would appear as part of daytime programming for children; while the sudden, out-of-thin-air, appearance of a magician in the studio, upset about not being able to perform his sleight of hand magic tricks on the radio, only adds more fuel to the perplexity that ensues in the radio drama. In an attempt to rationally understand the storyteller's initial intrusion into the live broadcast and her desire to tell a fairy tale at this hour of the evening, the artistic director, Hans Flesch, tries to calmly figure out the situation in order to reestablish order and continue the planned programming. But the broadcast's deterioration has already been triggered and only worsens with the mysterious surfacing of the magician, who makes his presence known amid the tumult and confusion through a clear and distinct, though unearthly sounding, voice, which is offset by the sounds of a vaudevillian-style whistle and a single drum beat: "Everyone do whatever comes to mind! The station has gone crazy."[71] What ensues is a jumble of jump-cuts from the mainstays of the early radio's offerings (instrumental concerts, operatic music, economic news, story hour, mailbox), beginning with the fairytale that the storyteller had been wanting to tell so desperately: "Once upon a time there was a radio subscriber who was content with everything offered to him by the broadcaster — that was a long time ago...."[72]

The self-reflexivity of the piece provides a rare voyeuristic opportunity for the audience, allowing them to be active accessories in the deconstruction of a broadcast, while also allowing the radio device itself to become an instrument in the creation of material for the radio medium. Since all radio programs in 1924 were broadcast live the possibility of such a disruption was always imminent but was always controlled by a very staid, very scripted approach to broadcast programming. The seeming spontaneity that Flesch plays with in bringing this piece to the air recaptures for the brief twenty minutes of its duration a sense of what pre-1923 radio transmission and reception must have sounded like before the radio became regulated as a centralized unidirectional broadcasting medium and standardized as a reception-only device. Both the storyteller's provocative prognosis and the magician's call to chaos offer alternatives that toy with this idea of keeping broadcast transmission and listener reception separate, that seek to upend the status quo of structured programming, and that spur on the continued artistic experimentation with the radio medium. Seeking revenge for not being able to ply his craft on the airwaves, the magician suggests an out-of-the-box approach:

> Why didn't you allow me to present my sleights of hand to the people over the broadcast transmitter; harmless, cheerful pieces of magic, which would have pleased them, I pleaded with you badly enough to believe me, when I said that radio listeners could become radio watchers by virtue of my power. You laughed at me! The people would have been able to see, yes, see doctor, all of these amusing things in their electronic tubes and in their detectors, in the same way that you see me standing here now. (To the microphone) Ladies and gentlemen, look firmly into your radio devices, into the filaments of your amplifier valves, on to the crystal of your detector — I will count to three — on three you will all see me....[73]

In a type of premonition of the televisual and through an eerily prescient treatment of the suggestive power of voice, the magician transforms the radio device into one capable of sonic illusions and audience participation via hypnotic vocalization. That the radio play *Zauberei auf dem Sender* teases out these types of innovations at such an early point in the medium's history, and that it does so within the framework of medial self-reflexivity, speaks to Hans Flesch's ability to discern new trends in the development of the medium, both conceptually and technically. Through his role as author/theorist of the piece, and his role as a character in the piece, he constructs a dialectic between establishing order through entertainment and promoting disorder through artistic innovation. In this sense, his only radio play draws out the radio medium's recent prehistory in its very deconstruction of a live broadcast. When it alludes to music originating from out of nowhere and the magician's powers of persuasion, it is speaking to government fears about unsanctioned use of the airwaves and the *Funkerspuk;* and at its core, when it thematizes the disruption of a broadcast, it is addressing legislative regulations setting limits on access to transmission and calling to mind issues of sound clarity and feedback distortion. In the end, both order and disorder win out. The evening continues with concert music in full swing, giving the subscribers and the government regulators their sanctioned entertainment; but at the same time Flesch advances his experimental ideas, developing a peculiarly radiophonic art form that plays with the long-held fascination with radio's ethereality, calls into question accepted notions of accuracy in program scheduling, and makes the technologies of transmission and reception the central players in artistic experimentation.

Friedrich Wilhelm Bischoff: *Hallo! Welle Erdball* (1928)

F. W. Bischoff served as director of the *Schlesische Funkstunde* (Silesian Radio Hour) in Breslau from 1929 to 1933. Together with Werner Milch he produced the radio drama *Hallo! Hier Welle Erdball: Eine Hörsymphonie,* which had its broadcast premiere on February 4, 1928. An experimental piece combining nursery rhyme poetry, allusions to sensational headline-style catastrophes, and satirical references to the increased capacity of the modern telecommunications landscape to unite remote locales and their newsworthiness, Bischoff and Milch's "aural symphony" helps to conceptualize an idea of a global listening practice, while it also experiments with new methods of archivization and delivery of individual sound elements and passages into the sound transmission process via prerecorded record albums and the use of film stock to capture sound in an editable and reusable format, and hence prompts one of the first uses of iteration within early German radio.

In fact, the example to be explored here is one iteration of this original broadcast and is called simply *Hallo! Welle Erdball* to distinguish it from the original. The only extant recording of the original broadcast from 1928, and perhaps the oldest surviving original German broadcast that exists on tape, it consists of two scenes — "Zeitablauf des Mannes K." (Routine of the Man K.)

and "Sensationen — Katastrophen" (Sensations — Catastrophes) — and a closing announcement, lasting a total of eighteen minutes, fifty-four seconds.[74] The catalog holdings of the Deutsches Rundfunkarchiv describe the relationship between the original and this version, broadcast in November 1929:

> With the radio drama "Hallo! Welle Erdball" we are dealing with a modified version of the radio drama "Hallo! Hier Welle Erdball!" recorded on stereophonic discs by Fritz Walter (Friedrich) Bischoff and Werner Milch; this "radio play symphony" premiered on February 4, 1928, in the Silesian Radio Hour, an audio recording of this broadcast version is not preserved.[75]

While there is some question about whether the first sequence on this audio recording belonged to Bischoff's original concept for the piece broadcast in February 1928, the nature of iteration and versioning introduced by this new technique of recording onto album, and archiving for later broadcast allowed for increased accuracy and sound quality, but it also made it possible that no two broadcasts of the piece would ever be exactly alike. When Reinhard Döhl, author, Germanist, and media studies professor, rightfully points out that the first sequence "Routine of the Man K." does not correspond to any existing text versions of the manuscript for Bischoff's full drama, he suggests that "it is a matter of a sequence from another production, perhaps not even one that treats Bischoff, which should still be investigated."[76] Yet there is another possible explanation that takes these new preproduction, archivization, and delivery methods into account. The closing commentary on the November 1929 broadcast recording makes it a point to focus on how the broadcast was delivered:

> You heard a scene from "Hallo! Welle Erdball" by F. W. Bischoff. It was reproduced with the help of four discs. The transition from one disc to another is supposed to proceed without any discernable breaks. The experiment was undertaken to establish if such a reproduction is an adequate replacement for an original radio drama.[77]

As Döhl also points out, this announcement indicates a moment of clear technical pride in the radio industry's ability to take advantage of these new methods in sound recording. But there is also a clear indication that this version of the broadcast was meant to test the process of seamless transitioning between the four recorded albums within the parameters of a live broadcast, in an effort to substitute recordings for live productions and allow for the eventual sharing of content between broadcast stations. In this experimental context, the technique of album transitioning is one step closer to an idea of mixing or sampling, and for an eventual uncoupling of the actual work of sound being broadcast from the text or script that represents it.

In addition to serving as a testing ground for recording sound onto stereophonic disc, Bischoff's 1928 radio drama also provided a focal point for experiments in sound production, which utilized new developments in film sound to produce a purely audio-based, i.e., image-free, film for transmission over the radio waves. Hans Tasiemka, a Weimar-era film and media critic, describes this new innovation: "It is thus a sound film without moving images, a photophonogram comprised of tone and sound."[78] This intermedial approach is the same used by Walter Ruttmann to create his 1930 film without images, *Weekend*. As we will recall from chapter 1, this highly successful audio piece interfaces Ruttmann's background as a filmmaker (montage editing techniques, innovative optical and animation work) with these new processes for recording aural components as light traces onto the edges of film stock. This optical sound recording procedure, developed by the Tri-Ergon Company, "relied on the use of a photo-electric cell to transduce mechanical sound vibrations into electrical waveforms and then convert the electrical waveforms into light waves. These light waves could then be optically recorded onto the edge of the film through a photographic process."[79]

In an essay dated 1931, but originating in 1928, Hans Flesch discusses the importance of the sound film — and by extension the stereophonic disc and the Stille-tape, which he alludes to in a footnote — for the production of radio dramas, seeing the process of sound recording allowed by each as acknowledging the mediatized aspects of communication that most radio play directors rarely take into account in their live broadcasts. The essay takes up some of the same threads from his earlier radio theoretical writings, mainly his continued assertion regarding the always-mediated nature of radio broadcasting. He writes:

> Today's radio drama director works too much in front of the microphone, and not enough from out of the microphone.... However, if he wants to create from out of the microphone, then there is a path that leads in this direction — activating a medium between artist and machine (the microphone), which makes the moral expression and the production of the artist with the machine appropriate. We believe that this medium is the sound film.... The primary characteristic of the machine is precision. If something artistic should emanate from a machine, then this primary feature must not be damaged. However, a radio drama, for instance, can never be performed with the types of precision demanded by the machine. This is possible when film is activated as intermediary, as it eliminates all contingencies, all disturbances, and all improvisations.... In the case of a radio drama recorded through this optical sound process, a shape can be created after playback through cutting, cross-fade(s), splicing, etc., which the director considers completely successful and then presents to listeners in the evening.[80]

Flesch couches his praise of this optical sound recording process in the enhanced abilities it offers the radio producer. Clearly issues of accuracy and precision are at the heart of Flesch's comments, but what accompanies them is a palette of new artistic possibilities for working with sound, which adopt and adapt a range of technical editing techniques from the film industry for purposes of radio. Tasiemka's more light-hearted piece about Bischoff's work also focuses on these borrowings from film, though he makes an important addition: "It is hoped that the National Radio Company will expand its radio drama archive using these methods as quickly as possible. It would also be beneficial, in good time, to think about the expansion of the archive with recent news reports. Bischoff has made the first step with this radio drama. Who will follow him?"[81] The archival function of this type of sound footage, be it cultural or journalistic in nature, increases the likelihood that a broadcast will not go unheard, while at the same time it decreases the production costs associated with live broadcasts. In addition, the creation of an audio archive prompts the extension of both a cultural memory and national memory through the radio producer's ability to draw connections to earlier events and provide moments of interacoustic referencing. It is in this arena of technical functionality and forward-thinking radio practice that Bischoff's aural drama demonstrates a level of experimental ingenuity, which also emerges in the performance of the piece through its engagement with issues of sensationalism and its suggestions for a critical listening practice.

Issues of sensationalism seem to go hand-in-hand with the emergence of new technologies, not only for the human catastrophes that result from the increase in dangerous potential housed in the speed and sharpness of their mechanisms, but also for the increased quickness with which these catastrophes were reaching the eyes and ears of the populace. That a disaster could occur halfway around the world and be reported on the next day on the radio waves certainly was an indication of progress, but it also was an indication of a growing mood of despair about the state of the world and led to discussions about increases in listener desensitization as the media of film and radio began to capitalize on sensational stories to sell their wares. As Döhl points out, the second sound excerpt from F. W. Bischoff's drama addresses what he refers to as "a mania for sensation"[82] that characterized the 1920s, but which should be pointed out, was not restricted to radio, but also played a central role in the media of photography, film, fiction, and newspaper journalism. At the core of this excerpt from Bischoff's drama are ironic depictions of the human predilection for extreme interest in another's failure, athletic prowess, or unfortunate accident followed immediately either by an equally extreme disinterest, or substitution of that initial interest by an event even more unfathomable than the last:

The day of sensations! The day of sensations!
Fred and Erna place first in the championship for the 66-hour dance.
Fred Groggi runs around the world in sixteen months, two days, three hours, twenty-one minutes, and seventeen and one half seconds.
The renowned coloratura singer Maria Polodi shoots her husband in the coatroom of the theatre and poisons herself with lipstick.
Sensations! Sensations!
The world consists of nothing, only of sensations!

The day of catastrophes! The day of catastrophes!
Immense earthquake in Japan! Two thousand people homeless!
A blizzard destroys the prosperous city Georgia in New Mexico!

At the bobsled championship in St. Moritz in an accident one,
    two, three, four, five, six, seven, ten heads crack apart.
Catastrophes! The world consists of catastrophes!
The world consists of nothing, only of catastrophes!
                    [00:08.25–00:09.46][83]

In the "Sensations — Catastrophes" sequence Bischoff illustrates the
nonsense of the world's rhythms, the headlines that demarcate the
pulse of a newly globalized media structure that overlooks in-depth
reportage and glosses over the possibility of connecting listeners vis-
à-vis the space of radio, and instead points only to gossip and news
as entertainment. Dieter Daniels points to Bischoff's radio drama
as both anticipating and coaxing a type of "global listening experience," through its invocation of news items from parts of the world
that propel the imaginations of the German listening public beyond
the routine of daily experience in the locales in which they reside.[84]
Daniels cites Bischoff's play, among others, as evidence for the heightened sense of "intoxication" that the radio medium provided its
listeners by permitting them access to a world outside their own. As
the final two sections of this sequence, Bischoff offers the following:

Stop! Stop! We don't understand each other!
We want life, you want poetry.
We abandon poetry, addicted, affectionate, and narrow.
We want, yes, we want truth, naked and stark!
There it is! — Where! — Here!
Help! — Hunger, hunger, hunger! — Mercy!
On behalf of the law: sentenced to death!

Change the channel! Change the channel!
Life exists in a thousand forms,
The truth is split into a thousand systems!
What should we do?
Change the channel!
You should change the channel, then you'll be part of the game.
One, two, three, the "Plumpsack" goes round.
                    [00:17.24–00:18.14][85]

Here two groups of listeners are at odds over what type of content the radio should broadcast: on the one hand the cold, hard realities of life, on the other the lulling metrics of poetry. As remedy, as antidote for this out-of-control spiral that listeners find themselves simultaneously attracted to and repulsed by, Bischoff recommends that they begin turning their radio dials to actively search out and engage with the system of truth they find most beneficial to them. In what might be described as a type of early resistance to the marketing ploys of entertainment radio, Bischoff orders the listeners to change the channel, to illustrate through their radio dials that they will no longer listen to what is being parceled out as content over the radio waves, and to demonstrate that they are still in control of the reception side of the broadcast. The confusion of the growing frequency jungle described by Daniels earlier in relation to transmission, spelled cacophony, disorientation, and overstimulation for many listeners on the reception side, and F. W. Bischoff's blend and montage of many voices in conversational verse in *Hallo! Welle Erdball* captures the modernist mood of fragmentation and incompletion that both accompanied and was itself produced and reproduced by new technologies like the radio.

Friedrich Wolf: *S.O.S. . . . rao rao . . . Foyn. "Krassin" rettet "Italia"* (1929)

Fast forward five years from the October 24, 1924, broadcast of Hans Flesch's radio play to November 8, 1929, when German author, dramatist, agitprop theater director, doctor, and script writer Friedrich Wolf (1888–1953) presented his *Hörspiel* — *S.O.S. . . . rao rao . . . Foyn. "Krassin" rettet "Italia"* — to a Berlin radio audience.[86] Ripped from the headlines, the sixty-four-minute drama is a progressive reenactment of events that took place in the spring of 1928 involving an Italian airship expedition to the North Pole led by General Umberto Nobile. It crashed on its return journey just north of the Norwegian island of Spitsbergen on May 25, 1928, leaving nine of the fifteen crew members stranded on an ice floe in the middle of the Arctic Ocean, while the other six were caught in the still-mobile gondola and never heard from again. An international rescue operation was begun after a Russian shortwave radio operator picked up an S.O.S. call from the group on June 2, 1928. Due to troubles in pinpointing the group's exact location this rescue effort lasted until mid-July of that year, when the men were rescued by the Soviet ice-breaker *Krassin* on June 12. Wolf's drama builds on Hans Flesch's earlier use of medial self-reflexivity through a celebration of the radio medium as a central instrument in the rescue efforts:

> It was not the impulse of a superman, not the "ethos" of a religious or civil mind that made this act of rescue possible, but rather the technologically quickened solidarity of the people. This solidarity formed a circle around this living example from the solitary radio amateur on the Murman coast, to the large broadcasting station in Rome, to the red tent of the ice floe and the pilot Tschuchnowski. It is a matter of fact that without delaying an action a completely different political system assisted an opposing political system in a fraternal manner. And this help was only possible by way of the most modern of communications media: through the radio! [00:01.51–00:02.51][87]

The notion of a "technologically quickened solidarity," which Wolf underscores here, highlights the immediacy of the radio and recalls the power of the solitary amateur radio operator surfing the airwaves for sounds from afar. In fact, the heart of the drama turns around a very nuanced mode of experimentation with how listener and broadcaster perceptions about radio communication have changed over the course of the six years since the inception of German entertainment radio. As the play begins, listeners settled into the evening comfort of their living rooms were confronted with the music of German-Jewish composer Walter Goehr, a frenzied and fantastical lead-in indicating unsettledness, shock, and deviousness. When coupled with the accuracy and authority of the announcer's description of the drama to be heard, Wolf's piece provides the edge-of-one's-chair authenticity that the tragedy of the airship *Italia* would still evoke in the minds and hearts of the radio listener one year following the actual events. After this lead-in to the piece, the drama continues with a litany of dispatches from remote radio stations across the globe seeking information about the whereabouts of the expedition. Beginning with the transmission station in Rome and continuing via Leningrad and New York and ending with the *Italia* expedition supply ship *Città di Milano,* these dispatches each commence with an announcement of the specific station's frequency number followed by a request for radio silence. Incidentally, the *Città di Milano,* a decommissioned

German ship paid as part of World War I reparations to the Italians, at one time assisted in laying transatlantic network cabling for the transmission of undersea communications, thus adding one additional layer of medial history to Wolf's 1929 radio drama. The announcements by the Rome broadcaster affect a pleading sense of urgency, while those from Leningrad and New York prefigure less concern, evidenced in each of these stations' interruptions of their regular evening programs of dance music to continue the service announcement begun by the Rome broadcaster. As the location of the transmission station gets proximally closer to the actual physical location of the stranded crew, the tone of the message becomes more acute, as signaled by the differences in the announcements made by New York and those by Leningrad and the supply ship. In one sense, the message being broadcast from the origin station in Rome requires the reception and retransmission of the message from other broadcast stations to be able to extend beyond its frequency range. Otherwise, it would be almost impossible to even think that the origin message would reach the stranded *Italia* crew in its remote geographical location in the Arctic. For that matter, without the sense of solidarity that must have existed among broadcast transmission stations regardless of nationality, it would have been equally impossible to ascertain whether the origin message had been received by the crew, or if they had sent a message back. The radio play calls attention to this fact through its incorporation of an amateur radio operator, whose pivotal role in the location of the *Italia* crew points to the former functionality of the radio device in the bidirectionality of communication. Where a pre-1923 amateur operator would have been able to both transmit and receive signals and sounds via his self-manufactured radio device, now this lonely amateur operator in a remote village on the Murman coast can only receive the S.O.S. calls of the crew stranded on the ice floe. Instead of being able to transmit back to the *Italia* crew from his shortwave radio that their calls have been heard, he can only write down what he has heard and telephone the authorities in Moscow. The "technologically quickened solidarity" has thus also become a technologically stultified one, since the radio's original transmission and reception capabilities have been downgraded.

While the radio served as a tool in the expedition's location, it also performed as a member of the rescue team and as a site where a dramatized version of these recent events could unfold. As an event that moved quickly from the realm of reportage to the realm of performance, the *Italia* tragedy contained all of the sensational elements that made for both an interesting news story and a compelling drama. While the world listened with bated breath in the spring of 1928, first for reports of the group's location, and then for news of the rescue efforts some six weeks later, Wolf's 1929 dramatization separates out, zeroes in on, and reproduces aspects of these events that seek to honor the decidedly Soviet role in the location and ultimate rescue of the group and promote a mediatized notion of world solidarity from the solitude and isolation of the men stuck on the ice, the amateur radio operator resigned to his position in his remote village, and the world's audiences tuning in on their radiosets in the isolation and bourgeois safety of their living rooms. As the first KPD member to be broadcast by the Berlin *Funk-Stunde,* this mythologization of the Soviet Union via the radio also opens up questions about the principles of nonpartisanship that guided the radio medium's creation prior to 1923.[88] Beyond its obvious political undertones, however, Friedrich Wolf's radio play builds upon Flesch's request for an art form that takes both the technical and functional sides of the radio device into account. Like Bischoff's drama, it plays with the notion of immediacy, choosing to focus on an event at the forefront of the listener's mind, but unlike the irony of Bischoff's piece, Wolf adapts the sensationalism of a tragedy averted into an event of nationalistic and world pride that allowed for a global, radio-centered, experience and a large-scale sigh of relief.

In 1930, six years following the broadcast of his only experimental creative piece and one year into his tenure as the director of the *Funk-Stunde* in Berlin, Hans Flesch commented:

> For the radio, this wonderful synthesis of technology and art on the route of transmission, the sentence applies: In the beginning was the experiment. Not limited to just the technical side, beyond the authenticity of physical forms, and the mechanical grouping receiver–transmitter–amplifier–microphone, the experimental has also moved into the pleasure of the attempt, and the presentation of this. Not only should the devices of transmission be reformed, but also the content to be transmitted; programming cannot be accomplished on the

top of one's desk. A bit of experience can help the program director anticipate this or that, however, in the same way that technology requires that the positioning of the orchestra, the chorus, or the soloist in front of the microphone not be schematically determined, but rather should be always newly tested, then unless new options are not constantly tested broadcast programming must likewise ossify.[89]

Clearly experimentation was the practice and the guiding principle that assisted Flesch in navigating between the provision of light entertainment popular among listeners and the need to develop the medium both artistically and technologically beyond mere reproduction. And it was an opinion taken up by several of his compatriots at the time, who were themselves actively pursuing the development of new types of content and urging new technical developments in their own positions as radio program directors, or were being commissioned by Flesch himself to produce innovative programming for the Berlin-based *Funk-Stunde*.

The "modern to the core" attitude of Hans Flesch, the technical innovation and ironic critiques of F. W. Bischoff, and the unveiled sociopolitical commentary of Friedrich Wolf are aspects that helped set these three radio producers and directors apart from their mainstream counterparts. But they are also aspects that would single them out for increased pressure from the government as the golden age of the 1920s transitioned into the sobering first years of the 1930s with the political maneuverings and street-level harassment of the National Socialists. The implementation of the November 1932 radio reforms in January 1933, spelled the beginnings of a National Socialist *Gleichschaltung* in the structures of power in German radio, and led to the ultimate dismissal (August 1932) and arrest of Hans Flesch (August 1933), the arrest and ensuing inner emigration of F. W. Bischoff, and the political exile of Friedrich Wolf, first to Austria, Switzerland, and France and then eventually to the Soviet Union.[90] In a speech titled "Schluss mit dem Korruptionsskandal im deutschen Rundfunk" (An End to the Corruption Scandal in the German Radio) delivered at the Berlin Sportpalast and broadcast on August 12, 1933, Eugen Hadamovsky, National Programming Director for German radio in the early years of the Third Reich, labeled their innovative contributions to the radio medium as "perversities":

> My comrades! With the incidents that have played out recently within the studios and around and through the radio itself, has ended the democratic era of the radio. And at the same time the era of the "radio Lilliputians" has also ended; those men who knew and saw only one horizon for the radio, namely, the horizon of their own personal welfare, and the horizon within the confines of their wallets. Ten years of systematized radio has brought us ten years of fossilized liberalism, ten years of spiritless, yet seemingly spirited perversities. . . . In short, for us, the radio is the sanctuary of our nation, and it should become the brown house of German spirit![91]

Along with their own physical removal from the world of radio went their dedication to innovation and experimentation with the radio medium, their ideas about the role and function of the radio within the sociocultural fabric of daily life, and their technical ingenuity in positioning the radio alongside the media of film, photography, and gramophone within the emergent media landscape in Weimar. With them also went countless others associated with the medium of radio, among them Bertolt Brecht, who will be a focus of the next chapter. Yet rather than being lost forever to exile, disappearance, or National Socialist rhetoric, their contributions to German cultural radio practice and in the arena of media theoretical discourse continue to influence radio practices today.

THREE

Don't Touch That Dial

Transmitting Modes of Experimentation from Weimar to Postwar West Germany

You small box, which I carried fleeing
So that its lamps wouldn't break on me as well
With care from house to ship, from ship to train
So my enemies could continue to speak to me

At my bedside and to my anguish
The last thing at night, the first in the morning
About their triumphs and my troubles:
Promise me not to fall silent all at once!
— Bertolt Brecht, "On the Small Radio"

The radio performs on several levels. Bertolt Brecht's panegyric to the radio casts one possible network of performances within the narrative framework of exile, positioning it as a unilateral conduit between the spectacular, triumphant hypernationalism of the National Socialists and the internalized, yet still very public, transitory space of his own forced exile.[1] The unlikely mobility of the radio not only upsets its traditional focal point in the security of the family living room by virtue of its own flight from the household, but also calls attention to its gossamer fragility when juxtaposed against the commanding voices of propaganda. The poem's sense of play between broadcast control, security, and national identity, on the one hand, and broadcast inaccessibility, vulnerability, and alterity, on the other, focuses attention on the radio as a site for profound cultural networking and mediation. At the same time that the radio operates in its established role as a broadcast medium, it also embodies trends in political and social upheaval, problematizes ideas about national identity, and helps to destabilize notions of space. While Brecht's poem historicizes the complex of events surrounding his forced political exile from National Socialist Germany, it also marks a volatile transition in radio technique, from one of intense artistic experimentation and theoretical musings to one of extreme state control, and signifies Brecht's move from active radio producer to active radio listener.

Brecht's loss of experimental possibility with the radio, when coupled with the twelve years of National Socialist domination of the country's airwaves, prompts questions not only about the disruption of Brecht's theories and experiments for the radio medium, but also about the revisions for radio in 1950s West Germany. This chapter looks at the practices of artistic radio experimentation begun in the early days of radio in the Weimar Republic and elucidated by Brecht in a five-essay series on radio theory. It also investigates the radio genre designs of Alfred Andersch in the immediate postwar era (1947–53), while also looking at a sequence of short radio lessons on cultural consumerism Andersch produced in 1959.[2] Both Brecht's and Andersch's work with the radio offset the period of National Socialist radio practice. While Brecht, in the years prior to World War II, recognized the collaborative and interactive potential of the radio medium and thus sought to push for developments within both the technical and artistic/cultural spheres of radio, Andersch attempted to revive and develop Brecht's ideas for radio following the twelve-year period of National Socialist stagnation. Andersch positions the broadcast listener as the central point of radio interactivity, as a point of information activation where radio transmission transforms the listener at the moment of radio reception into a producer, and in the process also transforms the radio from a device of passive transmission and reception to one of networked collaboration and interactivity. Yet, in practice, both Brecht's insights and Andersch's designs seem to fall on deaf ears, not for a lack of trying to change radio, but rather for the complexity of economic, political, and cultural regulation that was built up around radio within each of the sociopolitical climates it endured, namely, Weimar Republic democracy, National Socialist dictatorship, and postwar capitalism.

Brecht's poem to the radio was written in 1940 in the midst of his forced exile from Germany and some eight years after the publication of his last theoretical essay on radio. The poem, thus, marks both a movement away and a movement toward—away from the radio as a creative collaborative medium and toward the radio as a unilateral communication device; away from the experimental and toward the hegemonic. It is navigating the fine balance between maintaining the economic viability of the radio as medium (i.e., building a listener base, creating advertising revenue), and supporting artist access to the field of sound technologies offered by the radio as device, which characterizes the tone and thrust of Brecht's earliest radio theory pieces. The series of theoretical essays and fragments on radio broadcasting, which Brecht wrote and, in part, published between 1926 and1932, situates the new communications medium in Germany within the same contentious struggle, lauding and developing it as an experimental medium, while condemning the bourgeois tendency to see it only as a device of possibility. Brecht comments on this in a 1927 unpublished manuscript "Radio—An Antediluvian Invention":

> The bourgeoisie judges them [cities] only according to the opportunities it naturally can derive from them. Thus the enormous overrating of all things and systems which promise "possibilities." No one bothers with results. They just stick to the possibilities. The results of the radio are shameful, its possibilities are "boundless." Hence, the radio is a "good thing." It is a very bad thing.[3]

Brecht's criticism of bourgeois opportunism underscores a cycle of idea depletion, which transforms innovative possibilities into empty promises and repetitions. In Brechtian parlance the bourgeois idea of possibility does not engage the levels of innovation in order to develop them productively, but instead seeks to replicate already existing models of representation and, in the process, remove the prospect of other possibilities. In the case of the radio, Brecht fears that the excitement expressed over the possibility of hearing "a Viennese waltz and a kitchen recipe"[4] will ultimately allow the radio to be forgotten, that the bourgeois push to explore the radio's possibilities will drive it backward to obsolescence. Rather than supporting artistic or literary experimentation with the radio medium, this economy of regressive possibility instead hinders artistic access by promoting broadcasts, which are themselves reproductions of work for other media (concerts, theater productions, recipes). When Brecht writes, "I strongly wish that after their invention of the radio the bourgeoisie would make a further invention that enables us to fix for all time what the radio communicates,"[5] he is demanding nothing less than the development of a system of communication that elides the repetitive recycling of broadcast content offered in the bourgeois scheme of radio production and promotes instead innovative practices with the devices responsible for radio broadcast. In his December 1927 "Suggestions for the Director of Radio Broadcasting" he recommends, "You [the radio director] must build a studio. Without experiments it is simply not possible to assess fully your apparatuses or what is made for them."[6] While clearly illustrating the value of the experimental, this statement also demonstrates both the need for artistic access to the sound technologies of radio, as represented in the space of the studio, and the need for assessment of the broadcast productions and of the technology itself. Brecht's recommendation echoes that of Kurt Weill, a longtime associate, who comments on the important collaborative development of an experimental radio station at the Berlin School of Music in his 1927 essay "On the Possibilities of an Experimental Radio Station":

> The first and most distinguished task that an experimental radio station must approach consists in adjusting the basic attitude toward the radio to another level. The radio requires its own people; it must be more than just a welcome auxiliary income for otherwise interested artists; it can mature into its own independent branch of the arts if every activity in the studio meets the requirements [and explores] the possibilities of the microphone.[7]

Weill's commentary is significant for two reasons. First, it points to early trends in radio production as encompassing broadcasts developed by artists not conversant with the technology and materiality of the radio and makes a case for a radiophonic art that arises out of radio-specific conditions. Second, Weill's statement points to the importance of the studio microphone as the piece of technology central to radio broadcast and the creation of radiophonic art. This focus on the studio microphone suggests not only the fixed, immovable nature of early radio broadcast, but also that these early ideas of radio could not yet determine radio as something beyond speaking or performing into a microphone. Yet perhaps it is this very simplicity of having access to a microphone that would revolutionize radio, transforming it from a medium of pure substitution into a medium of communication, as Brecht suggests in his oft-cited essay "The Radio as a Communications Apparatus" (1932). For Brecht, the radio's function as a substitute for the stage, for the orchestra pit, for newsprint, and for the lectern builds a submissive listener base and encourages a passive reception of each of these media by removing the physical cues and community atmosphere implicit within each of them. Gone are the bodily and visual performance of stage and opera, the stirring sonic vibrations of the orchestral concert, the inkiness of the newspaper, and the sense of intellectual community of the public lecture. Instead, Brecht desires a radio functionality that builds community and collaborative practice, seeing within the materiality of the radio the possibility for building a network of listener-practitioners, a network in which "[the *technology*] must work according to the principle that the audience is not only to *be instructed* but also must instruct" (original emphasis).[8] Brecht elucidates this idea of a listener-practitioner network further in this same radio-theoretical essay:

> Radio must be transformed from a distribution apparatus into a communications apparatus. The radio could be the finest possible communications apparatus in public life, a vast system of channels. That is, it could be so if it understood how to receive as well as transmit, how to let the listener speak as well as hear, how to bring him into a network instead of isolating him. Following this principle the radio should step out of the supply business and organize its listeners as suppliers.[9]

Here we come to the heart of Brecht's musings on radio, and the modus operandi for his own experimental radio *Lehrstücke* (learning plays), produced in the late 1920s prior to his exile.[10] The move from distribution to communication, which Brecht posits, points to several issues and assumptions. Technically, Brecht's position requires an alteration in the radio device to allow it to function for both transmission and reception, while, socially, it seeks to build communities of information literate individuals capable of participating actively in the topical concerns of the day. In this applied description of his radio theory, Brecht adopts an early equivalent to an "open source" approach to the implementation of radio technology, in terms of both access and dissemination of information. The open source definition, as it is understood in the early twenty-first century in relation to software, is a multifaceted effort to provide access to both programming source code and to promote nonproprietary, interface-neutral distributions of software.[11] Brecht's designs for early radio (as technology and as medium) put forward similar specifications through the creation of both a technologically unrestricted radio and a listener-participant community, whose point of activation is based in the currency of sound, what Jonathan Sterne refers to as mediate auscultation.[12] In both instances, Brecht's theory relies on the assumptions that the radio community would see the benefits of technically retooling the radio device, and that the vast network of newly activated listener-practitioners would be capable of self-regulating against a cacophony of information. With respect to the network of listener-practitioners, Sterne's sense of the medical concept of mediate auscultation opens up additional avenues of inquiry into the epistemological power of sound. As participants in Brecht's network of channels, radio listeners would be both contributors to and consumers of sound-based information, requiring both a set of information literacy skills to filter, vet, and use the received aural information and a set of information technology skills to gather, create, and distribute their own radio-based productions. The radio becomes, then, a device that permits both the transmission and reception of knowledge, a device that mediates auscultation. In regards to the technical aspects of Brecht's theory, Friedrich Kittler, a contemporary German media theorist, has been quick to point out that Brecht's utopian designs fail to consider changes in German telecommunication laws from 1923:

> Brecht's radio theory culminated in the claim of transforming the radio from a distribution apparatus into a communications apparatus. Strange that Brecht called for a revolution in radio technology without also mentioning the counter-revolution nine years earlier. That the telecommunication laws of 1923 had converted the communications apparatus into a distribution apparatus had never occurred to him—to say nothing of state security as the reason for this measure.[13]

Kittler's October 1988 presentation "Artillery Waves" approaches Brecht's radio theory from a techno-historical or media ecological perspective, establishing a trajectory between the radio's arrival in the trenches and on the battlefields of World War I, the German state's regulation of the radio device in 1923, and Brecht's "open source" designs for the radio medium in 1932. Among this collection of short essays are Brecht's comments on his radio production *Der Ozeanflug: Radiolehrstück für Knaben und Mädchen* (Ocean Flight: Didactic Play for Boys and Girls).[14] The play itself details in allegorical form the transatlantic flight of Charles Lindbergh, combining music and sound effects with inner monologues by the pilot and by nature in the form of fog, a snowstorm, and fatigue. In this fashion the production locates the flight as a battle of technology against nature and the primitive. The collaborative efforts of the pilot and the machine in attaining their goal are reflected in Brecht's format ideas for the actual broadcast of the play:

> The other, *pedagogical* part (the Lindbergh role) is the text for the exercise: the participant listens to the one part [songs of the elements, the choruses, water and motor noises] and speaks the other part. In this way a collaboration develops between apparatus and participant in which accuracy is more important than expression. The participants speak and sing the text mechanically; they pause at the end of each line of verse; they read along mechanically as they listen to the text.... *The Flight of the Lindberghs* is not intended to be of use to the present-day radio but to *change* it. The increasing concentration of mechanical means and the increasingly specialized education — trends that should be accelerated — call for a kind of *rebellion* by the listener, for his mobilization and redeployment as producer.[15]

Brecht's prescriptive positions the listener into an interactive role with the radio apparatus, whereby the listener takes on the part of the pilot opposite a radio orchestra outfitted with noisemakers, instruments, and singers. His focus on exactitude rather than expression in the collaboration between the trainee and the apparatus provides the at-home listener an opportunity to better understand their role as deskilled, exchangeable labor. The performance of this radio experiment was meant to challenge the standard techniques of the radio to transform from procedures of pure reproduction to moments of collaborative production, in which the listeners become conscious of their passive, automated lives and are animated into action to change them, to become producers themselves, and to overthrow the processes of rationalization and specialization, which automate and deskill the workplace. But the production also likely capitalized on the mood of sensationalism and excitement palpable in Berlin, when a second American plane, just days after Lindbergh's landing in Paris in June 1927, would land at Tempelhof in Berlin. This event, which also marked one of radio's first live transmissions, was described by Berlin radio director Alfred Braun: "The excitement in the city was unparalleled.... Evening was upon us — and suddenly Berliners swarmed from all sides onto the Tempelhof landing field — according to the press, more than 100,000."[16]

Kittler's discussion of Brecht's radio theory culminates with a fairly quick commentary on *Ocean Flight* that foregrounds Brecht's celebration of Lindbergh's transatlantic flight, while also suggesting that Brecht did not take the opportunity to put his theories of the radio as communications apparatus into practice:

> Brecht's radio play *Ocean Flight* of 1929 celebrated everything possible in Lindbergh's first transatlantic flight — the airplane, the noise of the motors, the noise level, or the resistance to the elements of wind and water, but above all else, of course, the assistance of the nameless working class, without whom the engine would never have started.... In Brecht's *Ocean Flight* the communications apparatus simply did not appear as the basis of the entire flight experiment. It is no wonder that the dreamed for transformation from a distribution device to a communications device by Brecht's radio play had to fail. Brecht's horrible impression that the radio was an inconceivably old device, which would fall into forgetfulness, summarized brilliantly his own fossilized dramatization of a world war technology [the airplane].[17]

Kittler's critique of *Ocean Flight* wants to unsettle Brecht's theoretical musings on radio by pointing to his own practical engagement with radio production as a failed attempt to bring lasting change to radio. This criticism is lodged within an approach to technology that perceives the technical as a reserve, as an archaeological cache that maintains loyalty to its roots in the military-industrial complex. When Brecht claims, "*By means of constant, never-ending suggestions about better applications of the apparatuses in the interest of the many,* we must shake up the social basis of these apparatuses and discredit their application in the interest of the few" (original emphasis),[18] then Kittler's response is to demonstrate irrevocably the intricate connections between the radio and its military past. When Brecht celebrates Lindbergh's airplane in combination with survival against the natural elements, and the participation of the working class in the achievement of such an incredible technological undertaking, Kittler takes him to task for missing the relationship between the airplane and warfare. Yet it is exactly in the retooling of the radio that Brecht also seeks to retool this image of the airplane as a mechanism of war. Rather than seeing Brecht's theoretical claim as an evolution of the radio as technical device, and as a reorganization of the radio as artistic medium, which I believe is Brecht's intent, Kittler does not appear to make a distinction between the radio's function as device and the radio's function as medium, and instead sees the two as irretrievably linked to the radio's roots in warfare communication and warfare entertainment. These insights into the connection between radio and warfare also help form a transitional bridge between Brecht's artistic experimentation with radio in his *Lehrstücke,* particularly *Ocean Flight,* and the National Socialist philosophical approach to and use of radio from 1933 to 1945.

The physicality and material fragility of the small radio honored in Brecht's early 1940s poem, the acoustical mode of transportation Brecht carried with him into exile, stand in stark contrast to the hegemonic role radio had come to play in the National Socialist regime. Yet it is this very vulnerable device that permits Brecht to listen in on, to auscultate, the actions, words, and thoughts of his enemies back in Germany. Marshall McLuhan's allusion to the poem in his 1964 study *Understanding Media: The Extensions of Man* highlights what he sees as connections between radio's monopolistic effects as described by Paul Lazarsfeld, and its powers of enchantment — its "tribal magic" and entrancing "web of kinship" — with the rise of fascism.[19] In this instance McLuhan's citation of Brecht's poem is meant to provide an example of this enchantment, a moment in verse that ritualizes the radio device and casts it in terms of involvement as a medium that transports the listener from the crowded public sphere into a "private world." McLuhan, calling the radio a medium of "electronic implosion," claims:

> Radio affects most people intimately, person-to-person, offering a world of unspoken communication between writer-speaker and the listener. That is the immediate aspect of radio. A private experience. The subliminal depths of radio are charged with the resonating echoes of tribal horns and antique

drums. This is inherent in the very nature of this medium, with its power to turn the psyche and society into a single echo chamber. The resonating dimension of radio is unheeded by script writers, with few exceptions. The famous Orson Welles broadcast about the invasion from Mars was a simple demonstration of the all-inclusive, completely involving scope of the auditory image of radio. It was Hitler who gave radio the Orson Welles treatment for *real* (original emphasis).[20]

Invoking Orson Welles's 1938 radio adaptation and broadcast of H. G. Wells's science fiction novel *The War of the Worlds*, McLuhan draws out the intricate relationships caught up within National Socialist radio practice, German nationalism, and the dynamics of public involvement and private enchantment. Yet while Brecht's poem details his move into a private world of forced political exile, it should also be read within the context of his radio theoretical essays, which lends the poem the sense of lamentation Brecht most likely experienced when this forced exile also forced him to give up producing for the radio and become a solitary listener. What is missing in McLuhan's string of associations linking radio, tribalism, and the rise of fascism within the eight lines of this poem is an understanding of Brecht's theoretical and practical experimentation with the radio prior to the National Socialist takeover in Germany. Following McLuhan, Brecht's poem reveals the private listening experience that radio had become subsequent to his forced exile, and illustrates, as well, the intense involvement in Germany's public sphere that this private listening affords. Following Brecht's own theories of radio production, the poem also marks this move from radio producer to radio listener, but with the added factor of active collaboration in the listening experience. The significance of radio silence in the last line of the poem captures this sense of active listening. One has to wonder how Brecht would have employed the radio in exile, had his earlier theoretical musings about returning the radio to its roots as both a transmission and reception device been put into practice.

It is ironic that just one year following the publication of Brecht's last theoretical essay on radio, "The Radio as a Communications Apparatus" in July 1932, Joseph Goebbels, the Nazi propaganda minister, delivered a speech on August 18, 1933, which charted the new territories and lines of demarcation for Germany's media landscape. "The Radio as the Eighth Great Power," as this speech is known, was delivered at the opening of a radio exhibition and coincided with the National Socialist release of the *Volksempfänger*, or people's receiver, an inexpensive radio receiver that helped boost the number of households with radios from 4.1 million in May 1932 to 12.5 million by the same time in 1939.[21] Brecht's repositioning, both in terms of his exile and in terms of his move from radio production to radio listening, is the direct result of the new National Socialist agenda for radio, which also prompted the arrest and imprisonment of Hans Flesch, Alfred Braun, Kurt Magnus, Hans Bredow, and F. W. Bischoff, among others, in August 1933 for their innovations with the radio medium and their "oppositional character."[22] In fact, we have to look to November 1932 for initial evidence of a National Socialist radio policy beginning to take shape through a reorganization of the radio. These 1932 "Directives for the Reorganization of the Radio" (Richtlinien für die Neuordnung des Rundfunks) focused on returning the airwaves to delivering responsible, populist content that supported the ideals of homeland and family life, while reminding the radio directors and producers of the incredible responsibility they possessed:

1. The radio contributes to the life-tasks of the German nation. The natural ordering of people into home and family, profession and state should be supported and strengthened through the radio.

2. The German radio protects a Christian ethos and civilization as well as the respect for the honest beliefs of others. Those things that debase Christianity or endanger the customs and culture of the German Volk are to be banned from radio.

3. The radio serves all Germans inside and outside of the national boundaries. It connects ethnic Germans with the nation and allows domestic listeners to participate in the lives and fate of ethnic Germans elsewhere. The fostering of national identity is a duty of the German radio.

4. The radio participates in the great challenge of educating Germans as national citizens and of forming and strengthening the national thoughts and needs of the listeners.

Der Volksempfänger VE 301 W. Courtesy of Deutsches Rundfunkarchiv, Frankfurt am Main.

5. The work of the radio is to pay attention to and is to increase those virtues and products worthy of honor from the history of the German people and the German nation.

6. It is the task of all broadcast stations to nurture the mutuality of community of the German Volk. Thus, the regional stations act on the regional distinctions of their transmission areas and also communicate the rich traditions of the German ethnic groups and countryside.[23]

Ushered in by Chancellor Franz von Papen shortly after the elections of November 6, 1932, as a response to a perceived imbalance of power between the nine regional stations and the German government in terms of political partisanship and privileging of contemporary cultural trends, these directives demonstrate a fairly clear affinity with National Socialist rhetoric through their focus on nurturing the cultural, moral and religious aspects of their listeners' lives within a framework of traditional and racially sound values.

In his August 1933 speech, Goebbels echoes many of these directives, and sets out the role and position that the radio would take within the National Socialist agenda, stating, "We want a radio that accompanies the people, a radio that works for the people, a radio that serves as an intermediary between the government and the nation, a radio that traverses boundaries to give the world a reflection of our character, our life, and our work."[24] This section of the address packages the radio in a veiled rhetoric of both state control and *völkisch* hypernationalism. The radio is described here as a companion and tool for the German people, as a mediation mechanism between the Nazi government and the people, and as a device that would announce, honor, and propagate the true nature and future of the German people to the world. In another portion of the speech, Goebbels clarifies the types of broadcast the new radio would take on and the ways in which the radio would support Nazi ideology:

> We do not intend to use the radio only for our Party programs. We want room for entertainment, popular arts, games, jokes and music. But everything should have an internal relationship to our day. Everything should include the theme of our great reconstructive work, or at least not stand in its way. Above all it is necessary to clearly centralize all radio activities, to place spiritual tasks

ahead of technical ones, to introduce the leadership principle, to provide a clear worldview, and to present this worldview in flexible ways.[25]

Goebbels's statements about radio are relevant for a couple of reasons. First, they clearly demonstrate that the radio medium should tightly interweave Nazi policies of restructuring with activities that seek to regenerate the national German spirit. The combination of broadcasting light entertainment, games, and jokes while also demonstrating a commitment to the internal, spiritual ideals of the National Socialist zeitgeist put into motion many of the precepts of Weimar's conservative revolution. According to Jeffrey Herf, these conservative revolutionaries wanted to revive German *Innerlichkeit* (inwardness) while still embracing technology, and believed that "Germany could be both technologically-advanced and true to its soul."[26] The reconciliation of technology with the soul of the German nation would offset and remedy "the process of degeneration they [the conservative revolutionaries] felt was threatening the nation's body and soul" in the form of modernity.[27] Following this thread, Goebbels's intentions for the radio seek to simultaneously fold inward, isolate, and thereby nurture a mythic notion of German identity, while also forwarding policies of geographical expansionism, which are themselves based in these same ideas of German-ness. A studied look through the Deutsches Rundfunkarchiv catalogue of radio plays broadcast between 1928 and 1945 reveals a predilection for productions decidedly traditional, nationalistic and heroic: adaptations of Renaissance and classical German drama (Hans Sachs, Schiller, Goethe), memorials to World War I battles, allegorical plays in honor of work and fate, and dialect plays in Low German — all productions meant to fortify listeners' resolve and nurture a sense of nationalistic, identity.[28] That the radio should play the role of companion for its listening audience is interesting when taken in light of Goebbels's statements from this 1933 speech that point to administrative structures, the centralization of radio around the leadership principle, and a clear hinting at the consequences of what would happen if a station, broadcast, or producer were to "stand in its way [the party's reconstructive work]."

The structures of passive listening produced by this centralization around the leadership principle were paramount for the radio being transformed into the mouthpiece of the Nazi party. In his 1992 essay "Soundplay" Mark E. Cory comments: "Brecht was very clear on the dangers of passive listening, "concert" listening, which he felt could lead to a mind-numbing identification with a heroic individual."[29] Friedrich Kittler, in his 1986 volume *Gramophone, Film, Typewriter,* also refers to the power of sound technologies to enchant or lull the listener into a space of detachment, or intense involvement. Echoing Marshall McLuhan, Kittler points to the 1902 trademark of Berliner's gramophone company, which depicts a small dog with his ears cocked at the bell-mouth of a phonograph listening intently. The caption — "Die Stimme seines Herrn" (The voice of his master) — completes the trademark, and suggests the dog's obedience and loyalty to his master's broadcast voice.[30] The move made by McLuhan from Orson Welles's newscast simulation of the Martian invasion to Hitler's commanding voice over the airwaves parallels the move intimated by Kittler from the loyal and obedient dog listening to its master's recorded voice to household audiences on both sides of the Atlantic listening to Hitler's stadium-orchestrated speeches and Roosevelt's fireside chats.

In his very intriguing study of radio listening practices in the community of Hildesheim from 1923 to 1953, Andrew Stuart Bergerson traces what he terms convivial listening modes during the Weimar Republic years, and the subsequent association with "Nazi herrschaft [hegemony]" — what listening to the radio meant once the Nazis took power. Bergerson sites this transition within changes to the local public sphere: "It makes sense that Hildesheimers associated listening to the radio with Nazi propaganda, but not because of an increased volume of news or speeches. Rather, listening to *both* news *and* music lost its innocence during the Third Reich. Listening to the radio shifted from a normal aspect of everyday conviviality to an obvious tool of Nazi herrschaft" (original emphasis).[31] What once had been an experience that brought neighbors and communities together had now become associated with alienation and distrust, an activity that took place either in the privacy of one's own home, or one that was blared publicly out onto the swastika-draped market square. From the space of physical, but not aural exile, Bertolt Brecht's poem states the listening experience much more plainly, more openly: "so my enemies could continue to speak to me . . . about their triumphs and my troubles . . . ." It is then exactly this type of active listening, as opposed to concert, or passive listening, that separates Brecht's radio practice from McLuhan's and Kittler's investigations of the radio as purely a medium that involves and transports the listener into a private world, or a medium that "determine[s] our situation."[32] Instead the back-and-forth nature of Brecht's radio concept, returning the radio to its original technological capability of transmission and reception, not only acknowledges Kittler's critique outlined earlier about the links between radio and warfare technology, but also points to the collaborative, participatory possibilities that the radio device could bring to the radio medium.

Alfred Andersch's work with the radio, beginning in the late 1940s, signals a *Kahlschlag* (literally, clear-cutting) in radio programming. This new beginning for radio meant a retooling of the airwaves to broadcast collaborative transmissions, which, on the one hand, would abrogate the propagandistic and *völkisch* programs that dominated the National Socialist airwaves, and, on the other, could elide the sleight of hand machinations of consumer culture. Andersch's ideas for innovative and collaborative radio forms and his own insights about commercial control of the technology serve as touchstones for the changes in cultural radio production, which Brecht and his contemporaries sought to implement in their own experiments with radio prior to the National Socialist confiscation of the airwaves in 1933. It is within the development and implementation of these radio designs that Andersch's work with the medium not only anticipates the collage techniques used by contemporary radio artists in pulling a broadcast together, but also identifies and works through many of the issues related to the role of artists in the distribution and commercialization of their work. Alfred Andersch's radio work from 1947 to 1959 reveals a belief in the capacity of media technology to liberate and inform its audience. In an unpublished letter dated May 7, 1955, to Dr. Fritz Eberhard, then director of the SDR, Andersch comments on the duplicitous nature of the radio: "Your notion of radio as an instrument of monopoly as well as an instrument for the defense of freedom corresponds with my own."[33] Prior to serving as director of the SDR in the 1950s, Dr. Fritz Eberhard worked throughout his life to forward social democratic principles of governance, and during the Third Reich's formative years built an underground network of resistance activities until his exile in 1937. This comment about the bipolarity of radio from 1955 serves to highlight many of the new broadcasting regulations that had come into being in West Germany following World War II and leading up to the official withdrawal of Allied occupation forces in 1955.

Central to the new regulations were the adoption of models from Great Britain and the United States, which focused on public service broadcasting and the integration of inalienable rights to freedoms of expression and opinion via broadcast media. Contextualized largely in the politics of denazification or reeducation, these adopted models brought with them the creation of broadcasting councils to ensure that all broadcasting organizations would not be privatized, as they were during the Weimar period, nor be centralized under state/governmental control, as in the years of National Socialism, but rather would fall under public oversight in issues of accountability and diversity. At obvious issue here was the highly masterful use of the radio medium as a propaganda tool by the National Socialists, and it is this National Socialist legacy that prompted the inclusion of a constitutional article in the 1949 Basic Law for the Federal Republic of Germany specific to freedom of expression and censorship: "Every person shall have the right freely to express and disseminate his opinions in speech, writing, and pictures and to inform himself without hindrance from generally accessible sources. Freedom of the press and freedom of reporting by means of broadcasts and films shall be guaranteed. There shall be no censorship."[34] As Peter Humphreys points out, the Basic Law did not explicitly rule out the possibility of private commercial broadcast, nor did it establish a monopoly for public service broadcasting.[35] Yet the emphasis in Article 5 on freedom of expression, press and information without fear of censorship, when coupled with the broader notions of democracy and diversity initiated by the Allied occupation, provides a fairly clear pathway for the fledgling republic to follow with respect to continued decisions on broadcasting policy. In this context, Alfred Andersch's comment to Fritz Eberhard can be read either as a vindication of public broadcasting models for consistent support of the philosophies embodied in Article 5 of the Basic Law, which would safeguard against a more commercial monopoly with a producer/consumer model, or as a sentence against public service broadcasting and its own perceived monopoly on deciding about appropriate programming formats to support its mission of providing balanced and diverse content in the areas of information, education, culture, and entertainment.

Andersch's own approach to radio practice in the 1950s to comment on issues of political and social import and to support a new generation of young writers and intellectuals also assists in exposing the intimate connections between politics and technology. Although Andersch constructs in his daily productions for the radio an innovative and interactive template to deliver informed, informative, and thought-provoking content to his listeners, his capacity as producer still suggests a position of control. While his polyphonic approach draws together texts, sound resources, voices, and various content specialists to design a broadcast that considers numerous sociopolitical issues, the unilateral nature of radio technology still demands a producer/consumer model of information delivery. Andersch's implementation of the radio casts technology in terms of liberation, as a means for advancing the knowledge and critical skills of his audience. The central position of his at-home audience within this multidimensional framework carries each broadcast from a simple level of transmission and reception to one in which each listener becomes an active participant in the discussion initiated by the broadcast.

In his capacity as editor and host of numerous radio programs for five of West Germany's public radio stations — Hessischer Rundfunk in Frankfurt (HR), Süddeutscher Rundfunk in Stuttgart (SDR), Nordwestdeutscher Rundfunk in Hamburg (NWDR), Bayerischer Rundfunk in Munich (BR), and Südwestfunk in Baden-Baden (SWF) — Andersch implemented a technique of montage to create innovative and informative features for his listeners.[36] His creation of such programs as the *Abendstudio* (Evening Studio) for Radio Frankfurt (later Hessischer Rundfunk) and the *Feature* for NWDR expanded the role of radio beyond pure reporting to include literary and artistic productions. Both in his remarkably scant written musings about the radio medium and in his employment of the actual technology for broadcasting, Andersch develops a notion of the radio that assembles a montage of voices, sounds, music, texts, and specialists to collaborate in an open-ended and informed presentation of thoughts and reflections. In addition to the afore-mentioned *Abendstudio* and *Feature,* Andersch reflected on and developed a radio-specific artistic genre known as the radio essay for the SDR in the mid-1950s. Each of these radio forms mirrors Andersch's journalistic engagement with the fragmentary postwar climate, as their content weaves together the literary, artistic, and cultural elements with the material of the social, political, and scientific spheres to produce a pastiche that is at once reflective of the underlying motifs manifest in daily life and yet still remains open to input and discussion. In an unpublished manuscript Andersch details the philosophical concept behind the still experimental form of the *Abendstudio,* which draws attention to strategies employed by writers and intellectuals during the Third Reich:

> The escapist tendencies operating under the rubrics of the "eternal" and the "hyper-temporal" are to be rejected; they made sense during the Third Reich because they expressed a distance from the [political] system, but today they would signify the elision of exciting discussion. The "eternal" must result from those instances where topicality is measured with the highest benchmarks.[37]

The need to divorce the postwar radio content from the wartime tendency to use expressions that spoke to universal constructs and not historically specific issues is telling for a couple of reasons. First, and most importantly, it demonstrates Andersch's critical engagement with issues of topical concern and the foresight to know that his audience would also care about these same issues. Second, this statement serves as an implicit critique of his own wartime writings and reflections and in retrospect seems to justify his use of sublime nature metaphors to distance himself from the fascist political system.[38] In this regard, Andersch predicates that the *Abendstudio* should have "nothing to do with esoteric nonsense or endless artsy blather," but should instead take into account "[the place] of human beings within the postwar world with all of its problems and artistic formalist trends."[39] The broadcast of authentic, timely issues using experimental artistic forms combines provocative content that arouses the audience with an innovative application of the technical medium that tests the boundaries of traditional radio reportage, music performance, or dramatic presentation. The dynamic integration of established radio formats (radio play, conversation, reading, report) with artistic, scientific, and literary topics opens this content to new avenues of investigation not allowed for in a traditional reading: "In practice the literary and scientific fields, as well as their singular issues and formalist spheres, will continually overlap."[40] The intertextual and intermedial play that Andersch refers to here enable the radio to operate as a type of hypertext device, which permits the implementation of a multitude of texts and perspectives to weigh in on an issue. As the designer of a broadcast Andersch utilizes the various textual, tonal, and critical tools at his fingertips to trace the common outline of a specific topic. In this fashion, his audience receives multiple points of access to the issue being discussed. The position Andersch grants his *Abendstudio* listeners indicates their value in the design process. In his article "Bemerkungen zum *Abendstudio*" (Remarks about the *Abendstudio*) for the August 4, 1949, radio supplement for the journal *Frankfurter Rundschau* he writes about the ritual involved in listening to this program, I quote at length:

> The *Abendstudio* is a broadcast for listeners who only rarely turn on their radios. People who really want to gain something from the *Abendstudio* should take a short walk on Tuesday evening from 9:30 to 10:00 p.m. Afterward they should make a cup of coffee, dim the lamps (but not too much), and sit in a comfortable (but not too comfortable) chair. At 10:15 p.m. the radio can be turned on. If one follows these instructions, then they will wake up the next morning feeling fresh and stimulated and not exhausted.... The *Abendstudio* teaches that the most important words are those that are spoken spontaneously. For this reason it does not follow a "program"; its program is to listen to the mind in wherever it decides to go.[41]

Andersch perceives of the listening experience as one to be relished, as an event that one anticipates and must prepare for in celebratory fashion. Although the detailed listening instructions that he outlines in this advertisement seem somewhat controlling, they depict the type of listener Andersch imagines while producing and creating broadcasts. Through picturing his target audience in this manner, he ensures that each radio program's objectives match the level of intellectual competence he assumes of them. On another level, these instructions are meant to train his audience to listen between the lines, to be cognizant of the spontaneity of the technical medium. It is often in the arbitrariness of language, in those areas that cannot be scripted, that the essence of an issue is understood. In a world of increased progress where outcomes and results are of utmost importance, Andersch states in an almost ironic tone: "If Professor X, Journalist Y, and Poet Z sometimes need an hour to leave an issue completely unsettled, then the *Abendstudio* has fulfilled its purpose. It has shown, that a problem existed."[42] In addition to planting the seeds of discussion in the minds of his audience, Andersch also provides them with a set of tools to cultivate the issue in the context of their daily lives. These tools include a critical vocabulary, a set of viewpoints from varying specialists, and a hypertextual design format that enables exploration of related issues and perspectives.

This same design concept informs Andersch's work with the *Feature* at the NWDR from 1952 to 1954 and with the radio essay at the SDR from 1955 to 1958. In both positions Andersch was able to fine-tune his understanding of the process involved in adapting the literary and artistic realms to the radio medium. With his move to Hamburg in 1952 to join the radio team led by Ernst Schnabel, Andersch began his editorial responsibilities with the *Feature*. In one of his only radio-specific publications for the journal *Rundfunk und Fernsehen* Andersch enumerates further his application of the radio to broadcast literary and artistic content over the airwaves. In this essay he problematizes the concept of the *Feature*, not only for the radio industry's borrowing of an English term, but also for the confusion involved in specifying its meaning. In the attempt to define its aspects he privileges the *Feature*'s formal character over content:

> The term "Feature" never means the content of a subject; rather it means the way in which it appears, from "making," "form," and "appearance," through the "facial aspect" of a person or the "fashion" of a person, to the "special inducement" of newspapers and radio. It thus means the form of a subject, not the subject itself, whereby indeed, as in the appearance of a person, sometimes form and content can be identical.[43]

The artistic value of this radio genre arises from its form. The process involved in making/designing a *Feature* contains those elements that entice both the producer and the consumer. In the constructing of an argument, in the piecing together of content lies the adventure of the *Feature*-form. Andersch approaches the *Feature* always as a work in progress, adaptable to any given situation. The importance of content is incontrovertible, but in the display/design/style/delivery of that content lies the power to incite, inform, educate, and invigorate one's audience. Andersch praises the *Feature*'s ability to gather together and commingle a variety of broadcast sources and formats:

> Due to its exclusively formal and thus mediatory or instrumental character, the feature can spread over all possible types of broadcasts. It engages the boundaries of the report, of reportage, of the presentation of social, psychological, and political issues. Since it is form, and thus also art, its resources are unlimited; they extend from journalism to poetic writing, from rational description to the surreal reach into the dream, from the deliberate elucidation of topicality for immediate use to that type of poetic penetration of human community.[44]

Of particular interest in this definition is the *Mittelhaftigkeit* (mediacy) of the *Feature*'s form, its ability to act as a medium for conveying meaning or information. In its very tenuousness the *Feature* seamlessly transcends the bounds of established genres and styles to extract, play with, and apply those formal elements it finds especially effective. Andersch's own inclusion of music, literature, criticism, and politics in any one broadcast allows for a montage of constantly shifting discourses, which is reflective of the new information society. However this "Montage-Kunst par excellence" can only be as effective as the person producing it, since the design requires skills and know-how to draw out those features of the content important for the understanding of the target audience. In our explication of Andersch's designs for the radio we have again arrived at the audience. All three series cite the at-home listener as the gauge by which to measure the design of any specific broadcast. Each incorporates a type of collaborative agency, a notion that intermeshes a range of perspectives to produce a broadcast that informs and provides a point of access to intellectual and cultural discussion. Based on an idea of intertextuality, each show combines textual excerpts (quotation, reportage, readings, poetry, and anecdote), voice (announcer lead-ins, interviews, conversations), sound (background noise, musical interludes, and sound effects), and a host of content specialists (authors, critics, and professors) with the skills of critical thought to piece together a dynamic and collaborative broadcast.

In a similar vein, Andersch's creation of the radio essay for the SDR calls upon the same free-spirited elements of montage. Given the confusion engendered by the term *Feature* in the types of broadcasts being grouped indiscriminately beneath it, Andersch felt it necessary once more to tailor the ideas behind his collaborative work with the radio. In the *Funkkurier,* a newsletter produced by the SDR, Andersch describes the radio essay as:

> a very special form, and above all it is one of the few authentic artistic forms, which has developed in radio. The word "essay" characterizes the term along two threads: it distinguishes it from the radio play...and it brings to it the lively character of the experiment and its openness to all possibilities. At its peak, which is only seldom achieved, the radio-essay is a poetic document of the reality of our world, and of the lives of people within it.[45]

Perhaps in an attempt to rescue or resuscitate the dynamic and immanent qualities of the *Feature,* which he claims has been turned into "a vague collective term," Andersch again centers his attention on issues of form versus content when discussing the radio essay. Where the *Feature* acquired its special characteristics from within the act of production, the radio essay originates specifically from the thought and skill of the poet. In order to prevent its commodification by what Andersch continually referred to as the "cultural machinery of press and radio,"[46] he regulates its attainment, citing its peculiar nature and its cogent need for possibility as hindering its appropriation by the culture industry. In contrast to the now vague collective term of the *Feature,* the open experimental character of the radio essay resists being compartmentalized into a neat concept prone to marketing. The capacity of the radio essay form to hinder co-optation recalls one of Andersch's earliest poems "Fünf Sonette" (Five Sonnets).[47] In this poem Andersch posits a form that is gained through the subject's act of inward contemplation, a deep reflective moment that offers a space of constancy amid a world full of noise and distraction. When taken in light of Andersch's set of instructions for listening to his radio broadcasts outlined earlier, there are some striking similarities. The listening ritual of a leisurely walk, a hot cup of coffee, dimmed lighting, and a comfortable chair creates a space and a mood conducive to intellectual activity. Unlike the visual space of the cinema, where the cinemagoer relinquishes control to the projector and the screen, the aural space of the radio-centered living room remains in the control of the listener, who can, at any time, turn the radio off: "The *Abendstudio* restores to its listeners the invaluable knowledge that radios can also be switched off."[48] Of course, the possibility exists that the cinemagoers can walk out as they please, but the mesmeric effect of the projected image coupled with the economic investment paid at the door, makes this unlikely.

Even with fine-tuning the operative definitions of his radio program genres, Andersch's note to Eberhard about the economic and cultural monopoly enjoyed by radio in 1950s West Germany still formed a critical realization that his capacity as a radio broadcaster magnified the intensity of consumerist culture. This prompted a group of radio commentaries he titled "Denk-Zettel für Kulturkonsumenten" (Thoughts for Cultural Consumers), broadcast on the BR between January and September 1959 as part of the series *Nachtstudio* (Night Studio).[49] Andersch's commentaries investigated the state of art and literature, and the position of the author/artist in a machinated consumerist society. Navigating between the poles of monopoly capitalism and communicative freedom represented by the radio required the type of active critical thinking Andersch addresses in his definitions of his three radio series. Andersch's succinct description of the radio essay as a "a poetic document of the reality of our world, and of the lives of people within it"[50] that continually remains open to a full range of possibilities, anticipates many of his insights about art and aesthetics set forth in this series. Unlike his hour-long creations for the *Abendstudio, Feature,* or the radio essay, these fifteen-minute reflective pieces do not combine excerpts from text, music, or critical perspective from studio guests, but rather consist solely in Andersch's own observations:

> I would like to note, that my comments are not to be taken as lessons [*Denkzettel*],... but rather as thinking-notes, that is, with a hyphen between the thinking and the note, as notes to meditate on. They are actual slips of paper for scrawling on,... notes to questions that I myself am not all that clear on, sudden ideas, questions, sketches....[51]

The content of these broadcasts concentrates on the daily situation facing German artists as they negotiate between the realms of art and culture. Facets of this negotiation include the quiet but noticeable exodus of a handful of writers, poets, artists, and musicians to other countries, the politics of architectural and art historical restoration based on decisions made by *Kulturbeamten* (cultural agents) rather than *Künstler* (artists) and the false realities ushered in by the facades of the culture industry. The delivery of these short commentaries via the radio illustrates Andersch's intent to educate a broader public, which was also the goal of the *Nachtstudio* series:

> The audience to be addressed is not just any elite group, but rather every open-minded individual who actively participates in the events of the world into which he has been placed. The radio, unlike any other media outlet, is in the position of being able to immediately inform millions of people from all educational backgrounds and social strata, at all hours and in all locations, about events and ideas.[52]

With this claim in mind, what we gain from Andersch's commentaries is a more grounded and broader understanding of his polemic about the role and position of art in society, since the radio medium requires him to set aside the predilection for essayistic abstraction for the sake of clearer, more illuminative, and thought-provoking examples.

His ruminations suggest that artists in West Germany occupy a very special position vis-à-vis the social construct of culture. Under the heading "Deutschland und seine Künstler" (Germany and Its Artists) Andersch accounts for the curious self-exile of many artists (himself included) to other countries and to marginal regions within Germany ("a nest in the Lüneberger Heide or on the outskirts of West Berlin").[53] Since he cites such physical emotions as *Widerwillen* (dislike), *Missbehagen* (uncomfortable feeling), and *Beklommenheit* (trepidation) toward German culture as their (and his) reasons for leaving, it is important that we look more closely at Andersch's definition of culture:

> Nowadays the artistic concept of culture has become a sociological one; whenever the word "culture" is used, then it is done so almost exclusively in two senses: as a socially administered institution, and as an industrial enterprise. The approach of seeing art and culture as identical is entirely old-fashioned.[54]

Culture, no longer synonymous with art, is now the object of an industrial operation with administrative ties to political and social institutions. Instead of culture consisting of the entire spectrum of creative works put forth by a group of people, it has been endowed with bureaucratic and machinelike qualities and utilizes its relationships with the art world as inroads for its subversion. In this relationship, the work of art becomes fodder for the machinery of culture:

> Without a doubt we can still find the original work of art inside the innermost core of these institutional and business notions of culture, though modern culture does not attend to it as a creative axis from which it draws its strengths. On the contrary, modern culture directs all of its efforts to encasing the work of art in administration and production, to secluding its dangerous properties, to sterilizing its effect, and to subjecting it to a process of general stabilization. And it does this all the more, the more culture is industrialized and administered.[55]

The vividness of this image provokes and exposes the intricacies of the modern culture industry. The power of art no longer resides in the creative potential of an idea of an original but rather in the breakdown of the original into safe, easily digestible, and reproducible components — a simulacrum par excellence — and the neutralization of its potential to subvert or incite. The impact of the culture industry on West Germany's cultural fabric is felt and seen in the architectural surfaces of Germany's cities and in the lack of support for the performing arts. In another of these commentaries, "Denk-Zettel," he relates what artists encounter upon leaving their homes to walk through their city. The cultural politics of reconstruction, when coupled with the quick economic recovery of the 1950s, created an atmosphere of equally quick restoration from which "the spirit of history, of a life lived, of originality, has disappeared."[56] Instead each rebuilding project is outfitted with interchangeable *Attrappen* (templates) that can be erased and reproduced on a whim, which divorces them from their historical context, functionality, and originality: "the new buildings appear like impersonal products of an abstract organism known as 'reconstruction.'"[57] These biting critiques of art and culture in the throes of West German economic recovery are one illustration of how Andersch attempted to counteract what he perceived as a monopolization and administration of the cultural sphere through industrial concerns and quick economic growth. It is strange to note, that concurrent to this series of commentaries in 1959, the federal government of Christian Democratic chancellor Konrad Adenauer was attempting to push through a draft revision of the broadcasting law, which would create a second national television channel with commercial rather than public interests, and with direct oversight and ownership by the federal government rather than by the levels of public oversight put into place to assure diversity and cultural pluralism among the broadcasting stations following World War II. Referred to by Peter Humphreys as "Adenauer TV," it was clearly a move toward more, not less, federal monopoly of the airwaves, and a clear evidence of the duplicitous nature Andersch detected within the broadcasting sector four years earlier.[58]

While Bertolt Brecht's theories for an experimental radio were disrupted by the National Socialist rise to power and Alfred Andersch's designs for a collaborative radio during the postwar-1950s were subsumed and thus diluted by the machinations of West Germany's quick economic recovery, each open the radio up to the possibilities of interactive, audience-centered programming that commercial broadcasts and prevailing technical standards had not yet acknowledged. The instances of radio silence that characterize each spatiotemporal moment of this study's investigation are telling for the ways in which they cast each respective listening audience. Bertolt Brecht's exile signaled not only the disruption of his radio experiments, but also his move from radio producer to radio listener. The possibility that his small radio would fall silent signifies, as well, Brecht's last endeavors with the radio medium. For the radio listeners in Andrew Stuart Bergerson's study of listening practices in the Third Reich, radio silence becomes synonymous with the move from convivial, public listening conducive to discussion to secluded, private listening. For Alfred Andersch turning the radio off, allowing it to fall silent, promotes intellectual reflection and participation in the topical issues of the day, a possibility that was nonexistent during radio's retooling for propaganda. From these theories, genre designs, and experiments both Brecht and Andersch provide the radio a realm of possibilities beyond pure reception, a realm which opens the radio to collaboration and interactivity.

FOUR

Opening the Radio Up
Tactical Media and Alternative Networks

Cyberspace. A consensual hallucination experienced daily by billions of legitimate operators, in every nation. . . . Unthinkable complexity. Lines of light ranged in the nonspace of the mind, clusters and constellations of data.
— William Gibson, *Neuromancer*

The electronic age . . . takes control out of your hands and puts it into the will of another, whether that other is called God or Magic or The Corporation or The Government.
— Vito Acconci, "Public Space in a Private Time"

The radio, as we have seen, opens up a realm of utilitarian possibilities for entertainment, for communication, and for information transmission. In doing so, it takes advantage of naturally occurring electromagnetic frequencies to create points of access to our homes, our automobiles, our public squares, our places of work, and wherever the portability of sound finds us. When coupled with the unidirectional configuration of broadcast, the omnipresence of these electromagnetic waves sanctions a purely hierarchical approach to telecommunications media like radio and television. However, artistic and theoretical experimentation with the radio medium has long sought to dismantle these hierarchical approaches, to circumvent the myriad government regulations, legislative policies, and broadcasting standards put into place to control transmission access, reception capability, and content practices. Through the development of radio-specific genres, the integration of sound elements and noise to create montage and blending effects, the intermedial intersection with other media techniques (film, Internet, phonograph, etc.) to expand the radio's functionality, and the unfailing move to increase and engage listener interactivity with the realm of broadcast, experimentation with the radio medium in the context of German cultural broadcasting has consistently chipped away at these regulations and standards that have upheld longstanding notions of radio broadcast simply as a venue for entertainment. And it has transformed the radio into a medium for collaborative, thought-provoking art projects. As the radio continues to grow as an artistic medium — interfacing with the technical and artistic functionalities of other media, as in the Atau Tanaka example, engaging with and amplifying a rich history of sound media through the implementation and simultaneous creation of archival material, and responding to the notion of broadcast as entertainment — it also searches out operative modes to continue to open the radio up to provide a set of critical solutions to sociopolitical and cultural issues ranging from technical access for artists, transmission practices for broadcast, and multilayered approaches to the creative process itself. The radio's survival into the twenty-first century has brought with it new delivery methods in the form of satellite broadcasting based in subscription models, and new transmission techniques utilizing digital formats, while experimental approaches to the medium have adapted to explore tactical uses of the medium in the form of pirate radio broadcasts, agitprop techniques and community radio practices for both artistic and sociopolitical resistance related broadly to ideas about access, physical and virtual spatiality, and a growing global telecommunications infrastructure. As we will explore shortly, these three threads of a critically engaged radio practice form the background and foundation for artistic and social experiments that interrogate the nature and function of public space within the context of an already arrived and ubiquitous electronically based information space.

William Gibson's futuristic musings on cyberspace in his 1984 novel *Neuromancer* and Vito Acconci's artistic reflections on the role and function of public space in the early 1990s, which begin this chapter, each demonstrate the growing impact of electronic telecommunications infrastructures on how human beings experience space.[1] Acconci detects an increasing movement away from a democratic and oppositional idea of public space that results from immediate access to information offered by the electronic age, while Gibson's notion of cyberspace imagines a complex, interwoven system of innumerable data connections that simultaneously link together the external knowledge stores of human thought and demarcate an interiorized, transcendent nonspace of reflection or hallucination. Both utilize metaphors of spatiality to underscore an increased preoccupation with information spaces, which in Acconci's terms transforms a perception of informational freedom into a type of informational surveillance by a hierarchically structured other, and in Gibson's mind opens up a utopian moment of informational bliss. Gibson's ideas point to two categories of information, embodied as rationalized, concrete data or disembodied as abstract, imaginative contemplation — information for sale and information for thought: and cyberspace is the product of both. As a spatial concept comprised from a convergence of telecommunications networks, this account of cyberspace anticipates the significance of quick data flow for the 1990s global information economy, while, at the same time, it reminds us of the important role of the human mind, the human intellect, to imagine in nonspatial terms, to visualize outside the bounds of perceptive constructs.

Acconci's thoughts, however, point to a darker side of information access, one that hinders engaged moments of collaborative resistance by supplanting the desire for social or political change with a virtual idea that all needs are being met. Where Gibson's fictional world celebrates those hackers illegitimately jacking-in to the wires and data connections of the telecommunications infrastructures that comprise the immateriality of cyberspace, Acconci's world of public space laments this very loss of physical contact between people within those very structured and sense-filled spaces, where a democratic exchange of ideas once occurred without fear of surveillance and without fear of losing one's physical body to the immaterial data spaces of the electronic realm. Combining the playful subversiveness of Gibson's hackers with the cautionary suspicion of Acconci's public man elicits an approach to tactical media that is mindful of the very real, very physical problems faced by communities the world over, while taking advantage of dissident modes of media and telecommunications infiltration to unsettle a dominant paradigm of media infrastructure and draw attention to these very problems. The radio offers just such a model through its ability to connect its users (both as listeners and as practitioners) to a space of consciousness and intellect — its ability to capture and remediate those modes of thought and structures of knowledge, which often get lost behind long-held notions of radio broadcast as simply a medium for news and entertainment.

The focus of this chapter explores the medium's continued navigation of broadcasting standards and regulations in the context of an emergent European media policy with the growth and development of the European Union, and looks specifically at three examples that implement a tactical media practice in their considered use of the radio medium to question the viability of such policies. As national and informational borders continue to become more porous with each iteration of the European Union, and as common political, economic, social, environmental, and educational issues spill over these very same national borders, a realization about the intimate connections and delicate balances within the space of Europe arises, which points to the increased need for collaborative models of communication and problem-solving. Each of the following examples explore questions of nuclear power, migration, and asylum within a radiophonic framework, detecting in the structures of radio broadcast and transmission a territory of unbounded space accessible through the radio as medium and the radio as device — a territory of democratic potential and collaborative reflective thought. While the first presents a sociopolitical example involving pirate radio broadcasts connected to the antinuclear movement in West Germany in the late 1970s and early 1980s, and the subsequent two examples examine two separate artistic broadcasts dealing with issues of political asylum and wartime migration, and both supported by the Viennese art radio project known as Kunstradio, all three find common ground in their use of a strategic or resistant media practice to emphasize local issues not receiving attention in the global media and in the positioning of their radio practice in the transnational border regions of West Germany, France, and Switzerland, in the case of the first example; Italy and Austria, in the second; and Austria and Serbia, in the case of the third.

Toward a European Media Policy: Pirate Radio and the Case of Radio Dreyeckland

Hans Bredow provided the first justification for developing the radio and allowing it to become a national medium in 1920s Germany: to provide pleasure and motivation for the hardworking, yet economically depressed German people, essentially to provide entertainment and forgetfulness. Hans Flesch, in his early theoretical writings, creative work for the medium, and support of artists and musicians outside the mainstream positioned the radio outside the realm of substitution for and replication of live events in order to theorize and develop a radio-centered art form, which would take advantage of the specifically radiophonic attributes of the emergent medium, its regulatory and developmental history, and its technical functionality, while also distinguishing its place in the existing media landscape of film and gramophone. Flesch's contemporaries, F. W. Bischoff, Friedrich Wolf, and Walter Ruttmann, followed his lead by pushing the envelope of what was conceivable for radio-centered art productions through an innovative mixture of technologies and techniques from other media, and a persistent metacritical approach to the medium itself to help expand it and explore a range of possibilities beyond its perceived role in entertainment broadcasting. Bertolt Brecht's radio theoretical writings and fragments are one part progressive foresight, one part nostalgic desire. His call for transforming the radio into a two-way communications device, for reactivating its former abilities as both an instrument of transmission and reception, can certainly be read as a clear criticism of governmental broadcast regulation legislating the design and sale of radios with only reception capabilities to offset issues of interference and to safeguard against transmissions of an antigovernment nature. However, Brecht instead saw the democratic potential of a bidirectionality in broadcast through the provision of listener interactivity, and listener production possibilities, such that all radio listeners and radio producers would serve both roles simultaneously. Brecht's exile and the dismissals and/or exiles of our other Weimar-era radio pioneers (with the exception of Ruttmann)[2] coincided with the autumn 1932 reforms that consolidated economic and programmatic control of broadcasting to the central government, and merged National Socialist rhetoric and broadcast regulation into a radio practice that served as a seamless mouthpiece for Hitler's speeches and a German hyper-nationalism of mythic proportions.

The politics of radio in the immediate post-1945 media landscape were bound up in the social and political processes of denazification being experienced by other governmental and social institutions following the war. This mirrors, to a certain extent, the same type of regulatory behavior based on a fear of unsanctioned broadcast and interference apparent following World War I, with the primary difference being the administrative and regulatory oversight by the four occupying powers, which also meant four separate approaches to broadcast governance until 1949 with the formation of the Federal Republic of Germany and the German Democratic Republic. In this postwar context radio producers, like Alfred Andersch, created new discussion genres to engage a wide range of sociopolitical and cultural views in formats, which sought to recapture the innovation of Weimar-era cultural radio practice and to animate the Brechtian vision for multidirectional transmissions. While Andersch identified the tremendous democratic potential of the medium he also acknowledged the incredibly complex mechanisms at work within it that inextricably linked the broadcast medium with the cultural industrial forces of postwar capitalism. Andersch's comments about these contradictory, yet mutually beneficial, functions of the radio echo Hans Flesch's earlier desire to steer the radio away from its sole consideration as an entertainment device and toward its innate role as an artistic medium, and they also anticipate the critical media theories put forward by Hans Magnus Enzensberger, Andersch's one-time program assistant with the radio essay at the SDR from October 1955 through March 1957.

Enzensberger's theories are important to consider in the context of this chapter because they center on understanding and providing a progressive and operative media-based solution to the "consciousness industry" (*Bewusstseins-Industrie*), an expansive reworking of the Frankfurt School's *terminus* "culture industry" à la Theodor W. Adorno and Max Horkheimer to include not just culturally homogenous goods that follow a capitalist logic of production, but also processes that could be defined through their initiation of media networks as filtered through consumer consciousness.[3] As put forth in his influential essay "Constituents of a Theory of the Media" (1970), Enzensberger understands this system of mediated networks as universal and convergent, creating something similar to the type of rhizomatic structure described by French poststructural theorists Gilles Deleuze and Félix Guattari:[4]

> With the development of the electronic media, the industry that shapes consciousness has become the pacemaker for the social and economic development of societies in the late industrial age. It infiltrates into all other sectors of production, takes over more and more directional and control functions, and determines the standard of the prevailing technology. . . . All these new forms of media are constantly forming new connections both with each other and with older media like printing, radio, film, television, telephone, teletype, radar, and so on. They are clearly coming together to form a universal system.[5]

When coupled with the convergent properties and control functions of electronic media, Enzensberger's reconceptualization of the culture industry to include the import of behavioral consciousness and structures of the intellect begins to assume even more sinister characteristics of a type of consumer surveillance, while it also anticipates the types of informational and technical alignments necessary within security, telecommunications, transportation, and financial infrastructures to facilitate globalization.[6] Enzensberger's response is to invoke Brecht's earlier utopian vision for radio broadcast as a tool for political mobilization utilizing, again, a one-to-many functionality of broadcasting technology, which Enzensberger sees as one part of a larger puzzle to support a socialist resistance to mainstream media policies and practices through the persistent initiation and application of a strategic media practice. He writes:

> Anyone who expects to be emancipated by technological hardware, or by a system of hardware however structured, is the victim of an obscure belief in progress. Anyone who imagines that freedom for the media will be established if only everyone is busy transmitting and receiving is the dupe of a liberalism

which... merely peddles the faded concepts of a preordained harmony of social interests. In the face of such illusions, what must be firmly held on to is
that the proper use of the media demands organization and makes it possible.
Every production that deals with the interests of the producers postulates a
collective method of production. It is itself already a form of self-organization
of social needs. Tape recorders, ordinary cameras, and movie cameras are already extensively owned by wage-earners. The question is why these means
of production do not turn up at factories, in schools, in the offices of the
bureaucracy, in short, everywhere where there is social conflict.[7]

Enzensberger warns about production for production's sake that
arises out of an unconsidered use of technology. Emancipation and
social progress will not occur by virtue of the gadgets themselves,
which already contain within them the ideas behind their proper
use and function. Thus the idea of repetition, which Hans Flesch
was actively trying to move the radio away from in the 1920s, and
which Alfred Andersch was concerned about in the subsumption of
his discussion-based programming formats by other broadcasting stations in the 1950s, is an area where a more engaged application of
these technological structures and production methods needs to focus
its attention. French economist and music theorist Jacques Attali
likens this process of repetition to a type of "autosurveillance," which
he describes in the context of computerized music:

> The synthesizer, together with its integration with the microprocessor... tells
> us an enormous amount about society, embodying the two axes along which
> some future social evolution is alone conceivable. On the one hand, it recon-
> tains music by programming it: you play, to be sure, but you only pretend
> to play or create, and the freedom of play is in fact incorporated within the
> machine itself. This is what I have elsewhere called autosurveillance; it is also
> auto-production, inasmuch as you only seem to be doing things yourself, while
> in fact you are now only imitating the machine, which produces music in your
> stead. Autosurveillance is here the first phase: it guides you, if you make a
> mistake it corrects you; and this is the first option, the first great possibility of
> social evolution, that of the imitation of the machine. It is the second option
> that is then the truly liberating one, where the machine on the contrary serves
> as the instrument of a diffused and disseminated creativity.[8]

Attali offsets this process of repetition — the "preordained harmony
of social interests" in Enzensberger's text and the self-sufficient and
self-contained individual of Vito Acconci's public space — against the
process of composition, which also has pathways back to the model

of socialist media practice Enzensberger sets up in his essay. The series of utopian ideas, theoretical possibilities, innovative formats, and
media-based practices, which arrived with and developed from the
birth of radio, always have to be interpreted against the background
of governmental regulations, legislative policies, and broadcasting
standards that accompany the radio's growth. This constant shadow
relationship between the regulator and the regulated provokes criticism of these approaches as being too idealistic, or as ultimately
and unwittingly reproducing that which they set out to criticize —
the process of imitation, the unquestioned, uncritical buy-in to a
template-style approach to technical use, Attali's autosurveillance.
For Attali, composition provides the emancipation that Enzensberger
is looking for by allowing the machine to open up distributed networks along which both the products and process of creativity can be
dispersed and taken up by others for their own performative repertoire: "to compose is to take pleasure in the instruments, the tools of
communication, in use-time and exchange-time as lived and no longer
as stockpiled."[9] Perhaps Attali's idea of composition encompasses
what Enzensberger pictures as "networklike communications models
built on the principle of reversibility of circuits . . . a mass newspaper,
written and distributed by its readers, a video network of politically
active groups,"[10] while also initiating a two-fold notion of William
Gibson's cyberspace as a network for disseminating both marketable
information and creative, critical thought.

This is a key point, since no matter how much one wants to establish an alternative approach to media, no matter how much one
theorizes about protecting creative work from the processes of the
consciousness industry, there is still a loop-design in place that always
already presupposes the existence of regulatory mechanisms that tol-
erate and require innovation, and that always already transforms the
idea of an autonomous artwork into an art object and ultimately
into an art product. Yet within Attali's notion of composition, and
Enzensberger's networklike communications models there are equally
compelling modes of experience, modes of creative thought, and
modes of interactive communication, which respond to these globalized processes by opening up temporary, durational (time-delimited)

spaces of performance, which because of their spatiotemporal impermanence are able to elide these very inveigled processes that are built-in as components — however invisible, however inaudible — of the media systems themselves. These more tactical approaches to media use, particularly in the area of broadcast, take their cues from both the pre-1923 historical origins of radio broadcast with amateur radio operators, who built their own transmitters and receivers, and from an increased use of pirate radio practice, which grew out of a variety of social and environmental movements in 1970s West Germany. One example of a pirate radio practice that initiates these tactical media strategies can be found with the contemporary noncommercial community/free radio station Radio Dreyeckland (RDL) in Freiburg i. Breisgau, which has its origins as a pirate transmitter within the antinuclear movement located in the transborder region of France, Germany, and Switzerland. The development of RDL from its beginnings as an illegitimate pirate radio transmitter to its current status as a legal radio broadcaster within the framework of community/free radio provides a foil for following the levels of interarticulation between Enzensberger's network models, Attali's compositional approach, and Acconci's public man for purposes of political resistance and social change, as well as for helping to chart the changing course of media policy in West Germany in possible anticipation of a European media policy within the framework of European Union market integration in 1992.

Dreyeckland began its illegal pirate broadcasts in 1977 under the French name Radio Verte Fessenheim (RVF), and the German Radio Grünes Fessenheim, and characterized itself under the rubric of a *freier Sender* (free transmitter), which should not be confused with the term *freies Radio* (free radio), for which Dreyeckland would later receive a license and a fixed frequency in 1988 from the regional state government of Baden-Württemberg as part of a softening of the state controls on public broadcasting.[11] The three names associated with the broadcasting group point to its function as an open network of communication for the broader environmental movement, its more specific origins in the anti–nuclear power movement begun in the early 1970s, and the location of several of its autonomous underground antennas along and across the national borders of France, West Germany, and Switzerland, the regional borders of Alsace, Baden, and Basel, and the dialect regions of Alsatian, Alemannisch, and Basler Schwyzerdütsch. The history of RVF/RDL as a transborder network of clandestine radio transmissions is intimately tied to a supraregional identity that finds common ground through its shared experience of the region's environmental terrain and its mutual facility with a regional vernacular:

> Little was known about a common culture or history of the people from Baden, Alsace, or north Switzerland when environmentalists from all three countries joined forces across borders in order to fight against the expansion of the chemical and nuclear industries in the Upper Rhine region. The roots and foundation for the survival of Radio Verte Fessenheim/Radio Dreyeckland are also connected with this transborder struggle against nuclear reactors and chemical plants. The history of our radio is embedded in the processes of political development of the region and can only be understood in this context.[12]

To a certain extent a public identity, mobilized around issues of local and regional importance, is formed from these common experiences and simultaneously helps to shape an alternative public sphere to provoke a multiple array of responses to issues of common concern. Unlike the mainstream press, which supported the concerns of industry only in making these plants profitable and viable sources of energy for the region, the environmentalists used the radio medium to offer alternative opinions related to safety issues, healthcare, and environmental damage. For twelve minutes on June 4, 1977, at 7:45 p.m. this larger notion of a supraregional identity found a common voice with the first publicly announced broadcast of RVF from the location of an occupied nuclear energy tower in Heiteren, an Alsatian community near Fessenheim, site of France's oldest nuclear power plant, which had begun operation in March of that year. Over the course of the next four years, other demonstrations and actions against chemical and plutonium factories and plans to build other nuclear reactors ensued, accompanied by weekly broadcasts reporting on activities related to these demonstrations and occasional live broadcasts from factories occupied by striking workers or construction sites where other nuclear reactors or chemical plants were being built.

Structurally the pirate broadcasts also began to grow, adding antennas in all three regional areas (seventeen by 1979), broadcasting in three languages (French, German, and Alemannisch), expanding broadcast content beyond environmental concerns to include broader questions of social welfare (squatter's rights, homelessness), and focusing editorial responsibility for production of broadcasts to each of the "studios," which also began broadcasting local programming before the simultaneous broadcast for the entire "Dreyeckland" region was put on the air. From an organizational perspective then, the pirate broadcasts were produced by a loose network of correspondents spread out over the entire region, who would work together in local editorial teams to record their contribution onto tape, which was then shuttled around the region to clandestine locales in the region's forested areas for transmission. The economics of redaction, the geographies of frequency ranges, the technical specifics of production, and the politics of pirate transmission and reception are described in a booklet accompanying a documentary audio recording edited by Christian Scholze titled *Radio Grünes Fessenheim:*

> Usually the broadcast is produced one or two days before it is transmitted. Only for very urgent reasons and events in progress do we broadcast live, i.e., the broadcast goes directly via microphone into the ether. Our sound studio would most likely make every radio professional's hair stand on end: two simple reel-to-reel recorders, two cassette recorders, a record player, three good microphones, a headset, and a small mixing board.... A telephone adapter makes it possible for us to edit directly into the broadcast the newest information.... Broadcasts are never done directly from the studio. For this we have small, mobile transmitters, which are deployed at many different locations. The coverage of a device is large, fifty kilometers and more. The mountains of the Black Forest and the Vosges range benefit us in this respect.... A complete VHF-transmission system consists of a transmitter, a small battery, a cassette recorder, a microphone for live broadcasts, and a VHF-antenna. Radio Fessenheim now has more than twenty complete transmitters ready for operation, very small ones with one watt of power, and larger ones with twenty-five watts of transmitting power.[13]

The separation of broadcast production and broadcast transmission into several decentralized locations obviously assisted in avoiding detection by police and postal inspectors, who were well aware of the RVF's illegal broadcasts, and from September 1977 on were actively searching out transmission sites with helicopters, and disrupting their on-air broadcast frequency using a humming interference signal. However, following Vito Acconci's reflections on the nature and function of public space, this decentralization also supports a more democratic use of the broadcasting space established along the transmitter networks and signal antennas set up by the collaborators of RVF. According to Acconci, the public space does not have to create a unified collective mind-set in order for it to be considered democratic:

> The piazza remains democratic when people break up into clusters. Groups of people form territories, as if over a vast plain. The cluster is small enough that it doesn't need a leader: each person in the cluster has the chance to talk for him- or herself, without asking for it, without needing to be granted the privilege of talking.[14]

Although Acconci demonstrates that this rendering of public space into autonomous territories eventually evolves into something larger, thus requiring organization and thus dispersing democratic potential once again, his description also illustrates the importance of public space serving as a transitory space through which moments of transgressive thought and action can occur before ultimately being taken up by the mechanisms of Enzensberger's consciousness industry. When seen in the context of pirate radio practice, this transitoriness takes its energy from the fleetingness of sound, from the compositional ability of the production team to splice in the most recent information coming from the site of a demonstration, and from the adrenaline-based playfulness of illegal transmission. Yet it is also this transitoriness that presented a direct challenge to the public-service broadcasting monopoly that had marked the media landscape in West Germany since the end of World War II. While the initial irregularity of RVF's broadcasts and the movement of final production tapes to any of its clandestine transmission stations contributed to their not being caught by the authorities, RVF argued that the location of their broadcast signal on the radio dial between 100 and 104 MHz signified the availability of those frequencies for broadcast and that the low-wattage output of their transmitters posed no threat of interference to other stations.

In 1981 Radio Dreyeckland, as the transmitter had now become known, began the process to legalize the radio in the region of Baden, where it had established a permanent production team in Freiburg. Encouraged by François Mitterrand's election in France and his suspension of all prosecution of community/free radios, the RDL-collaborators in Alsace developed permanent studios in several locations (Colmar, Mulhouse, Strasbourg, Haguenau), which allowed them to move away from the unidirectionality necessitated by pirate radio practice to incorporate listener opinion and discussion via telephone call-in, and those on the German side of the border to escape criminal prosecution through the origination of broadcast transmissions from these transmitters in France. These activities also contributed to RDL's reconceptualization of its role. It acknowledged its roots as a medium for distribution of information and for mobilization of the region's citizens in the context of the environmental and anti–nuclear power movements, but saw its role growing past one of support and point of contact for these specific political movements to one that developed a critical voice for the region through direct lines of contact with the listeners, and their initiation as radio producers themselves. This signaled a move away from pirate radio practice in terms of broadcast production, but not in terms of transmission, which remained strictly separated from the editorial side of the project. These shifts in radio practice also generated changes in definitional approach — to transform from being an open or free transmitter to being supporters and practitioners of community/free radio. Free radio defines itself as an independent, open medium, which "pursues non-commercial, grassroots, socially based radio that engages critically with existing social issues"[15] and supports the creation and cultivation of a *Gegenöffentlichkeit,* or alternative public sphere. In a declaration announcing the start of broadcasting from Freiburg in April 1985 members of RDL described the ways in which this practice of community/free radio cultivates a notion of the alternative public sphere:

> Overall Free Radio in the Federal Republic is today not reality, but rather utopia. Only Radio Dreyeckland has had the fortune to be able to try a portion of this utopia: a radio that functions as a community radio under the supervision of its listeners; a radio that is not privately owned by a few, but rather is the property of all those who make its existence possible; a do-it-yourself radio taken up by all listeners, female and male; a radio with open access for all — so far at least visible via telephone and public editorial meetings — with easily manageable technology; a radio that ultimately breaks through news blackouts, that elucidates rather than soothes, in that it provides debates and

lively dialogue in place of journalism that is watered down and based in official statements.[16]

This change in direction also necessitated that RDL begin broadcasting in the Freiburg area, because the philosophies behind community/ free radio really suggested that production and transmission be directly connected to the listeners who were the central constituents of the broadcasts. Rather than continuing to be cautious by broadcasting from its French partner station in Colmar, this meant returning to illegal, but proximal broadcasts.

Crucial to this notion of *Gegenöffentlichkeit* are those aspects of a liberally minded media practice, characteristic of Bertolt Brecht and Hans Magnus Enzensberger, which focus on open access to technologies of production, such that consumers of media products (i.e., listeners to radio, viewers of television, etc.) are provided with an avenue for entering into discussions and expressing opinions within the forum of these electronic public spaces, and thus become producers themselves. Programming mirrored issues of importance to the local community and offered insights on sociopolitical issues from other parts of the world: squatter's rights, issues related to the unemployed, gay rights, women's radio, children's radio, reports from Central and South America, the peace and environmental movements. And all of this was accomplished through an editorial structure consisting of teams of collaborators or autonomous groups that rotate their members out, thus ensuring that any one program does not become associated with one individual person or group of people. RDL's 1985 decision to move back into a position of illegitimacy to pursue the tenets of a community/free radio practice, in order to assist in establishing an alternative public sphere to that being offered and supported by the mainstream press and public broadcasting, brought with it increased police raids, surveillance, arrests, and criminal prosecution for broadcasting illegally. Even on the heels of police crackdowns throughout 1985 and into the spring of 1986 and three criminal prosecutions in September/October 1986 for violation of laws regulating the operation of a communications system (*Fernmeldeanlagengesetze*) RDL continued broadcasting and pressuring for a legalized frequency through repeated applications to the

Regional Office for Communication (Landesanstalt für Kommunikation) for a broadcasting license, and through petitions and street demonstrations in Freiburg demonstrating support for a locally operated, regional community radio. Following two years of these types of activities, RDL was granted a license and a permanent frequency (102.3 MHz) on November 23, 1988.

At the same time that RDL found itself in the midst of a progressive embrace of community/free radio practice by the local community and a regressive confrontation by regional and federal state authorities for the very same reasons, media policy in the Federal Republic was also looking at reforms to dismantle the monopoly held by public broadcasting and open the field to private and commercial interests as well, which were part of a larger European trend to open up regulatory hurdles to commercial interests looking to capitalize on open frequencies and establish enhanced consumer services based on the future potential of a "new" media economy — and many Western European governments were happy to oblige. These reforms caused considerable political and public debate in West Germany centered on the nature and function of public broadcasting and how these historically decided upon broadcasting structures would continue to provide accountability with the addition of these new private, for-profit television and radio stations. As Peter Humphreys clarifies, these structures of accountability provided West Germany with a model of broadcasting unique to Western Europe:

> The accountability mechanisms for broadcasting marked German public-service broadcasting as a distinctive model. For obvious historical reasons, it was more self-consciously democratic and pluralistic than many other systems.... The principal democratic/pluralistic feature of the German regulatory system was the key role played by "broadcasting councils" within the individual regional broadcasting corporations.... These broadcasting councils each contained varying numbers of representatives from "socially significant groups" such as cultural bodies, churches, employers associations, trade unions, and so on, along with political representatives. This "internal control" assured that the channels were "internally pluralistic."[17]

The fear that this level of accountability to democratic and pluralistic values in broadcasting would fall by the wayside with the institution of private commercial broadcasting was quelled by a ruling handed down by the Federal Constitutional Court in November 1986 in response to a new media law in Lower Saxony from May 1984 permitting commercial broadcasting, which gave the state government sovereignty over allocation of new broadcasting franchises; and this raised some concerns related to the decentralization of broadcast that followed World War II.[18] The importance of this ruling lies with the Court's finding that several of the Lower Saxony media law's provisions did overstep too much in locating regulatory oversight with the state government, and thus hampering these mechanisms of accountability. But it also provoked significant changes in West Germany's media landscape, namely the suggestion and subsequent implementation of a dual broadcasting system, with room for both the continuation of an internally regulated public service broadcasting sector and a deregulated private commercial sector, which did not need to meet the same standards of diversity or balance of programming required of public broadcasting.

In the context of our discussion of RDL and other Free Radios popping up around West Germany, these media policy reforms and the creation of a dual broadcasting structure are important factors to consider, since their noncommercial approach to broadcasting limit their categorization in either of the sectors, while their small budgets and lack of financing would also keep them out of the competitive process involved within the private commercial broadcasting sector, and thus continued to make it difficult to legally acquire a broadcasting license and frequency. Instead, in the framework of the liberal media theory put forward by Enzensberger, Jürgen Habermas, Oskar Negt, and Alexander Kluge, the community/free radios interpreted their alternative media practice and support of an alternative public sphere as building a third pole within this dual broadcasting system.[19] Although it would take some time before this idea of a third pillar within the existing broadcasting structure would find resonance within state and federal media policy, it has started to become a significant factor in varying levels of decision-making related to the development of the telecommunications landscape in Germany, primarily as a result of increased influence of the Bündnis 90/Die Grünen political party on the national level. One example is the November 1996 preliminary report of an independent commission charged with investigating the economic and social factors of the media within

Germany's move into the information economy. This preliminary report focused on issues related to freedom and diversity of opinion, the aspects of competition within the media sector, and more specifically on changing ideas about radio and the necessity for regulation within new media. It also contains an appended draft preliminary report from Bündnis 90/Die Grünen, which expands on issues related specifically to broadcasting policies and the expansion of the dual broadcasting structure into a triadic structure that integrates local experience into the media landscape, stating, "The triadic broadcasting system means that private, noncommercial program offerings should be made available. It is these types of programming that truly give the term 'private' its meaning. As with the private sphere, these formats are geared to the community of the citizens, and are thus integrated, local offerings."[20] While these insights are presented in an appended draft to the commission's preliminary report (which would lead one to ask how independent the commission was in the first place) and could thus be seen as being utopian or idealistic with respect to the actual role of community/free radio, the arguments presented do reflect a more progressive atmosphere at the national level, not only with a view to furthering an open domestic policy in these areas, but also, as the draft report suggests, "to minimize the already existing gap to our neighbors [e.g., The Netherlands],"[21] thus highlighting the need to maintain a competitive edge within the sphere of policymaking that demonstrates a broader, more open-minded approach to broadcasting regulations, and positioning Germany, rightfully, as a leading player in a larger idea of a European telecommunications media policy.

Radio Dreyeckland's transition from pirate radio broadcast to free radio broadcast marks not only a transition from an illegal occupation of frequencies to support specific social movements to a legitimate permanent frequency to support the creation and maintenance of a locally infused, alternative public sphere; it also signifies the continued need to navigate the delicate balance between meeting regulation standards and defining the parameters of alternativeness for the purpose of self-definition. By shedding its pirate status to promote a grassroots approach to media practice called for by Brecht and Enzensberger through the activation of listeners in the production process itself, but without the power to change the actual policies regulating the media landscape other than through continued existence, Radio Dreyeckland is positioned in this liminal space between doing right by the law and doing right by its media philosophical approach. In contrast, media theorist Geert Lovink offers a notion of sovereign media, which attempts to exist outside the bounds and regulations of communication through listener alienation and the performative composition of the mix: "The penchant for mixing represents the transition from alternative media, which are still trying to fill a lacuna in the existing supply, to sovereign media, which have detached themselves from the potential listening audience.... Sovereign media are fallout from the 'emancipation of the media,' and they abandon the communication model."[22] Lovink's description of sovereign media suggests that proponents of an alternative media have not gone far enough in abandoning the communication structures they are attempting to critique, but rather end up reproducing these same models and regulatory structures that fix them in place. Instead his sovereign media exist only for themselves, only for a potential audience of none. The utopian undercurrents that flow through this idea of media are difficult to avoid and point to the improbability of actually being able to detach themselves from a consumer model or abandon fully the structures of communication.

Sounding Out Austrian Radio Space

While the majority of contemporary mainstream and nonmainstream radio listeners would likely not think twice about the prerecorded origin of their radio programming, in the case of the former, nor beyond the broadcasts of nonconventional music (classical, jazz, opera) or the occasional documentary-style report reminiscent of much National Public Radio broadcasting, in the case of the latter, beginning in the 1980s the budding world of telecommunications art, which accompanied the more readily accessible computer networks and global telecommunications systems, began to explore the possibilities of a broadcast- or radio-enabled space for artistic purposes. And, as evidenced by the next two examples of this study, these telecommunications artists continue to do so, to the extent that the disembodied voices and sounds of radio space have begun to inhabit the predominantly economic realm of data space normally associated with these global information infrastructures. That the radio and its technologies of transmission and reception have enjoyed a relatively long history as both a viable medium for artistic expression remains uncontested. That the radio be positioned within a range of a/synchronous communication devices and techniques (telephone networks, web-based messaging applications, live audio streaming, etc.) as a method for connecting artists and their varying sound projects in a network of broadcast space, however, is an idea that continues to ride the waves of the cutting edge.

Broadcast weekly since its inception in 1987 on the Ö1 cultural channel of the Österreichischer Rundfunk (ORF), the Viennese Kunstradio program has produced a range of artistic broadcasts that can be loosely described as exploring the edges and finely tuned detail of sound production, sound transmission, and sound reception as elements within a full range of artistic production (visual art, sculpture, text, performance art, and sound art) vis-à-vis the medium of radio. Two broadcast projects, in particular, serve as the artistic focus of this chapter: the two-part series *Europa Report* 1: "In Transit," and *Europa Report* 2: "Between the Cities" from 1989 and 1991, respectively, and *Other Voices — Echoes from a Warzone* from April 1999.[23] Each of these broadcasts engage conceptually with the varying practical (read: real) and theoretical issues of globalization in the context of the growing European Union, and more specifically with a range of political, social, economic, and cultural connections between Vienna and Eastern Europe. Given Austria's geographic location in central Europe, and with Vienna's long imperial history as center of the Austro-Hungarian empire, these broadcast projects also provide a medial and artistic layer to understanding and shaping Austria's role in contemporary critical discussions about issues of migration, national identity, and the framing of ideology within post-1989 Europe. Where the 1989 and 1991 series *Europa Report*,[24] orchestrated and performed by the group Radio Subcom, explores various geographical points and economic sites where human movement and information flow occurs (airport transit halls, market squares, border crossings, cargo shipyards), in order to auscultate larger global questions of asylum for economic/political refugees, the 1999 project *Other Voices — Echoes from a Warzone*,[25] arranged by artist and DJ Gordan Paunović, amplifies the cityscape of thoughts and sounds of Belgrade and its people immobilized by NATO's aerial bombing response to Serbia's leader Slobodan Milosević and the war in Kosovo.

The nonhierarchical broadcast structure and the overarching theme of migration taken up by each of these projects speak to the movement of information and bodies across networks and crossings to create or establish a cultural presence, when the possibility of physical movement and physical presence is hindered by spatio-temporal distance, or by political, social, and economic regimes of power. Allowing mobility to occur through the flow of information, marketable goods and services, and signals, rather than through the movement of physical bodies across national and international boundaries, points to a set of larger research questions about the links between information as a commodity, network globalization and connectivity, and artistic access to these invariably closed systems. How does the subtraction of the physical body from within an exchange of ideas lead to changes in information reception? That is, does the removal of the physical body trigger the transformation of intellectual thought into information, and subsequently into commodity? How does information for thought become information for sale? And what role does artistic experimentation play in this intertwining of communication and economics? These are viable questions that inform and are informed by these three live performance broadcasts. Exploring thematically the varying issues surrounding migration, the two-part *Europa Report,* and *Other Voices* each work by forming interconnected networks of broadcast stations, points of interactive access for its various audiences, and intermedial networks of sound-based input and output, and in the process they work by subverting broadcasting practices of standardized content and transmission procedures, and effectively demonstrate that alternatives to a globalized telecommunications structure and homogeneous cultural content are possible.

Radio space, or broadcast space, draws together notions of an immaterial space known as the ether, the physics of electromagnetic frequencies, the clarity of disembodied sound, and the receptiveness of the listening subject to create a space of performance. This performance space transcends the physical limitations of the performing and listening body, blends the notional ideas behind the performance repertoire and the relational powers of the listening experience, and splices these out-of-body interactions onto equally immaterial and inaudible electromagnetic frequencies to be captured and broadcast by very real, very material, and very technical devices such as the radio receiver. When radios still had dials what we encountered in the tuning process was an eerie sort of journey through the ether, a fantastic jaunt of disconnected voices, music, and electronic sounds until the clarity of the searched-for channel came through. This encounter with radio space highlights its immersive capacity, the ability to draw listeners in and engage them. In the introduction to his recent study media arts professor Joe Milutis describes the ether as:

> At once the attic of the universe in which antique and broken, unrecorded, or unheard transmissions can be found, and it is the misnomer for the wireless-seeming tangle of ports called the "Ethernet" that resides in the basements of institutional space and facilitates local area networks.[26]

Here he establishes a delicate connection between the elusive, diaphanous qualities of this nonspace and the fleeting resonance of sound, reminding us that for early radio practitioners and enthusiasts the ether served as a loose archive for both already uttered and conveyed sound and for sound yet-to-be-heard and mediated either through the parameters of broadcast or those of the listening experience — in a certain sense these are sounds in their natural state, sounds that exist within a field of electromagnetic frequencies and wavelengths. And, misnomer or not, Milutis links the nonspace of the ether with the technocultural embrace of ethereality in the creation of cyberspace, and in doing so highlights the ether as a networked space, where the crisscrossing of wires, ports, and signals, demonstrative of the global telecommunication infrastructure, have been marking out territorial claims in a type of electromagnetic frequency land grab or foreclosure on URL "etherfront" property using tactics reminiscent of eminent domain. Industrial designers Anthony Dunne and Fiona Raby also note this territoriality in their volumes *Hertzian Tales* and *Design Noir*. They situate their research at the juncture between the immaterial world of electromagnetic frequencies and the material world of electronic objects, defining the proximal space of electromagnetic radiation that escapes from electronic objects as hertzian space. Citing hertzian space as "a medium for carrying information, an invisible alternative to wires and cables,"[27] Dunne and Raby comment that attempts to make this space habitable, to account for it in the design and architecture of new buildings and other objects, is becoming increasingly more difficult given this territoriality:

> Like other "natural" environments, the electromagnetic spectrum is constantly under threat from commercial over-development. Unsurprisingly, industry views hertzian space solely as something to be bought and sold and commercially developed for use in broadcasting and telecommunications. The spectrum is highly regulated by the state and nearly all uses of it require a license — unauthorized use is viewed as trespassing. The high value of electromagnetic real estate has encouraged the government to explore radical plans to raise billions from the part privatization of the spectrum. If these plans go through, it will revolutionise the allocation of spectrum to media, telecommunications and public sectors. Not-for-profit and community-based organisations will find it more and more difficult to compete for access with aggressively commercial companies.[28]

Yet even within this corporate and governmental divvying up of the ether and the electromagnetic frequency spectrum, and in the increasing move to create larger zones of immaterial wealth, where economic and knowledge transactions take place virtually, an experimental, artistic, and operative mode exists that seeks to access and transform this space of regulated telecommunications into an unrestricted space of networked performance. It is in this vein that the Austrian Kunstradio project, formed under the direction of Heidi Grundmann, strives to connect artists with the often inaccessible technical infrastructure of radio. In her essay "Radio as Medium and Metaphor" Grundmann writes:

> *Kunstradio* had to do with artists who saw themselves as the initiators of media-based processes and which logically understood its role not as the regulator of access to the radio but as an entry point to the means of production and transmission provided by public radio; as a clearing-point at which strategies were developed in partnership with the artists for avoiding bureaucratic restrictions within the institution itself.[29]

While the politics of artistic access are extremely important for an understanding of the Kunstradio project's raison d'être, it is in their manifesto about the nature of radio as a communications medium, and the nature of radio as an artistic medium, that this idea about radio space is adapted along the contours of simultaneity and interactivity it implicitly sets into motion:

TOWARD A DEFINITION OF RADIO ART

1. Radio art is the use of radio as a medium for art.
2. Radio happens in the place it is heard and not in the production studio.
3. Sound quality is secondary to conceptual originality.
4. Radio is almost always heard combined with other sounds — domestic, traffic, TV, phone calls, playing children, etc.
5. Radio art is not sound art — nor is it music. Radio art is radio.
6. Sound art and music are not radio art just because they are broadcast on the radio.
7. Radio space is all the places where radio is heard.
8. Radio art is composed of sound objects experienced in radio space.
9. The radio of every listener determines the sound quality of a radio work.
10. Listeners hear their own final version of a work for radio combined with the ambient sound of their own space.
11. The radio artist knows that there is no way to control the experience of a radio work.
12. Radio art is not a combination of radio and art. Radio art is radio by artists.[30]

Conceptualized by telecommunications artist and Kunstradio collaborator Robert Adrian, the manifesto points to radio space not as a space regulated by issues of quality or tied to a fixed studio but rather as a fluid, transforming, and transitory space dependent on the networks of relationships it mediates between artists, their radio art concepts and sound objects, and their listeners. Each of the points in this constellation initiates encounters with and within the space opened up by the medium of the radio, yet the twelve points of the manifesto clearly situate listening and the position of the listener as the point where the experience of radio art occurs — for example with point two: "Radio happens in the place it is heard and not in the production studio" — and becomes intricately tied to the sounds and the unique spaces of each individual listener — here, point ten: "Listeners hear their own final version of a work for radio combined with the ambient sound of their own space." Conceived in this way, radio space allows temporary spaces of performance to develop that put both artists and listeners on equal footing in the transmission and reception of a radio art piece, and moves the value of the piece away from its technical point of transmission in the studio, and away from an idea of art objects selling as art products in the art market, and toward its point of reception with the listener — in effect restructuring the commercial broadcast paradigm from one based in the marketing of information through time-specific standardized formats to one based in the interchange of knowledge without privileging these formatting concerns.

Robert Adrian's manifesto about art radio theorizes the position and role of the audience in the art process. The expansion of the networked electronic space to incorporate outlets via radio broadcast to an audience of dispersed listeners became possible as advances in network technologies continued to grow, and as radio itself began to explore areas of convergence with computer-based and satellite networking. The stage was thus set for the types of technically and artistically experimental broadcasts that Kunstradio wanted to produce and support — broadcasts that explore the very nature of knowledge and information in the ever-changing landscape of telecommunications technologies, fold in ideas about artist and audience interactivity that move beyond the emptiness the term has come to represent in standard infotainment models, and splice these together for a deeper understanding of how artists use broadcast space to field geopolitical issues surrounding migration, work with and resuscitate them notionally and conceptually, and transmit them back as broadcast for audience reception and engagement.

Radio Subcom: Pirate Radio
and Experimental Artistic Practice

In a 1993 presentation on Orson Welles's 1938 radio play *The War of the Worlds,* Friedrich Kittler commented on the standardized format that commercial radio had cornered itself into:

> Nobody listens to radio. What loudspeakers or headsets provide for their users is always just radio programming, never radio itself. Only in emergencies, when broadcasts are interrupted, announcer voices get stuck in the throat or stations drift away from their proper frequencies are there at all any moments to actually hear what radio listening could be all about.[31]

The idea of a distant, primordial realm of sound only rarely heard transforms the radio from its role in traditional broadcasting with set programming standards, scheduling structures, and reception frequencies into an exciting device, a type of sonic window onto a wealth of new sounds and sound collages, an entry point to experiments in sound. For Kittler, radio is no longer what it was once regulated to become, a device for reception-only of commercial productions.[32] On the contrary, contemporary radio artists from around the world have begun to experiment with these traditional notions of radio as a reception device by cracking it wide open to expose the myriad wavelengths, frequencies, and bandwidths that comprise radio's multiple, yet often inaudible, uses. In her essay "Radiokunst" Heidi Grundmann draws attention to several experimental radio projects that challenge traditional commercial radio output.[33] One such performance group is Radio Subcom, a two-person nomadic audiovisual broadcasting studio based in a Mercedes bus that is outfitted with both the latest in digital technologies and with appropriated and found parts, which are then fashioned or repurposed as broadcasting technologies. In addition to Radio Subcom's methods of radio production, Grundmann also points to Canadian media artist Michael Snow and his use of short-wave radio to synthesize and rebroadcast the panoply of noise that resides in radiospace. What these two examples demonstrate is a tendency in contemporary Kunstradio to move beyond the producer/consumer model of cultural production and to focus instead on allowing the technology to come through as the primary player in their experiments, which removes the artist from the equation and engages the listener at a primal level, confronting her with the tones, vibrations, and noise normally filtered out or "mainstreamed" by commercial radio frequencies. As the Kunstradio project makes clear in their twelve-point "Kunstradio Manifesto," control over the experience of a radio work is an impossibility preempted by the proximal soundscapes of each individual listener. As radio artists, Snow and Radio Subcom never claim ownership to the works they produce, seeing themselves as thinking agents, as stopovers, within the routing of information, where their own take can be added to the mix before sending it back out into the network.

Radio Subcom included Austrian media author Armin Medosch and Swiss music performer Oil Blo. Armin Medosch describes the group's function as a type of "recycling station for clichés," seeing their mobile audiovisual studio on wheels as a production unit for this reworking or reactivation of already regurgitated and meaningless content:

> The sounds that emanate from the radio are overused expressions; their significance is bound to learned listening habits. Radio Subcom grabs hold of these clichés, changes them through means of sound-based technologies and shifts their context, so that they acquire a completely independent meaning from their original intent. The radio becomes a recycling station opposed to a media-based pollution of the environment. From preserved sounds, comparable to salvage materials like scrap metal or used paper, pleasing new products are made.[34]

For Radio Subcom commercial broadcasting has calcified the way in which radio is listened to, the public's listening habits are, in effect, preprogrammed. In a hyper-actualization of Kittler's remarks, mentioned earlier, Medosch and Oil Blo unsettle the accepted flow of information and commonplace of commercial radio through defamiliarizing the contextual meaning of a sound bite or cliché, and rebroadcasting it as part of a larger sound collage with a specific geopolitical focus. This resuscitation of radio and other media content, those elements that members of Radio Dreyeckland referred to as watered down journalism, forms the foundation of Radio Subcom's approach to a new radio aesthetics, which combines a creative use of sound technology and a rethinking of the currency of information:

Information is a central theme of our age. Radio Subcom expands it into artistic dimensions. Networking, coordination, the immaterial art of communication, the revaluation of the quality of the data stream through a poetic consciousness. Information is a responsibility that should find an auditory outlet on a wide basis through alternatives and proposed solutions of art. The art of intermediation and the mediation of art need support and collaboration for the design of their infrastructure and their forward-looking ideas.[35]

Both parts of Radio Subcom's *Europa Report* series take their substance from the acceleration in the politics of harmonization within the European Economic Community. The adoption of the 1985 Schengen agreement dismantling internal border controls between participating countries and the implementation of the Single European Act in 1986, which established the goal of achieving a common market by 1992, focused on increased collaboration and cohesion in the economic and technology sectors to institute free movement of goods and services, as well as greater partnerships in supranational integration in the areas of social rights, health care, and the environment. These mid-to-late-1980s agreements and policies eventually led to more than economic integration, culminating in the creation of the European Union in 1992 following the ratification of the Maastricht Treaty. Central to the Schengen accord was the development of rules and definitions related to asylum and illegal immigration, and the creation of a shared information system containing data about specific individuals, vehicles, or objects reported stolen, which is supplied by each of the Schengen member states. The first part of Radio Subcom's *Europa Report* series "In Transit" was performed in 1989 at the Ars Electronica Festival and broadcast that same year on November 23 as part of the Kunstradio program. Also commissioned by the Museum of Contemporary Art in Los Angeles for their 1989 radio art series "The Territory of Art," the approximately twenty-four-minute, thirty-one-second piece begins with the phrase "This radio program is authorized by the new European security forces." In the context of Schengen and the transient mode of audiovisual collection that characterizes Radio Subcom's radiophonic production, this opening phrase offers both a critical dig at the new hierarchical systems of information enhancing Europe's internal border crossings and a playful stamp of approval to the piece about to be performed and heard.

That a modified Mercedes bus, painted dark green with a white stripe around the middle and Radio Subcom lettered upward, containing a panoply of electronic devices, and weighed down by these same devices, would not draw attention at border controls in the late 1980s, requiring more extensive background checks and searches, is absurd, and Subcom cleverly acknowledges this fact within this opening salvo. The piece consists primarily of industrial-type sounds, cryptic and ominous vocal modulations, the hum and forward progression of various transportation sounds, and sporadically interspersed announcements reminiscent of the emergency broadcast system. The piece ends on an ironic tone with the inclusion of what can only be described as a tourist-brochure style inducement for a future Europe:

> Good old Europe: Let's enjoy a Europe without heavy industry and other sources of pollution. Europe, in which the economy and the ecology are no longer at ends, since the production and recycling have achieved a perfect cycle. We can enjoy daily the increase of our national income through our technology parks. We are proud of our large and sanitary, restored and rebuilt cities — they stand as an example to all.[36]

Here Armin Medosch provides a glimpse at a future European simulacrum, a vision of a sanitized, efficient, and hyperreal state of official media-centered happiness. Yet the promotion of a new Europe based in policies of economic, informational, and political collaboration is cast in a pall of utopian progress, suggesting that an all-too-quick embrace of a technological and media-based panacea would have just as negative an impact on the living environment as heavy industry. The changing economic landscape of Europe, transforming from an economy based in heavy industry to one based in networking (information, data, communication, media), also brings with it a change in effluvial by-products, categorized as pollutants in the case of heavy industry, and as information overload or low signal-to-noise ratio, in the case of networking. This idea of the purity of signal being hindered by the plethora of background noise, which comprises our daily encounters with the media landscape, forms the operative mode behind Subcom's approach to a radio practice (the cliché recycling described above) that seeks to return the medium to a level of authenticity through composition:

Up to now radio has consisted of newspaper journalism with acoustic input. With the implementation of the technical installation described here, the period of subjective, composed language based solely on authentic recordings can begin. Language and sound in the composition of a radio program merge into an insoluble object, which can be grasped as a meaningful message only in its entirety, and thus consequently rescue the medium's authenticity.[37]

In this respect, Radio Subcom sees its artistic role in radio production as one that simultaneously unfetters information from its packaging in journalistic sound bites or advertising lingo, and reactivates it for critically engaged discourse. "In Transit" serves as both a provocative reminder and as an uncanny premonition of the ways in which the media transforms public perception, while at the same time is equally transformed by official government policy. Radio Subcom's desire to rescue the radio medium, to resuscitate its deep-seated authenticity as a medium that communicates, and thus as a medium that questions, is also a desire to uncouple communication from governmental sanction and return it to a space of creative and vocal potential.

The Kunstradio broadcast of Subcom's second sound piece in the *Europa Report* series — the fourteen minute, fifteen second "Between the Cities" presented on February 28, 1991 — is preceded by a note from Oil Blo that contains a postscript suggesting an appropriate volume level for the listening audience: "The volume level is presumed to be used for listening or not listening. Thus the listener's volume control should be turned accordingly to gentle."[38] Here we have an interesting confrontation, one that pits audience vs. audience, one that casts radio as an active interface rather than as a passive listening device, and one that exposes a type of *Feind im eigenen Haus* (internal enemy) in its disjunctive integration into the ORF program. Oil Blo's warning to place the volume on *leise* (quiet) may be, on the one hand, an indication that the information about to be presented is so shocking that it is best to encounter it softly — perhaps a portent of the listeners' delicate constitutions. On the other hand, the documentary and "mix" style of the piece is so "other" to a more typical cultural radio broadcast that the decibel level may need to be softened for this particular type of broadcast. Suggesting the appropriate volume to listeners also serves to remind them that they themselves control at least one aspect of the radio broadcast, and thus reminds as well, at least at a tacit level, of the radio's former transmission capabilities before it was retooled for reception only. Finally, this postscript also calls attention to the institutionalization that the radio piece is about to undergo in its adaptation for broadcast on the ORF. To fit such a short audio work into a forty-five-minute time slot requires additional material, and this is one way in which the monopoly of the ORF is able to exert some of its power. Heidi Grundmann comments on this relationship between Kunstradio and the ORF, and the type of artistic experimentation that the relationship engenders:

> Of course, there is still a wide range of approaches [for radio art] — also in central Europe, which are provoked, for example, by the prevailing conditions of local media policies that do not provide independent access to radio waves to marginalized or underground groups. For many years artists from any number of groups have reacted to this... and have developed a counter-image to the existing media political situation: this image contains the possibility of artists (and other marginalized groups) being able to broadcast independently and to develop a radio aesthetics that corresponds to their own needs and that is not governed by the rules and conventions of institutionalized (state-owned) radio.[39]

The issues of access and the types of contemporary experiments that Grundmann describes here are also components within Radio Subcom's work. The group's live performances and productions for radio combine practices in tactical media, methods of pirate radio, and techniques of agitprop theater with original rap, spoken text, and archived sound and video clips to create an alternative sound-based snapshot of current political and social issues in Europe. The concepts of pirate radio and agitprop theater are themselves each layered with their own traditions of cultural signification, subversive application, and community identification. Pirate radio methods often involve either a mobile or easily/quickly transportable set-up of equipment, which is either found, pieced together, modified from other parts, or "borrowed." Matthew Fuller, in an essay on the media ecology of pirate radio, provides an economy and workflow of a typical operation:

> The most grinding work of a pirate operation is in maintaining transmission sites. Renewing equipment after busts, finding new locations for studios, links and aerials. Financial attrition as equipment gets eaten up in seizures is one way that the airwaves are kept locked-down.... Pirates operate without prescriptive demands, working instead with their inverse: at what level of cheapness

will things still run, how disposable can the gear be made in order that when it is seized another can be put into play as soon as possible?[40]

Even within this underground world fraught with the possibility of getting busted, Fuller locates the attraction to pirate radio not in the fear of getting caught, but in the commitment to the process and the sense of group subcultural identity it provokes: "There is a phenomenology of cash flows, of the libidinality or dullness of the work of broadcast, of setting signals loose to evade capture, but that are yet received, a sense of a technico-aesthetic life inventing and re-sensing itself through the process."[41] The importance of retooling or repurposing equipment, of unleashing broadcast signals onto commercial wavelengths, is also seen within the work of urban agitprop artists, who appropriate mainstream cultural motifs and public uses of technology (surveillance cameras) and recast them in moments of live street theater. These somewhat fleeting moments of disruption and alternatives to established public space and public broadcast bring to tactical media a much more practiced engagement with a notion of globalization as the "immense enlargement of world communication, as well as of the horizon of a world market"[42] — not only in a practical sense of understanding the workings of network and broadcast infrastructure, but also in a playful sense of letting commodified information loose, of allowing knowledge to shed its informational veneer and to be available for reflection, no longer information for sale, but information for thought. With linkages out to Jacques Attali's notion of composition, Geert Lovink refers to the playfulness of production as a theory of mixing. Writing in the context of Amsterdam's numerous pirate radio and autonomous radio channels in the 1980s, Lovink describes the approaches of DJs working within a culture of appropriation, mixing, and setting loose:

> They [the mix shows] represent nothing and no one. Mixers create their own sound universes which stretch infinitely far in both length and breadth. They bob about in a sea of free time. Duration is the essence of their concoctions. If the mix is subjected to the time dictate, then it turns into a live scratch or rap, making do without the glamour of a performing artist. These live performances have traces of genius. A fleeting masterwork is born there and then, and evaporates into the ether afterward. A careless attitude to copyright is an important precondition. Rummaging in the world media archive is not compatible with the constitutional state. But the latter excludes free radio.[43]

This captures the elements of improvisation, moment-specific performance, and an approach to the archive as preexisting source but not as proliferation, which run through Attali's notion of composition. What is key to Fuller's insights on pirate radio practice, Lovink's theories of the mix, and Attali's composition is these very time delimited ideas of duration that are couched within equally unbounded notions of space. And, although Attali's work is not specific to the radio medium, it is the techniques of broadcast that open up compositional performance to the specificity of the temporal and the immateriality of the spatial.

The mobility of their modified Mercedes bus and the assembled nature of their radio equipment lend Radio Subcom an aura of transgression — crossing both national boundaries and national radio bandwidths to produce and transmit their radio art pieces. This nomadic, itinerant collection and rearticulation of sound retools the notion of the archive as occupying a historical, temporally fixed, and spatially permanent position, while also capturing a sense of sound as a fleeting and imprecise reflection of our daily experience with it. Here Medosch describes the importance of sound technology for their work, and locates the value of this work in the process of producing radio, in the process of mixing:

> Creative use of sound technology is a further important component of the radio aesthetic represented by Radio Subcom. Oil Blo uses a mixture of the newest digital audio technology and machines from the stone age of radio technology: vocal mixes using an old thermionic amplifier, vocal alienations on a guitar effects pedal from the early 1950s or cheap pre-amps, tape-scratching and other "primitive" methods; ... Radio art is not a special category of conventional radio; rather it is the art of making radio independently.[44]

In making the process of radio production the object of radio broadcast by removing the spatiotemporal limitations imposed by commercial radio programming, Medosch and Oil Blo return to the radio some of the excitement of the unknown that Kittler mentions nostalgically. The use of radio as tactical media is readily apparent in the making of the *Europa Report* 2: "Between the Cities" piece, produced in the fall of 1990 and performed live at the RAI/Audiobox Festival in the southern Italian city of Matera. The material for the performance piece was collected in Milan, in the tenuous atmosphere of a *besetztes Haus* (a squat) and the sense of restlessness and heightened sensitivity that such a situation produces. The underpinnings of the radio broadcast stem from longer conversations with two occupants of the house, and even though much of the interviews no longer remains in the final product, segments from them are looped in as hook lines, as repeated fragments of particularly descriptive moments of dialogue.

The subject of these conversations centered primarily on the occupants' experiences as part of Milan's subculture, specifically in their knowledge of the *Centro sociale,* a group of autonomous cultural centers in Milan and northern Italy, and various issues that occurred in association with them, or which were bubbling to the surface at the time in Milan. Examples include the Mafia's attempt to use the centers as distribution points for the sale of heroin, the problems with housing, social assistance programs, and xenophobia in association with an influx of North African refugees: "Ask the North Africans who are sleeping on Piazza Vetra in Milano / Ask them about Europe in 1992 / Ask the Pakistani in London / Ask them about Europe in 1992 / Ask the Romanians / Ask them / Ask the people on the street how they feel from the heat of the global warming";[45] the fallout from an arson fire in a squatter house where three hundred people regularly spent the night; and a violent 1989 strike by police to vacate the Centro sociale Leoncavallo: "Milan: 1989 the occupied communications center Leoncavallo was vacated by a brutal police raid. The last European underground holdouts are disappearing. As artists we are asked to decide if we want to establish ourselves through art, or if we want to voluntarily go into the underground."[46] While Naomi Klein, in her 2002 volume *Fences and Windows,* describes Italy's social centers as "windows — not only into another way to live, disengaged from the state, but also into a new politics of engagement,"[47] the immediacy that Radio Subcom brings to their 1991 performance and broadcast not only presents issues related to the activist function of artistic production and distribution, but also suggests that behind the shiny glass surfaces Klein sees ten years later is a deeper, richer, perhaps more engaged history that deserves to be sounded out. With Milan and her daily news stories as the geopolitical epicenter,

Radio Subcom interweaves larger issues of importance on a continental and global level: the social and economic impact of the opening of Eastern Europe: "The revolution will not be televised, unless of course television causes the revolution — the opposite is true in Eastern Europe — a successful coup of international entrepreneurship";[48] and the anxieties surrounding the creation of a unified Europe with a single currency: "Poland, East Germany, Hungary, Czechoslovakia make themselves free, wanted to be a part of the community, so terribly. Now they feel that they are cheated, terribly mistreated, no human rights, no social security, no strong economy, everything for the multinationals, nothing for the population. Fuck everything."[49] Each of these rap commentaries on local and global events are enmeshed within an overarching critique of mainstream media — the role of media as public relations and entertainment — media as big business:

> The role of the media: the Internet has thrown its fiction over reality like a giant glass cover. The Internet, the electronic environment, consists solely of pure public relations. All concepts — information, entertainment — have become inferior since the arrival of public relations. The differentiation between fact and fiction has become senseless: hostage-taking, war, terror attacks can no longer be considered in themselves as politically motivated, but rather as side effects of big media business.[50]

With loops such as "police control, capital control," "piu fascist" (more fascists), "united Europe in 92," and "war looks good on color TV" as well as information and commentary provided in the form of rap music threads, Medosch and Oil Blo draw attention to the rhetoric of mainstream opinion makers and seek to give a voice to the minority who do not have the hi-tech toys of the media, nor their attention. "Between the Cities" captures the reverberations of information, recognizing the global to local flow of data that is consistently negotiated through mainstream media and reversing it, such that the local embodiment of information is cast in relation to the global, not necessarily superseding it, but positioning it as an equal part in the production of knowledge. With its focus on Milan street culture, on its representatives' reception and interpretation of global media events, of its perceptions on how a united Europe will play out in 1992, Radio Subcom's media performances engage the issues of globalization as they apply to the opening of markets in newly liberated Eastern Europe and from the perspective of a minority class. Frederic Jameson, in his essay "Notes on Globalization as a Philosophical Issue," writes:

> The former socialist countries have seemed largely unable to generate an original culture and a distinctive way of life capable of standing as an alternative, while...in the third world the older traditionalisms are equally enfeebled and mummified, and only a religious fundamentalism seems to have the strength and the will to resist Americanization. But here the operative word is surely *seems;* for we have yet to see whether these experiments offer positive social alternatives, or merely reactive and repressive violence.[51]

Radio Subcom's piece suggests that the movements that brought about change in the East were swept cleanly away by a desire of the West to have these new markets, that in the global media frenzy surrounding the expulsion of communism the alternative voices that Jameson misses did not have the opportunity to express themselves in the net cast by the global media. The piece ends with a message that has obvious parallels to Jameson's statements: "There are only two directions: one is leading toward central Europe, toward the centers of money, power, and tech-knowledge; the other direction is an endless trip through the slums of the Third World."[52] Whatever effective role experimental art radio can play in mediating discussions on globalization or in providing alternatives to the dominant paradigms of mainstream media will remain an open question. The idea of an information economy that embodies itself in the form of cellophane-wrapped bites is challenged by such artistic experimentation with media as that of Radio Subcom. Subcom turns traditional/nostalgic notions of radio on their head. On the level of production and performance, in the process of radio making, their media performances delve into the postmodern mythos of globalization — the celebration of difference and cultural pluralism. Their focus on Milanese street culture to engage larger European questions of economic and social/cultural unity, and their remediation and appropriation of radio, in content and in technology, poke numerous holes into the promises of global networking, global economy, and global communication. That radiophonic space, like Gibson's cyberspace, can be envisioned as an alternative reality to mainstream information, as a place where information can resume its shape as thought, provides some interesting directions for radio to develop.

Radio Art and the Sounds of Displacement

On the evening of April 29, 1999, NATO Operation Allied Force began its thirty-seventh day of air operations with "the single most intense period of attacks over Belgrade."[53] That same evening in Vienna from 10:15 to 11:55 p.m., Kunstradio, a program on the Ö1 cultural channel of the ORF, broadcast a live mix by Serbian radio artist and Radio B92 founding member Gordan Paunović, described as a hundred minutes in support of the free voice of Radio B92. Radio B92 began broadcasting as an independent and experimental youth radio station in Belgrade in May 1989 under the direction of Veran Matić. By 1999 it had established itself as the highest rated station in Belgrade and had become the primary source of current affairs programming for ANEM, the Asocijacija nezavisnih elektronskih medija (Association of Independent Electronic Media), a consortium of thirty independent broadcasters in Serbia. Under the Milosević government the station was banned numerous times, culminating in its takeover on March 24, 1999, the day NATO began aerial bombing over Belgrade. The Kunstradio project's sponsorship and broadcast of Paunović's live performance supported worldwide efforts in assisting Radio B92 to continue its broadcasts via Internet and other radio channels as Radio B2–92.[54]

Paunović's live radio broadcast and subsequent CD remix *Other Voices — Echoes from a Warzone* (Vienna/Belgrade, April 29, 1999) perform on several levels. They mix audible threads from within the ten-year media landscape that emerged in Serbia between 1989 and 1999. They trace the development of community-based radio and artistic practice within the Milosević era and tease out connections between the creation of alternative media spaces in support of democratic change in Serbia and the neglect of these media spaces by the global media event that arose around Operation Allied Force, the NATO response to the conflict in Kosovo in the spring of 1999. They document those other voices that get lost or silenced in this folding together of repressive media policy on the one hand and the loss of local identity and local response created by an influx of global media conglomerates on the other. And, finally, they demonstrate the collaborative interplay between the two cities of Vienna and Belgrade, inextricably linked through their common geographical, cultural, economic, and historic ties to the Danube, and now also linked through the intermeshing of their respective soundscapes.[55] In the performances marked by Paunović's live broadcast and CD remix, the flows of information between Belgrade and Vienna along Internet channels, diary excerpts, email correspondence, and radio waves stand in for the people of Belgrade, as they are caught between a minimized degree of mobility and the impossibility of movement. In the context of Gordan Paunović's radio performance, how are tactical appropriations of these global telecommunications infrastructures providing new modes of interchange within the cross-border region between Vienna and Belgrade? To this end, how is the historical riparian network between Vienna and Belgrade via the Danube being recast in terms of electronic signal flow?

Gordan Paunović's radio art piece and the Kunstradio program's role in its broadcast provide an exceptional example of how artistic experimentation with the radio medium manages to break in to the globalized space of radio transmission and to help reposition and amplify the voices and ideas lost or ignored within these globalized information networks. It is this actual materiality of the radio, the radio as instrument and the radio as medium, that forms the substance of today's radio art. Heidi Grundmann clarifies these types of experiments in the context of the Kunstradio program and its institutional support by the ORF in her mid-1990s essay "But Is It Radio?":

> The position of *Kunstradio* — however marginalized — inside a public radio institution has made it possible for artists to exploit not only the institution's technical resources but also its mainstream program formats. There have been projects where artists were able to infiltrate other programs and/or channels of the ORF beyond the late-night ghetto, inserting radio-art into Ö3, the pop music channel, or into one or the other of several regional channels. Such interventions outside of the gallery-like space of the weekly national radio-art program are most successful when they are not announced/perceived as art but are left to be incidents in the public space of everyday radio, anticipating

an audience of passers-by who may or may not stop or hesitate for just a brief moment of irritation or even reflection.[56]

Grundmann points to the playfulness involved in the broadcast of radio art. With terms such as "infiltrate" and "intervention" to describe the methods used by Kunstradio-supported artists to broaden their audience base beyond the late Sunday evening times-lot provided to the program by ORF, Grundmann's essay highlights what happens when the roles of technician and artist come together in the realm of radio production. Clearly, the types of productions supported by Kunstradio through its provision of artistic access to the technologies of radio seek to interweave radio's original function as a military relay device and its consumer function as entertainment device. In this sense, the military's use of the radio for tactical reasons is repurposed through the playfulness of these radio artists in order to challenge the assumptions set up by the various broadcasting and transmission standards of commercial radio and also to invoke or play out the types of experimentation suggested by Bertolt Brecht in his oft-cited series of early radio theoretical essays, such as artistic access to broadcasting technologies, listener interactivity, and development of genres specific to the materiality and technique of radio.

The live broadcast of *Other Voices* engages these modes of experimentation with the radio device through its performative routing of unique threads of information, each with their own specific spatio-temporal set of source histories and cultural reverberations or echo effects. The intertextual and intermedial play between these individual components of the overall broadcast prompt both the listener and the creator of the broadcast to think more critically about the relationships between each source of information, while also requiring them to delve more deeply into the respective trace histories of each source. In this sense, Gordan Paunović never claims ownership to the work, seeing himself instead as a thinking agent, as a stopover within the routing of information, where his own take, his own interpretation of the materials, is added to the mix before sending it back out into the network, or in this case over the radio waves. In total, twenty distinct verbal and artistic sound elements were utilized in the live broadcast.[57] This combination of ambient sound and personal documentary details the quick physical change of Belgrade's skyline and the slow process of coping with the impending loss of one's home, one's city, one's identity. Paunović's mixture of tracks from archived music productions, voice overlays, essay commentaries, and live Internet and audio feeds helps to trace these moments of changing experience and displacement of identity.

The live broadcast itself serves as a moment of self-referential tactical media practice, an idea of media that seeks in some way to appropriate the more traditional channels of media as relays of power and use them as relays for dissent and disruption.[58] The live piece begins with a reading of a short essay by Radio B92 founding editor Veran Matić entitled "Schaffung des Informationsraums: 'Commando Solo.' " As the lead-in component for Paunović's live broadcast mix, Matić's essay introduces themes related to postmodern military practice and telecommunications into the broadcast space of the radio piece. Written during the NATO intervention in April 1999 and sent to the Kunstradio studios just two days prior to the live broadcast, the essay takes NATO's use of hybridized weapons combining high-powered bombs and imaging technologies to task and problematizes the use of captured images and recordings from these hybrid devices by mainstream journalists to provide popular backing for NATO's involvement. Among these are discussions about the Commando Solo aircraft to establish an alternative information space through military jamming of civilian radio and television airwaves, as well as the melding together of smart-bomb missiles and cameras to provide logistical and video analysis of targets being bombed:

> The only evidence offered to us as the sole truth is from the camera located in the cone of the missile, which hits its target. The day-to-day recurrence of the same or similar photos acquired through these cameras transforms journalism into a superfluous occupation, since the sole truth originates from the cone of a missile. In this way brutal homicides and destruction become easily tolerated video games.[59]

For Matić, the idea that the 'truth' behind the success of the NATO intervention resided in a quick media consumption of images captured by smart bombs as they headed toward their targets demonstrates the failure of mainstream journalism to critically engage with the reality of the situation in Serbia and the war in Kosovo, and turns the thirty-plus days of NATO bombing into a video game reminiscent of the first Gulf War. To put it more plainly, the global media event prompted by the NATO response to the Kosovo conflict in spring 1999 overlooks and diminishes the local experience of that event. These ideas about the hybridization of warfare technologies and telecommunications networks and about the disappearance of any human experience of the NATO bombing in mainstream media coverage serve to emphasize the artistic possibilities inherent in radio as foregrounded by Paunović's radio art piece and by the Kunstradio program's role in its broadcast. In June 1999, during production of the CD remix, Paunović writes:

> Mainstream media, following guidelines from political establishments on both sides, transformed the reality into a huge propaganda stageset. Beyond the Potemkin villages of the big TV networks, there was another life going on — a life of people who spent years and decades fighting totalitarianism and nationalistic hatred with the power of their expression and creation. Writers, sound artists, radio personalities, media workers, journalists and musicians, suddenly became collateral damage of the war in Yugoslavia.[60]

Paunović's motivation for producing this radio performance piece centers on the artists, writers and media producers who were denied access to the technologies of media production by both the Milosević media state and its broadcasts of the Serbian war and the large television corporations and their broadcasts of the NATO intervention. The function of Matić's essay as epigraph serves as a justification for Paunović's own creation of an alternative information space via the live radio and Internet streaming broadcasts. In this regard, Paunović accomplishes the same type of takeover of radio space that the Commando Solo aircraft has been developed to do militarily. Yet what Paunović's tactical use of the radio medium adds to the mix are the varying threads from spoken text and sonic elements that evoke the emotive atmosphere of Belgrade in April 1999, as well as traces of the historical, cultural, and political engagement with the post-1989 dissolution of Yugoslavia.

What is missing from the publicly proliferated media landscape surrounding the Serbian war in Kosovo and NATO's intervention are the haunting sounds of air-raid sirens, the explosions generated by the aerial bombings, and the rationalized stories from those entrenched in Belgrade's cityscape, all of which arise as elements in Paunović's work. As the website associated with the live version of Paunović's piece points out, the broadcast is structured around three recurrent sound elements: a live audio stream of sounds of the NATO bombing picked up by a microphone hanging outside a window in Belgrade on the evening of April 29, original recordings of a one-minute air-raid alarm from Belgrade sent to the studios in Vienna via an Internet feed, and excerpts from an orchestration by Arsenije Jovanović titled *Concerto grosso balcanico*. Although the broadcast is bounded by the spatiotemporal limitations set up by commercial radio programming timeslots, Paunović's use of these live sound captures and integration of excerpts from topical texts allows the broadcast to transcend its hundred-minute time limit and also transforms the radio from a conduit of transmission and reception to a device that transports its listeners to the streets of Belgrade through a live, point-to-point flow of information. The noise of the bombings captured from the microphone and the air-raid alarm taken from the Internet feed evoke the immediacy of Paunović's piece, while the use of Jovanović's earlier sound project invokes a sonic archaeology of the war in the former Yugoslavia. This 1993 soundscape is a disturbing triptych, which blends the sounds of war with the anxious stirrings of animals (sheep, dogs, and wolves) confronted by these very human sounds.[61] The creation of a CD remix, released in March 2000 to coincide with the anniversary of the beginning of the NATO intervention, emphasizes this function of the live broadcast as archaeological cache or archive and provides Paunović the creative and reflective time necessary to engage with a particular facet of the longer hundred-minute live broadcast. The relationship between the live broadcast and CD remix as one of archive and iteration is one that could continue ad infinitum, and it is one that positions the live broadcast as having the quality of rawness, as a never before heard, never complete, and never deceased sonic snapshot of events occurring in Belgrade in the spring of 1999.

At the center of the CD are voiced excerpts dated from March and April 1999 from two electronic diaries. One is by Jasmina Tesanović, a forty-five-year-old writer, filmmaker, and feminist activist and the other was written by Slobodan Marković, a twenty-one-year-old computer science student at the University of Belgrade, independent media activist and founder of the online Serbian *Internodium* mailing list, which addresses issues of open access to Yugoslav (.yu) cyberspace.[62] The electronic format of both diaries illustrates two important details. First, it points to the importance of the Internet for the sharing of information from two of Belgrade's citizens during a time of war, which Geert Lovink contextualizes in his essay "Kosovo: War in the Age of the Internet" in terms of the extensive media vacuum that had arisen around the NATO intervention:

> It was hard to grasp that an entire region inside (Southeast) Europe is being turned into an information black hole.... What the Internet was left with were Serbian witnesses, diaries, personal accounts, mainly from educated urban citizens. Immediately, while the first bomb load was dropped, the Internet diaries started to pop up. Their psycho-geography is limited, by nature, by the very definition of the genre. They did not produce theory or a critical analysis of politics and the war situation. Add to this situation the semi-personal touch of e-mail, and presto, you get an odd, once in a lifetime mixture of paranoia, reflection, pathetic pity, waves of despair, worrisome productions of subjectivity, with here and there valuable pictures of the everyday life under extraordinary circumstances.[63]

Although Lovink's commentary argues that the personal nature of these Internet diaries makes them in some way less valuable theoretically and critically, I want to suggest that it is exactly their personal overtones, their documentary character, that makes them accessible to the Internet medium, and transferable to the medium of radio broadcast. In this context of war and atmosphere of despair the realm of the personal necessarily becomes the locus of knowledge production, and the foundation from which more critical and theoretical analyses can take shape. And herein lies the second important aspect of these diaries' respective electronic formats, namely, that they help to illustrate once again the radio's transformation from a device for reception only into a medium that interactively engages its listeners and its source feeds in an intellectual, cultural, and sociopolitical network of idea exchange. In a certain sense, both Tesanović's and

Marković's diaries can be viewed as early blogs, or weblogs, which themselves are types of textual broadcasts of information. The entries used from Slobodan Marković's email postings originated from his own personal submissions to an Internet-based mailing list known as the Syndicate Mailing List, which was formed in January 1996 as a "loose affiliation of artists, curators, networkers, writers and festival organisers, most of them from Eastern Europe, who are working in the field of electronic- and media-art."[64] In contrast, Jasmina Tesanović's diary began its unique life on the web almost by accident. As the publisher's note to the 2000 American publication of the diary explains, Tesanović did not personally post her diary entries to the web; rather a friend in Sweden took the step of sharing her personal writing with the world Internet community:

> Hours after NATO started bombing Yugoslavia, Jasmina Tesanović received an e-mail from a friend in Sweden, who wanted to know how she was doing. Jasmina didn't have time to write back, so she sent entries from her diary. Her friend, the writer Ana Valdes, posted Jasmina's diary entries on the web site of a magazine she wrote for. Within a week, the diaries had been posted anonymously on fifty web sites, translated into several languages and sent in emails throughout the world.... The diary of an anonymous woman from Belgrade had become everybody's diary.[65]

Unlike Marković, who knowingly posted his observations on the NATO bombing to the web, Tesanović's diary experienced its anonymous online celebrity through a more grassroots approach to media activism. Both diarists were able to garner a wide audience outside the boundaries of Belgrade and Serbia through utilizing the inherent networks associated with the Internet infrastructure, which facilitated the level of resonance that both achieved in a very short amount of time. With Marković's computer science background and active interest in supporting open artistic and media access to networks in Yugoslav cyberspace, as well as his involvement with media arts groups in Eastern Europe, it is not surprising to understand the reach that his email postings found, nor the types of discussions they informed on several electronic lists in Europe and beyond.[66] In Tesanović's case the language of her diary entries propelled their movement along Internet streams, and this language, as we will see shortly, is informed by her involvement with feminist activist groups like Women in Black and their focus on the situation of women in the various wars in the former Yugoslavia.[67] In much the same way that the live feeds of sounds from Belgrade during the bombing add to the immediacy of the live radio art piece, the echoes of discussion and transmission generated by both of these diaries during the height of NATO activity add a sense of timeliness and urgency to Paunović's piece as well.

Paunović's implementation of the two electronic diaries for his versions of *Other Voices* — his adaptation of them through translation (into German in the case of Marković's entries, into English in the case of Tesanović's), his staging of them as individual channels for mixing into the live radio broadcast, his enlivening of their written thoughts through dramatic vocal readings, his placing of them into the electronic soundscape that represents the city of Belgrade on this one particular evening in April 1999 — reveals the importance of electronic signal flow as a substitution for the physical body, whose movements are restricted or disrupted by both the technologies of war and the technologies of global telecommunications. Both textual documentaries offer eyewitness testimony to the war in Belgrade — commentaries on the absurdity of NATO's missile targets and the civilian-based casualties that resulted from them, and rationalized observations of the developing chaos percolating around them. While Marković's email transmissions recount in emotional detail the nightly destruction of NATO bombs in sarcastic and ironic tones, Tesanović's diary captures the human experience of the war in interstitial terms — of Belgrade's citizens caught between moments of sanity and nervous breakdown, caught between local compulsive patriotism and global compulsive guilt, and caught between the isolation of staying put and the anonymity of being displaced. In the first voiced excerpt from her diary listeners to the radio broadcast experience the reasoned paradoxes of this war — the human players set against the backdrop of the world that causes it. Dated March 26, 1999, at 5:00 p.m., the entry responds to NATO's first sortie of air strikes against Yugoslavia just two days earlier:

> I hope we all survive this war and the bombs: the Serbs, the Albanians, the bad and the good guys, those who took up the arms, those who deserted, the Kosovo refugees traveling through the woods and the Belgrade refugees

traveling through the streets with their children in their arms looking for non-existing shelters when the alarms go off. I hope that NATO pilots don't leave behind the wives and children whom I saw crying on CNN as their husbands were taking off for military targets in Serbia. I hope we all survive, but that the world as it is does not.[68]

Tesanović's remarkable ability to name and empathize with each group of people involved in the Kosovo war, regardless of their ethnic background, refugee status, or NATO involvement, points out that the degree of separation between perpetrator and victim so important in past instances of war is no longer a distinction that can be made in the age of a telecommunications-based war. Seeing images of their future attackers on CNN, watching the movements of Serb and Albanian troops on state-run television, hearing about the migration of Kosovo refugees from independent broadcasts and seeing the nervous wandering of want-to-be refugees in Belgrade with their own eyes provides a continuum between the insanity of imagined war and the calm concreteness of the real war. Tesanović clarifies this balance in the same entry from March 26:

Today is the second aftermath day. The city is silent and paralyzed, but still working, rubbish is taken away, we have water, we have electricity. But where are the people? In houses, in beds, in shelters. I hear several personal stories of nervous breakdowns among my friends, male and female. Those who were in a nervous breakdown for the past year, since the war in Kosovo started, who were very few, now feel better. Real danger is less frightening than fantasies of danger. I couldn't cope with the invisible war as I can cope with concrete needs: bread, water, medicine. And also, very important: I can see an end. Finally we in Belgrade got what all the rest of Yugoslavia has had: war on our territory.[69]

Fear of the unknown, of how the war would be played out, is now replaced with a knowledge of how the war would affect their lives. There is a certain spatiality involved in knowing more about how one's life might end. This is a sense of space that becomes progressively smaller, that limits physical movement and reduces the possibilities of expression. That Paunović places Tesanović's dramatized voice within a surrounding audio stream of air-raid alarms, exploding bombs, and chilling cries in the night, expands this sense of spatiality by positioning Tesanović's words as the unspoken thoughts of every citizen of Belgrade in the surrealist buffer of a city experiencing the loss of its most basic infrastructure. Not included in the radio broadcast, but available on the Kunstradio website, is her diary entry from March 31:

> Fear has entered in my mind: I don't know if I dare think what I do, I cannot cope with reality: is it possible that we are all sacrificed for somebody's lack of political judgment, or worse, madness. I am censoring my thoughts afraid to think in personal tones, afraid to be heard, judged and executed. The conflict is escalating, the atrocities are daily happenings.... My head and language are getting stiff, they have to incorporate all these controversial meanings; I despise getting along in war, no space for feminine language, no free space.[70]

One week into the NATO intervention, the nightly bombing and the daily Serbian war are taking their toll on her sense of self, and her sense of place within the world. Language is becoming other, transforming as her reality is transformed and not allowing her to write and think as she desires. Tesanović links the ever-decreasing sense of space, freedom of movement, and freedom of thought with equally decreasing possibilities for language. Here, her comment that there is "no space for feminine language, no free space" reminds us of her engagement with feminist-based NGOs, and with the founding of the first women's publishing house in Serbia called "94." However, this comment does not mean she is somehow giving up her feminist perspective; on the contrary, the importance of this feminist work for her sense of self and her sense of well-being is still a factor in her continued existence in the bombed city of Belgrade. This statement underscores, as well, the absurdity of being in a city that is being watched by the whole world, but whose citizens are not being listened to. The situational specificity of living in a city that is being attacked by NATO airplanes and barraged by Milosević propaganda has made her painfully aware of the lack of a space where such a feminist perspective is viable, or operational as a valid alternative viewpoint to bombs or half truths. In the entry from April 12, Tesanović reflects on the prospect of leaving Belgrade, her friends, her streets, her habits, her language — and becoming Other:

> I couldn't go to sleep last night, finally I took a tranquilizer, there it goes, I started to. I postponed all these weeks the use of drugs to stay normal, but I see that no normal person can stay normal without drugs, if you want to stay here. I do not want to go, I do not want to leave my city, my friends, my

streets, my habits, my language. I do not believe in Other. I understand those who left, out of fear, out of needs, I could have been one of them too, but I want to stay. Friends from all over the world offer me flats, money, help. But the only thing I need from them and from others all over the world is to try to stop our war.[71]

We hear the resolve in her voice, and again the steadiness of her words places a balance between the two wars that she and her fellow citizens have to locate themselves in, the Serbian war and "compulsive patriotism" during the day, and NATO intervention and "compulsive sense of guilt" at night. In the final three spoken excerpts dated April 20, April 23, and April 26, we come face-to-face with this interstitial existence, with the impossibility of what Zygmunt Bauman terms "degree of mobility—the freedom to choose where to be":[72]

April 20, 1999. Now, what is my cross: NATO bombs, Serbian patriotic death. OK, between compulsive patriotism and compulsive sense of guilt, I guess there is no way out. It would take another life to do so.[73]

April 23, 1999. Just yesterday I thought, now everybody is fighting for our souls, of us Serbs led astray, all these televisions, local and international. We even receive American leaflets from the planes telling us about us. Not even the Colorado teenaged killers could draw attention from our educational program.[74]

April 26, 1999. I do not feel safe with the NATO or any other bombs, NATO being the only ones I know. I do not feel safe without bridges, in a boat, on a horse, on a bicycle, against NATO airplane[s]; I do not feel safe without schools, universities, libraries, against highly technological NATO countries. I am not afraid, not anymore, we are beyond good or evil by now, but my legs simply tremble, when I hear the NATO or any other planes with bombs above my head.[75]

Tesanović's personal diary documents her slow move into war, into isolation, into silence and then her steady return back to identity, to community, and to expression. These last three clips evidence this narrative arc and also demonstrate Tesanović's realization that her mobility is restricted, in both a physical sense of movement and in an intellectual sense of sharing ideas and reflections. The strength of this work of radio art lies in Gordan Paunović's ability to amplify the steady, deliberate, and balanced words of Jasmina Tesanović, to turn the creative impulses of these journalists, musicians, and writers, who have been labeled "collateral damage," back into the expressive forms of engagement they were originally intended to be. Her Internet-based diary and its place within Paunović's radio mix allows her to extend her body beyond the limitations of its physical nature, allows her to circulate her thoughts and knowledge outside the imposed boundaries of war-torn Belgrade, and allows her to take a position as an engaged global citizen. The collaboration between Paunović and the Austrian Kunstradio project to draw attention to these "other voices" not captured by the global media network highlights as well an engaged use of tactical media. Where a culture of fear is readily compounded by the global media event surrounding the conflict in Kosovo, the type of tactical media practice evidenced in Paunović's and Kunst-radio's live broadcast allow for a different type of globalized network communication to occur, one that is not founded on easily digestible sound bites and the marketability of information, but rather one that mixes together a multiplicity of knowledge inputs and serves a wide range of outputs. The sounds of displacement — the fear of a disembodied identity that forms the heart of the broadcast's two diaries, the constant air-raid sirens that creep into the background of the listener's minds — make the realities of this war audible, recordable, and traceable, and transpose local experience, local identification with the war, onto the European and global imagination.

While the notions of travel, exile, homelessness, and displacement each presume a relocation or dislocation of a physical body, charting this type of movement in the late twentieth century requires an additional investigation into the ways in which information, documentation, and surveillance stand in for the physical body. As Zygmunt Bauman puts it,

> In the world we inhabit, distance does not seem to matter much. Sometimes it seems that it exists solely in order to be cancelled; as if space was but a constant invitation to slight it, refute and deny. Space stopped being an obstacle — one needs just a split second to conquer it.[76]

In an epoch of globalized economies, media states, and convergent telecommunications networks, mobility and movement assume characteristics of instantaneity, where the distances of time and space become imaginary, as equally traversable by immobility or staying put, as they are by physical movement. Gordan Paunović's implementation of these diaries into the ethereal flow of radio broadcast and Internet transmission opens a viable network space in which the power of Tesanović's words addresses the hegemonic forces that are keeping her physical body restricted: the nightly NATO bombing, the omnipresent weight of the Milosević regime, and the quelling silence parsed by the constant din of commercial Western media. David Morley, in his study of the media's impact on notions of home, identity, and nationhood, suggests that:

> Traditional ideas of home, homeland and nation have been destabilized, both by new patterns of physical mobility and migration and by new communication technologies which routinely transgress the symbolic boundaries around both the private household and the nation state. The electronic landscapes in which we now dwell are haunted by all manner of cultural anxieties which arise from this destabilizing flux.[77]

Morley's study raises issues concerning the human experience of the intertwining of global economic practice and new communication technologies, and the ways in which these macro-level structures provoke "the radical intrusion of distant events into the space of domesticity."[78] Here we have to expand on our earlier question concerning the transformation of intellectual thought into information and ask how this information is subsequently transformed into commodity. How does information for thought become information for sale? The trajectory of artistic and technical experimentation represented by the three projects discussed in the parameters of this essay demonstrates the power of a networked radio space in opening up lines of communication and collaboration between artists to circumvent traditional modes of radio broadcasting and bypass regulations seeking to limit access to networks within the global telecommunications infrastructure. The freedom to move information within these networks, but not to move or create knowledge, maintains them solely for the economic structures of globalization. The experimental modes of communication and thought behind the *Europa Report,* and *Other Voices* broadcasts and performances appropriates the channels and relays of these same telematic networks and opens them up as a temporary autonomous zone of performance and dialogue that taps into the immaterial realm of artistic consciousness, provides possibilities for artistic collaboration, and transmits engaging, thought-provoking broadcasts back out into radio space for access and continued dialogue by the listening public.

The Longevity of Radio and the Impermanence of Sound

> This is the greatest miracle of wireless. The omnipresence of what people are singing or saying anywhere, the overleaping of frontiers, the conquest of spatial isolation, the importation of culture on the waves of the ether, the same fare for all, sound in silence.
> — Rudolf Arnheim, *Radio: An Art of Sound*

> Radio happens in sound, but I don't believe that sound is what matters about radio. . . . What does matter is the play among relationships. . . . So radio is most captivating as a place, but a place of constantly shifting borders and multiple identities, a no place . . . where voices can gather, mix, become something else, and then disappear into the night.
> — Gregory Whitehead, "Radio Play Is No Place"

These are two very different and differently utopian approaches to the radio as artistic medium. Rudolf Arnheim's 1936 musings celebrate the radio as a vanguard medium able to leap across national borders and provide the intimacy of sound to spaces of isolation and silence in an almost conquistadorial fashion, while Gregory Whitehead's 1994 framing is much more about the multiplicity of radiophonic space and the innumerable relationships allowed to thrive within it.[1] Both invoke the obvious pairing of radio and sound to describe the medium and the material it delivers, but Arnheim privileges the role of sound in that pairing more so than Whitehead, who looks instead

164

to the radio as medium and the alternate and ever-changing notions of spatiality it initiates vis-à-vis sound as communicative substance. Arnheim wants to conquer socioeconomic, cultural, and political distance/isolation through the democratic potential of sound and its enframing through radio, while Whitehead understands this same potential as residing in the radio's ability to assemble a range of possible relationships through the currency of broadcast. In this sense, both position the radio as the center of a mediatized and transgressive utopian moment yet with differing viewpoints on whether the utopian moment is achieved through the centrality and ubiquity of sound and the unidirectionality of centralized broadcast or instead through the dispersive network potential of the radio medium irrespective of the content being broadcast. For Arnheim the longevity of radio depends on the permanence of sound, its pervasive role in the communication of ideas, while for Whitehead the longevity of radio acknowledges the unique impermanence of sound in the active creation of those relationships he so clearly favors. This short comparative exposition between the work of perceptual theorist Rudolf Arnheim and audio artist and writer Gregory Whitehead and their respective excerpted comments on the nature of radio and sound facilitates a number of ideas with respect to the study at hand. First, and foremost, it allows us to take a step back from the specificity of the case studies provided in the core chapters of this volume, in order to reflect once again on some of the broader issues at play in the connective tissue between and among these individual chapters. Second, the exposition provides us with a type of mapping that plots the development of the radio medium in the German context at two crucial points in its history: in the midst of its early growth as a medium of national concern and national pride, and in the midst of negotiating its identity within a plethora of supraregional and globally networked telecommunications media. Finally, it engages with the changing practices of cultural radio production unique to each spatiotemporal moment and in the process sheds some additional light on the ways in which both theorists and practitioners of an alternative radio practice have continually negotiated throughout the existence of the radio as an emergent medium the legislative standards governing the radio's use in order to articulate and put into practice the types of experimental modes we have explored throughout the course of this volume.

Call it what you will — but a transgressive, tactical, or alternative media practice with respect to German cultural broadcasting necessitated an experimental turn away from the duplicative nature of the government-sanctioned entertainment broadcasts which characterized the earliest days of German radio, and a concerted effort toward creating innovative program designs, intermedial content, and technical prowess to leverage radiophonic space for acoustic artists. Granted, all practices with the radio medium in our earliest examples could and should be considered experimental, since the subtle division between mainstream consumer tastes and avant-garde cultural practices had not yet fully developed in these early years, although the distinctions did begin to sediment rather quickly as broadcast consumers demanded consistency and cohesion in their programming, and as broadcasting standards and legislative policies governing the radio became more fine tuned. This always tentative and porous boundary line between the mainstream and the experimental forms the logic that provokes and drives the technical, artistic, and legislative development of the radio medium. It is a logic opposed to a traditional understanding about the unidirectional practices of broadcast, invoking instead a multidirectionality reliant on the back-and-forth feeds between the mainstream and the experimental, seen, for example, in the practices of mix culture along intertextual and intermedial trajectories.

Each of the examples from the history and contemporary presence of German experimentation within the realm of radio sound that we have explored in this volume serve as guideposts and illustrations of this logic, demonstrating an economics and politics of cultural currency that acknowledges the existence of a foundational symbiotic relationship between the experimental and the mainstream. Here pioneering radio figures from the 1920s like Hans Flesch, Friedrich Wolf, and Friedrich Bischoff were cognizant of the importance of artistic and technical experimentation with the radio medium in order to expand radio offerings beyond duplicative programming and to legitimize the radio as an artistic medium within the Weimar cultural and media landscapes. While it could be said that these early examples of artistic experimentation with the radio assisted with the development of the medium and with the shaping of a mainstream conception of radio culture simply by virtue of their being the new kids on the block, the rich media theoretical discussions started by Flesch and Bertolt Brecht have helped shape artistic radio practice and furthered theoretical debates in media and literary studies by taking up insightful critical threads about knowledge creation and information consumption, listening practices and interactivity, artist access, intermedial cross-pollination, and questions of spatiotemporality, which show up consistently and perpetually as points of departure and contention for both radio artists and radio/media theorists throughout the span of time represented in this volume. Here Alfred Andersch's attempts to create unique and innovative program designs in German postwar radio that would engage the listening audience on a level of intellectual interactivity and elide their co-optation by the larger market forces of the culture industry, take their notional cues from the radio theoretical work of Bertolt Brecht, while his own practical work with the medium in the form of critical commentaries and essay-style, roundtable discussion programs employ the type of montage, multivocal/multiperspectival approaches borrowed from cinema that came into being in several of our earliest case studies.

Acknowledging the duplicitous nature of radio broadcast as both monopolistic and liberative, Andersch ultimately desires to have it both ways: maintain a marginal space of artistic and programmatic experimentation with the radio medium, while also diving into the midst of discussions in cultural politics about the nature and autonomous role of art within a semantics of cultural consumerism. The Andersch example is instructive for this very layering of duplicity — in terms of the new semantics being associated with notions of art and culture, and in terms of the multidirectional feeds between mainstream culture and artistic experimentation. In many respects Andersch's radio work in the postwar 1950s serves as a tempering transitional voice between the utopian naïveté of both Rudolf Arnheim's 1936 and Gregory Whitehead's 1994 descriptions of radio practice, in that it recognizes equally the radio medium's highly charged political relevance and its capacity for cultural impotence. Andersch offers us a highly critical voice respective to the short, but definitive history of German cultural broadcasting that sought to navigate the radio medium beyond its role as a communications and entertainment medium that supported a sense of national consciousness or national pride and a highly critical challenge to contemporary radio artists to interweave into their radio practice equally crucial negotiations with the hierarchical structures of broadcast. These levels of transparency in the making of artistic broadcasts likewise translate into a deeper understanding of the mechanisms in place to legislate broadcasting policy, regulate technical innovation, and standardize broadcasting practice. Our more contemporary examples thus demonstrate a dissolution of the customary one-to-many paradigm of transmission and reception methods and instead offer a many-to-many approach through the incorporation of tools and group practices that place broadcast at everyone's fingertips, regardless of their position in the producer/end user model of cultural consumption. Here the pirate broadcasting and reception tactics of Radio Dreyeckland, the agitprop production and dissemination techniques of Radio Subcom, and the networked streaming audio techniques and intermedial/intertextual performances of audio artists like Gordan Paunović and Atau Tanaka provide additional transgressive modalities for an alternative and experimental radio practice to help counter the varying and shifting discourses at work in the realm of telecommunications regulation.

The mutually beneficial and interwoven relationship between experimental practice and mainstream culture, however, begins to disentangle itself with the presence of these more stultifying affiliations with the structures of power that seek to regulate both the technical and content parameters of broadcast. Provision of access to the tools of transmission or the tools of production is most often accompanied by suspicion and questionable knitting of the brow on the part of governmental regulators. Issues of national security, safeguarding of economic viability, and the data mining of sensitive information are all offered as reasons for governmental or private control over these types of global telecommunications infrastructures. As we have seen, these are not issues limited to our contemporary world of emergent media; rather they exist at every historical juncture where new media have materialized, including that of the radio medium in the German context. We witness them in the years leading up to the birth of entertainment radio in 1920s Weimar as responses to the political and economic fallout of World War I and the transition to a shaky democracy. We see them in the early 1930s with the rise of the National Socialists and the linking of cultural radio transmissions with the spiritual and folkic perseverance of German culture and the sanitizing of the airwaves of content deemed avant-garde and degenerate. We observe them at the beginnings of postwar capitalism in West Germany, where the vocabularies of reeducation and denazification guided an idealized retooling of the radio in order to provide structures of oversight to defend against the type of dictatorial control of the medium experienced during the Third Reich and to provide access to a framework of open discourse and freedom of expression. And, finally, we see them in the initial supranational stirrings of the European Union and the desire to create an equitable media policy cognizant of multiple broadcasting scenarios that would provide for an economically competitive telecommunications infrastructure within the individual member countries.

Where mainstream culture instantiates these aspects of legislation and regulation as a filtration system for broadcast content, practitioners of an experimental mode of broadcast and transmission see them as points of origin for an infiltration of these very systems of content and user surveillance. Irrespective of the innate value of these three operating modes, this is not a dynamic that occurs in hierarchical or successive stages; rather it is one that occurs simultaneously in an assemblage of transgressive, regressive, progressive, and reactive behaviors, which seek to either sediment and make permanent the materiality of sound and its broadcast and reception, or to unsettle and disrupt these same attempts in an effort to unhouse and revivify the immateriality and impermanence of sound. The radio as medium and framework of broadcast thus resides in a type of transitory relationship between the cohesion and recognition of programming genres needed to sustain the mainstream, and the innovation and unpredictability of sound that enlivens and excites the experimental. This long history of radio experimentation and harmonization, marked by transgressive modes of practice and negotiation of varied systems of regulation and broadcasting standards, is ultimately one that also captures the radio as a medium that adapts to the impermanence of its political, economic, and legislative surroundings, and thus ensures its longevity.

Notes

Introduction

1. Friedrich Kittler, "Die letzte Radiosendung," in *On the Air: Kunst im öffentlichen Datenraum,* ed. Heidi Grundmann (Innsbruck: Transit, 1993), 72–80, here 72.

2. Douglas Kahn, "Radio Space," in *Radio Rethink: Art, Sound and Transmission,* ed. Daina Augaitis and Dan Lander (Banff, Alberta: Walter Phillips Gallery, 1994), 95–114, here 95.

3. Brandon LaBelle, *Background Noise: Perspectives on Sound Art* (New York: Continuum, 2006), xi.

4. Kate Lacey, *Feminine Frequencies: Gender, German Radio, and the Public Sphere, 1923–1945* (Ann Arbor: University of Michigan Press, 1996), 11n12.

1. Wiretapping the Beast

1. Jackson Pollock, interview with William Wright, The Springs, Long Island, New York, late 1950, broadcast on radio station WERI in Westerly, Rhode Island, 1951. *Jackson Pollock: Interviews, Articles, and Reviews,* ed. Pepe Karmel (New York: Henry N. Abrams, 1999), 20–23, here 20.

2. Walter Ruttmann, "Malerei mit Zeit," in *Walter Ruttmann: Eine Dokumentation,* ed. Jeanpaul Goergen (Berlin: Freunde der deutschen Kinemathek, 1989), 73–74, here 74. For the convenience of the reader, I will provide the German original of English translations in the note. All translations from the German are my own, unless otherwise noted. "Telegraf, Schnellzüge, Stenografie, Fotografie, Schnellpressen, usw., an sich nicht als Kulturerrungenschaften zu werten, haben zur Folge eine früher nicht gekannte Geschwindigkeit in der Übermittlung geistiger Resultate.... Hier liegen auch die Gründe für unsere verzweifelte Hilflosigkeit gegenüber den Erscheinungen der bildenden Kunst. Der Blick, der in geistigen Dingen immer mehr auf die Betrachtung eines zeitlichen Geschehens gedrängt wird, weiß mit den starren, reduzierten zeitlosen Formeln der Malerei nichts mehr anzufangen."

3. Atau Tanaka, *Frankensteins Netz / Prométhée numérique / Wiretapping the Beast,* Südwestrundfunk, www.frankensteins-netz.de (accessed February 23, 2002; site now offline).

4. Bertolt Brecht, "The Radio as a Communications Apparatus," in *Bertolt Brecht on Film and Radio,* trans. and ed. Marc Silberman (London: Methuen, 2000), 41–46, here 42.

5. Walter Ruttmann, *Weekend* (June 13, 1930), 11 min., 20 sec.; Deutsches Rundfunkarchiv, 2782389-01. mp3 audio file.

6. Quoted in Klaus Schöning, "The Contours of Acoustic Art," *Theatre Journal* 43, no. 3 (1991): 307–24, here 316. It is highly unfortunate that Schöning's article contains no bibliographic or citation information whatsoever, so the actual source of Braun's description cannot be given here.

7. In chapter 2, I explore F. W. Bischoff's acoustic film *Hallo! Welle Erdball!* from 1928, which also utilized the Tri-Ergon process. The process itself is also discussed in further detail here.

8. Walter Ruttmann, "Prinzipielles zum Tonfilm (2)," in *Walter Ruttmann: Eine Dokumentation,* ed. Jeanpaul Goergen (Berlin: Freunde der deutschen Kinemathek, 1989), 83–84. "Ich bin augenblicklich mit der Herstellung meines ersten Tonfilmes für die Tri-Ergon beschäftigt. Der Fall diese tönenden Filmes ist doppelt interessant, da die beiden modernsten Errungenschaften rein äußerlich ineinander übergreifen und zu einem Vergleich reizen. Mein Film umfaßt den deutschen Rundfunk und spielt auf allen Sendestationen, um von dort aus durch die schönsten Gegenden des deutschen Reiches akustisch und bildlich zu führen. Der bildlose Rundfunk und der tonlose Film sind zwei Gegensätze, die gegeneinander ausgespielt im anderen Sinne dem Begriff des Tonfilmes näherkommen. Die Möglichkeit der Fruchtbarmachung der Illusion und Phantasie liegt in der konträren Ausspielung von Ton und Bild."

9. Walter Ruttmann, *Berlin, Symphony of a Great City,* DVD (Chatsworth, Calif.: Image Entertainment, 1999), originally released 1927.

10. Brady M. Roberts, ed., *Constructing New Berlin: Contemporary Art Made in Berlin* (Munich: Prestel, 2006). Published in conjunction with the exhibition "Constructing New Berlin" shown at the Phoenix Art Museum and the Bass Museum of Art.

11. The Palast der Republik was built in the early 1970s in former East Berlin as the seat of the Volkskammer, the East German parliament. However, it also served as a destination for citizens to enjoy state-sanctioned art work, theatrical, and music events. It is currently being demolished to make room for a re-creation of the former Berliner Stadtpalast that originally inhabited the site.

12. Sabine Breitsameter. "What is AudioHyperspace?" *Audiohyperspace — Akustische Kunst in Netzwerken und Datenräumen.* Südwestrundfunk www.swr2 .de/ audiohyperspace/engl_version/info/index.html (accessed February 16, 2003).

13. M. P. McCauley, "Radio's Digital Future: Preserving the Public Interest in the Age of New Media," in *Radio Reader: Essays in the Cultural History of Radio,* ed. Michele Hilmes and Jason Loviglio (New York: Routledge, 2002), 505–30, here 508.

14. Atau Tanaka, "Composing as a Function of Infrastructure," in *Surface Tension: Problematics of Site,* ed. Ken Ehrlich and Brandon LaBelle (Los Angeles: Errant Bodies Press, 2003), 205–12, here 207.

15. Pollock, interview with William Wright, 21.

16. Donna Haraway, "A Cyborg Manifesto: Science, Technology, and Socialist-Feminism in the Late Twentieth Century," in *The New Media Reader,* ed. Noah Wardrip-Fruin and Nick Montfort (Cambridge, Mass.: MIT Press, 2003), 516–41.

17. Ibid., 519.

18. Ibid., 523.

19. *Wiretapping the Beast,* email to author, May 8, 2002.

20. Atau Tanaka, interview with the author, March 2003.

21. See Pierre Lévy, *Collective Intelligence: Mankind's Emerging World in Cyberspace,* trans. Robert Bononno (New York: Plenum Trade, 1997).

22. Atau Tanaka, "Composing as a Function of Infrastructure," 212.

23. Atau Tanaka, *Prométhée Numérique,* mp3 file, ISRC Fi-3AB-05-00001, © 2005 Aureobel.

24. Atau Tanaka, "Prométhée Numérique — Frankensteins Netz: Score to the Final Mix (2002)," *Audiohyperspace — Akustische Kunst in Netzwerken und Datenräumen,* Südwestrundfunk, www.swr.de/swr2/audiohyperspace/ger_version/ frankensteins_netz/ tanaka-partitur.pdf (accessed March 3, 2003).

25. For an example of the score from Walter Ruttmann's *Weekend* see Golo Föllmer, "Walter Ruttmann, 'Weekend' " Medien Kunst Netz, www.medienkunstnetz .de/works/ weekend/ (accessed May 30, 2006).

26. Sabine Breitsameter, interview by Eva Lauinger, "Radio meets Internet: Ein Gespräch mit Sabine Breitsameter" *Audiohyperspace — Akustische Kunst in Netzwerken und Datenräumen,* Südwestrundfunk, www.swr.de/swr2/audiohyperspace/ engl_version/programmes/interview.html (accessed February 28, 2003). "Zuhören ist ja etwas, was mit einer, ich sag mal, sehr reziptiven, in Anführungszeichen, zurückgelehnten Haltung zu tun hat. Man muß sozusagen die Dinge auf sich zukommen lassen. Ich glaube, daß wir in einer Zeit leben, und das Internet ist ja auch Ausdruck dieser Zeit, wo es eigentlich eher darum geht möglichst aktiv zu sein und möglichst was zu tun. Und, daß das schon glaub ich, eine sehr große Klippe ist, die jemand, der hören will, zuhören will, überwinden muß. Nämlich diesen, ich sag' s mal, Mut zu finden, sich zurückzulehnen, nichts zu tun, um mal zu sagen, ich wart mal, was jetzt kommt und hör mir das mal an. Ich nehme mir diese Zeit. Ja, und ich greife nicht ein. Es geht vielleicht gar nicht. Ich halte das für eine sehr wichtige, für eine sehr wichtige Sache. Und ich denk, in der Tat, daß so diese Interaktionsmythologie, die auch durch das Internet verbreitet wird, vielleicht auch Ideologie, Interaktionsideologie, die verbreitet wird, daß die natürlich dem Zuhören und dieser rezipierenden Haltung nicht unbedingt zuträglich ist. Jedenfalls glaube ich, ist es wichtig, das zu thematisieren, damit uns das Zuhören nicht verloren geht."

27. Sabine Breitsameter, "Acoustic Ecology and the New Electroacoustic Space of Digital Networks," *Soundscape: The Journal of Acoustic Ecology* 4, no. 2 (2003): 24–30, here 30.

28. Pollock, interview with William Wright, 20.

2. Between Military Innovation and Government Sanction

1. Alfred Braun, a radio director in Berlin, lists this historic broadcast in his "Kleine Chronik des Deutschen Rundfunks 1923–1932," in *Achtung, Achtung, Hier ist Berlin! Aus der Geschichte des deutschen Rundfunks in Berlin 1923–1932* (Berlin: Haude and Spener, 1968), 80–87. The first entertainment program was broadcast on October 29, 1923, at the Voxhaus at Potsdamerstrasse 4 in Berlin, and began with the words "Hier Sendestelle Berlin, Voxhaus, Welle 400." This broadcast consisted primarily in a combination of live chamber music performances and the playing of gramophone records, ending with the Vox recording of the German national anthem "Das Lied der Deutschen." Additional information about this first program evening can be found in E. Kurt Fischer, *Dokumente zur Geschichte des deutschen Rundfunks und Fernsehens* (Göttingen: Musterschmidt-Verlag, 1957), 72–73.

2. Heinrich Heine, *The North Sea,* trans. Vernon Watkins (New York: New Directions Books, 1951), 39–45. The German version of Heinrich Heine's poem can be found in *Sämtliche Schriften,* ed. Klaus Briegleb (Munich: Hanser, 1968), 1:192–94.

3. Braun, *Achtung, Achtung, Hier ist Berlin!* 9. The speaker referred to is Hans Bredow, who would become the first superintendent of the German radio in 1923, and whose writings will be looked at a bit further on in this chapter. "Lange bevor es einen Rundfunk gab, fand in Bremen eine Tagung der Deutschen Schiffsgroßreeder statt mit einem Referat über das Phänomen der drahtlosen Telegraphie. Die kritischen Einwände und Bedenken konterte der Referent in der Diskussion zuletzt mit dem Satz: 'Meine Herren, einst wird kommen der Tag, wo keines Ihrer Schiffe den Hafen verläßt ohne Sende- und Empfangsgerät, um in die Einöde der Weltmeere zu rufen und zu hören.'"

4. Heine, *The North Sea,* 39–42.

5. Ibid., 41–43.

6. Ibid., 45.

7. For additional information on the intertextual references for Heine's poem, see P. S. Barto's early piece "Sources of Heine's *Seegespenst*," *Modern Language Notes* 32, no. 8 (1916): 482–85.

8. Scholarship on film sound primarily focuses on the development of sound with respect to Hollywood film. For information specific to the advent of sound in European cinema, especially its economic underpinnings, see Douglas Gomery, "Economic Struggle and Hollywood Imperialism: Europe Converts to Sound," in *Film Sound: Theory and Practice,* ed. Elisabeth Weis and John Belton (New York: Columbia University Press, 1985), 25–36. On the competitive nature between film and radio in the American context, see Paul Young's recent study *The Cinema Dreams Its Rivals: Media Fantasy Films from Radio to the Internet* (Minneapolis: University of Minnesota Press, 2006). See especially his chapter 3, "Eating the Other Medium: Sound Film in the Age of Broadcasting."

9. Hans Bredow, "Dem 'Deutschen Rundfunk' zum Geleit," in *Aus meinem Archiv: Probleme des Rundfunks* (Heidelberg: Kurt Vowinckel, 1950), 15. "... um dem deutschen Volke etwas Anregung und Freude in das Leben zu bringen."

10. Emil Sehling, comp. "6/IV. Gesetz über das Telegraphenwesen des Deutschen Reichs," *Die civilrechtlichen Gesetze des Deutschen Reiches* (Leipzig: Veit, 1902), 200. This compiled volume of legal documents from imperial Germany is available through the Max-Planck-Institut für europäische Rechtsgeschichte Digital Library, "Literaturquellen zum deutschen, österreichischen und schweizerischen Privat- und Zivilprozeßrecht des 19. Jahrhunderts," http://dlib-pr.mpier.mpg.de/ m/kleioc/0010/exec/bigpage/"201532_00000215" (accessed October 15, 2005), which includes digital facsimiles of Sehling's text. "Das Recht, Telegraphenanlagen für die Vermittelung von Nachrichten zu errichten und zu betreiben, steht ausschließlich dem Reich zu."

11. Winfried Lerg does note that the law was adapted in 1908 when the technologies had developed to include wireless telegraphy. The law would again be revised in January 1928 with the adoption of the Gesetz über Fernmeldeanlagen (Law concerning Telecommunications). See Lerg, *Rundfunkpolitik in der Weimarer Republik* (Munich: dtv, 1980), 30.

12. Winfried Lerg, *Die Entstehung des Rundfunks in Deutschland: Herkunft und Entwicklung eines publizistischen Mittels* (Frankfurt a. Main: Knecht, 1965), 49. Königs Wusterhausen was the site of the first military broadcasting station. "Tatsächlich spielten Einheiten der Funkertruppe in den Tagen zwischen Krieg und Frieden eine besondere Rolle, als das Nachrichtenwesen der obersten Kriegsbehörde (Kriegsministerium) entglitten, aber noch nicht wieder fest in den Händen der im Frieden verwantwortlichen obersten Verkehrsbehörde (Reichspostamt) war. Koordiniert wurden die Selbstverwaltungsbestrebungen von einer Institution mit der Bezeichnung *Zentralfunkleitung (ZFL)*. Diese *Zentralfunkleitung* war am 9. November 1918 von Mitarbeitern der *Technischen Abteilung für Funkgerät (Tafunk)*, die der *Inspektion der Technischen Abteilung der Nachrichtentruppe (Itenach)* unterstand, gegründet worden.... Über die Station Königs Wusterhausen wandte sich die Zentralfunkleitung an sämtliche Stationen des innerdeutschen Funknetzes mit der Meldung, daß sie als Zentralsoldatenrat die Leitung aller Anlagen übernommen hätte. Man beabsichtige nichts Geringeres als ein von der Postverwaltung unabhängiges Nachrichtennetz aufzubauen."

13. Georg Ledebour (1850–1947) was a publisher and politician. An early member of Germany's SPD, Ledebour was a critic of the imperial government's leadership and social policies and was opposed to World War I. During the November Revolution he became the leader of the Unabhängige Sozialdemokratische Partei Deutschlands (Independent Social Democratic Party of Germany) (USPD), the independent faction of the SPD, and aligned himself with the Spartacists, led by Karl Liebknecht and Rosa Luxemburg, which would eventually break and form the Kommunistische Partei Deutschlands (Communist Party of Germany) (KPD). In mid-1919 he stood trial for his participation in the Spartacus revolt and was acquitted. For additional information on the revolution of 1918–19 see Erich Kuttner, *Die deutsche Revolution: Des Volkes Sieg und Zukunft* (Berlin: Verlag für Sozialwissenschaft, 1918); Marx-Engels-Stiftung, ed., *75 Jahre deutsche Novemberrevolution* (Bonn: Pahl-Rugenstein, 1994); and Eduard Bernstein, *Die deutsche Revolution von 1918/19: Geschichte der Entstehung und ersten*

Arbeitsperiode der deutschen Republik, ed. Heinrich August Winkler (Bonn: Dietz, 1998).

14. Georg Ledebour, ed., *Der Ledebour-Prozeß, Gesamtdarstellung des Prozesses gegen Ledebour wegen Aufruhr etc. vor dem Geschworenengericht Berlin-Mitte vom 19. Mai bis 23. Juni 1919* (Berlin: Verlagsgenossenschaft "Freiheit," 1919), 129, quoted in Lerg, *Entstehung des Rundfunks,* 47. "Ich habe damals die Auffassung gehabt..., daß es vielleicht doch gut wäre, durch das Wolff'sche Telegraphenbureau eine Meldung in die Welt zu schicken. Ich bin auf diesen Gedanken durch eigene Erfahrung gekommen, weil ich wußte, daß im März 1917, als die Kunde von dem Siege der russischen Revolution kam, auf mich nichts einen solchen Eindruck gemacht hat wie die Tatsache, daß diese Nachricht durch die Petersburger Telegraphenbureau verbreitet wurde.... Ich sagte mir weiter: wenn man jetzt durch das Wolff'sche Telegraphenbureau eine Meldung von dem Siege der Revolution herausgibt, dann wird das in der ganzen Welt geglaubt werden."

15. The term *Funkerspuk* appears to be a well-known term among German radio historians and media theorists, yet not one of the sources I've consulted cites the origins of the expression. Although Hans Bredow refers to the events surrounding the *Funkerspuk* in his 1956 memoirs *Im Banne der Ätherwellen,* vol. 2, *Funk im ersten Weltkriege, Entstehung des Rundfunks* (Stuttgart: Mundus, 1956), 104–9, most contemporary scholars of German radio history and theory cite Winfried Lerg's more historically engaged analysis, *Entstehung des Rundfunks,* 53. Lerg mentions the term in the context of the 1934/35 *Rundfunkprozess* (radio trial) against Hans Bredow. The Nazi-led trial brought several charges against leading figures of German radio from throughout the country, including Bredow, Hans Flesch, Kurt Magnus, Alfred Braun, Friedrich Bischoff, and many others. Lerg quotes from Bredow's defense documentation to demonstrate Bredow's opposition to the ZFL and their claim that the radio network should be kept separate from the telegraphic networks of the postal service due to their lack of technical prowess. Bredow instead saw the need to keep the communications network in "more secure hands." For additional information regarding the *Rundfunkprozess* see Birgit Bernard "Korruption im Rundfunk der NS-Zeit," *Rundfunk und Geschichte* 28, no. 1/2 (2002): 60–67; and Ansgar Diller, *Rundfunkpolitik im Dritten Reich* (Munich: dtv, 1980), 128–33.

16. Lerg, *Rundfunkpolitik,* 45. To complicate the picture even further, after the ZFL had been folded into the broadcasting structure, the military radio operators initially associated with its origin were left to fend for themselves once the system of broadcast communications had returned to oversight by the postal affairs ministry. Although they were much more technically skilled than their civilian counterparts, they were still seen as security risks and would not be tolerated by the new government. "Damit waren auf den Tag [9. April 1919] genau fünf Monate nach der Entstehung jener Zentralfunkleitung alle revolutionären Spuren im deutschen Funkwesen beseitigt."

17. These documents can be found in Lerg, *Entstehung des Rundfunks,* 367–75; and in Ingo Fessmann, *Rundfunk und Rundfunkrecht in der Weimarer Republik* (Frankfurt: Knecht, 1973), 258.

18. Bredow, *Im Banne*, 176–77. Bredow's impressions of the Versailles agreement, as it relates to telecommunications policy in the early Weimar Republic, can be found on pp. 112–14 of this memoir. "Während des Krieges war mit Rücksicht auf die Landesverteidigung in den kriegführenden Ländern die Benutzung eines Senders oder Empfängers für Private verboten gewesen.... In Deutschland stützte sich das Funkverbot auf das Telegraphen-Gesetz, und Ausnahmen wurden nur bei den konzessionierten und staatlich überwachten privatwirtschaftlichen Telgraphenbetrieben im Seefunk und Weltfunk sowie für Zwecke der Industrie und Forschung gemacht. Die Aufrechterhaltung dieser Einschränkung nach dem Kriege wurde nach aussen hin allein mit der Notwendigkeit der Geheimhaltung des öffentlichen Funkverkehrs begründet, in Wirklichkeit waren aber politischen Gründe entscheidend."

19. Lerg, *Entstehung des Rundfunks*, 367. "eine ganz ungewöhnliche Ausbreitung einer Abart der drahtlosen Telephonie" and "die beteiligten Reichsbehörden werden nunmehr Stellung nehmen müssen zu der Frage, ob und unter welchen Vorsichtsmaßnahmen ein derartiger drahtloser Empfangsapparat jedem Interessenten in die Hand gegeben werden soll."

20. Ibid., 367.

21. Bredow, *Im Banne*, 201. "Wir waren uns darüber einig, dass die Aufrechterhaltung des Empfangsverbots das Entstehen unzähliger ungenehmigter Empfangsstellen doch nicht verhindern könne. Zuerst hatten die früheren Kriegsfunker das Abhören von Nachrichten aus dem Äther als Sport betreiben. Schliesslich hätte eine Bastlerbewegung nach amerikanischem Vorbild auch die technisch interessierte Jugend ergriffen. Man wusste, dass es bereits Tausende von illegalen Empfangsstellen gab, ohne dass hiergegen etwas Ernsthaftes geschehen konnte."

22. Dieter Daniels, "Interaction versus Consumption: Mass Media and Art from 1920 to Today," in *Timeshift: The World in Twenty-Five Years,* ed. Gerfried Stocker and Christiane Schöpf (Ostfildern-Ruit, Germany: Hatje Cantz, 2004), 147.

23. Ibid., 146.

24. Ibid. Unfortunately, Daniels provides no citations in his essay to adequately credit an exact volume of Kittler's work. However, my own knowledge of Kittler's writings leads me to believe that Daniels is most likely referring to his volume *Gramophone, Film, Typewriter,* ed. Geoffrey Winthrop-Young and Michael Wutz (Stanford, Calif.: Stanford University Press, 1999). See especially his chapter on the gramophone for interarticulations between this early sound medium and the development of radio.

25. Fessmann, *Rundfunk und Rundfunkrecht in der Weimarer Republik,* 41.

26. The full or excerpted text of four of these documents related to the development of entertainment radio in Germany are reproduced in the appendices to Fessmann's volume, pp. 251–58. These are the March 1924 Verordnung zum Schutze des Funkverkehrs, the January 1928 Gesetz über Fernmeldeanlagen, the undated Genehmigung zur Benutzung von Funksendeanlagen der DRP für die Zwecke des Unterhaltungsrundfunks, and the October 1923 Verfügung Nr. 815, which, however, is referred to here as the Bedingungen für die Errichtung sowie den Betrieb von Rundfunkempfangsanlagen von 24. Oktober 1923 (Conditions for

the Construction and Operations of Radio Reception Stations from October 24, 1923). A facsimile of the Genehmigungsurkunde für Rundfunkempfänger (Approval Certificate for Radio Reception Devices) is reproduced in Lerg, *Entstehung des Rundfunks*, 372–73. Excerpts from the 1926 Richtlinien für die Regelung des Rundfunks and the November 1932 Richtlinien für die Neuordnung des Rundfunks can be accessed in Fischer, *Dokumente zur Geschichte des deutschen Rundfunks und Fernsehens*, 79–81, 85–87.

27. Fessmann, *Rundfunk und Rundfunkrecht*, 251.

28. Ibid., 258. "3. Änderungen am Gerät und seinem Zubehör, Lösung etwaiger Bleiverschlüsse, Zuschaltung irgendwelcher Teile, die geeignet sind, die Einstellung der Empfangswelle zu ändern, sind verboten.... 6. Die Aufnahme von Nachrichten anderer Funkstellen ist nicht gestattet. Mitgehörter fremder Funkverkehr darf weder niedergeschrieben noch mitgeteilt oder irgendwie verwertet werden. Der Inhaber der Urkunde hat seine Empfangsanlage bei Benutzung durch andere daraufhin zu überwachen und ihre Benutzung durch Unbefugte zu verhindern."

29. Bredow, *Im Banne*, 201. "Die Wehrmacht war daher bereit, ihre Bedenken zurückzustellen, wenn dabei die militärischen Interessen geschützt würden. Man war der Ansicht, dass auf Antrag Empfangsgenehmigungen erteilt werden sollten, aber zum Schutze des Funkverkehrs den Hörern und auch der Apparate-Industrie gewisse technische Bedingungen auferlegt werden müssten. Die genehmigten Empfänger sollten so gebaut sein, dass der militärische und postalische Funkempfang nicht durch Ausstrahlung von Rückkopplungsschwingungen gestört werden konnte. Ausserdem sollte das Abhören des militärischen Funkverkehrs in einem bestimmten, dem Wehrmachtsverkehr vorbehaltenen Wellenbereich technisch unmöglich gemacht werden."

30. Heide Riedel, *60 Jahre Radio: Von der Rarität zum Massenmedium* (Berlin: Deutsches Rundfunk-Museum, 1987), 13. Until frequencies were adopted, wavelengths measured in meters were most often used by radio stations to locate their signal on a radio dial. Medium waves along the electromagnetic spectrum are associated with AM radio or amplitude modulation. "Im Juli 1923 wurde ein Kompromiss erzielt: Der Industrie wurde die Einschränkung auferlegt, nur solche Empfangsgeräte zu produzieren, die nicht mehr als den Wellenbereich von 250 bis 700 m (Mittelwellen) aufnehmen konnten und außerdem nicht in der Lage sein sollten, Funkwellen selbst zu erzeugen und auszustrahlen (Rückkopplungsverbot)."

31. A digital version of the Radiokosmos Stuttgart advertisement can be viewed as part of a discussion thread on the radiomuseum.org website: Wolfgang Holtmann, "Radio-Experimentierkästen Kosmos," Post to Radiomuseum forum, www.radiomuseum.org/forum/kosmos_baukaesten_elektro_radio_radiomann_etc .html#post40570 (accessed September 17, 2007) "Solange die gesetzlichen Bestimmungen über den Liebhaber-Radioverkehr vom Oktober 1923 in Kraft sind, können wir vollständige Lehr- und Versuchsbaukasten oder einzelne Teile daraus nur ins Ausland liefern. — Inländische Schulen, die Apparate zu Experimentierzwecken brauchen, wenden sich am besten wegen Bezugserlaubnis an die zuständigen Postdirektion."

32. Bredow, *Im Banne*, 201. "Im übrigen wurde die Gefahr des Abhörens wegen der Verschlüsselung des Militärverkehrs nicht mehr allzuhoch eingeschätzt. Spionage konnte durch Verbote sowieso nicht verhindert werden. Dagegen lehnte die Wehrmacht die von geschäftlich interessierten Kreisen geforderte allgemeine Freigabe auch des Senderbetriebes an private Stellen ab, weil dann Verhältnisse entstehen könnten, die einen geordneten militärischen Funkverkehr unmöglich machen würden."

33. For an in-depth investigation of women's roles in broadcasting in both Weimar German radio and the radio in the Third Reich see Kate Lacey's excellent study *Feminine Frequencies: Gender, German Radio, and the Public Sphere, 1923–1945* (Ann Arbor: University of Michigan Press, 1996). See particularly her chapters 3 and 8: "Let Women Speak to Women! On Women's Radio in Weimar Germany" and "Finding a Voice: Women's Radio and the Evolution of Broadcast Talk," respectively.

34. Bredow, *Aus meinem Archiv*, 15. "In einer Zeit schwerster wirtschaftlicher Not und politischer Bedrängnis wird der Rundfunk für die Allgemeinheit freigegeben. Nicht länger soll er ausschließlich wirtschaftlichen Zwecken dienen, sondern es soll der Versuch gemacht werden, diesen Kulturfortschritt zu benutzen, um dem deutschen Volke etwas Anregung und Freude in das Leben zu bringen.... Das deutsche Volk ist wirtschaftlich verarmt, und es ist nicht zu bestreiten, daß auch die geistige Verarmung Fortschritte macht, denn wer kann sich heute noch Bücher und Zeitschriften kaufen, wer kann sich die Freude guter Musik und unterhaltender und bildender Vorträge gönnen? Erholung, Unterhaltung und Abwechslung lenken den Geist von den schweren Sorgen des Alltags ab, erfrischen und steigern die Arbeitsfreude; aber ein freudloses Volk wird arbeitsunlustig."

35. For more in-depth information about the history of broadcasting in the environs of Frankfurt a. Main, see August Soppe, *Rundfunk in Frankfurt am Main, 1923–1926: zur Organisations-, Programm-, und Rezeptionsgeschichte eines neuen Mediums* (Munich: Saur, 1993).

36. There is no single monograph, biographical or otherwise, devoted to Hans Flesch and his work with the early development of radio in Weimar-era Germany. Marianne Weil's 1996 documentary essay "Hans Flesch — Rundfunkintendant in Berlin: Ein Beitrag zu seinem hundertsten Geburtstag," *Rundfunk und Geschichte* 22, no. 4 (1996): 223–43, published on the anniversary of Flesch's hundredth birthday, provides a welcome addition in this area, but primarily concentrates on Flesch's effectiveness as director of the Berlin *Funk-Stunde* from 1929 to 1932. Other sources for a biographical sketch include the previously mentioned volume by August Soppe, *Rundfunk in Frankfurt am Main*; a short panegyric essay by Kurt Magnus, "Gedenken an Hans Flesch und seine Freunde," *Rufer und Hörer* 8 (1953/54): 409–15; and a book written by Flesch's niece Marlies Flesch-Thebesius, *Hauptsache Schweigen: Ein Leben unterm Hakenkreuz* (Stuttgart: Radius, 1988), which explores the family's history in the Nazi period and devotes the chapter titled "Eine unbürgerliche Existenz" to her uncle.

37. Weil, "Hans Flesch — Rundfunkintendant in Berlin," 223. "Eines einfallsreichen und experimentierfreudigen Programmgestalters, der zeitgenössische

Musiker wie Paul Hindemith [his friend and brother-in-law] oder Kurt Weill durch spezielle Auftragskompositionen für das neue Medium interessierte, der auf dem Feld des ja gerade erst entstehenden, 'Hörspiels' nach neuen 'funkeigenen' Formen suchte und der im heiklen Bereich des Politischen die Ansicht vertrat, der Rundfunk müsse sich den wichtigen Fragen der Zeit stellen und dürfe nicht ängstlich alles Kontroverse meiden."

38. I am greatly indebted to Friedrich Dethlefs and his staff at the Deutsches Rundfunkarchiv, currently located in Wiesbaden, for their wonderful assistance in helping me locate documents and early sound examples during a too brief week-long research visit in July 2004. I am also grateful to Dr. Wolfgang Hagen, lecturer in media studies at the Humboldt Universität in Berlin for sharing several electronic versions of Hans Flesch's essays with me.

39. "Der Unterhaltungs-Rundfunk: Vortrag von Dr. Hans Flesch," *Radio-Umschau: Wochenschrift über die Fortschritte im Rundfunkwesen* 1, no. 8 (1924): 185. "Der Redner [Flesch] ging dann näher auf die akustischen Veränderungen der Lautübertragung durch Radio ein und erhärtete seine Ausführungen durch die vergleichende Wiedergabe von Musik. Ein Geiger und ein Posaunist brachten im Saalbau einige Stücke zum Vortrag; dann wurden sie im Auto zum Senderaum im Postscheckamt befördert, und dort spielten sie die gleichen Stücke. Interessant war nun, wie sich die Reproduktion durch Radio (Lautverstärker) die Klangfarben der Instrumente veränderten, namentlich der Violine, und bei anderen Vorträgen war zu hören, wie vor allem das Klavier klanglich seiner Charakteristik verlustig geht, während das Cello fast garnicht verändert klingt.... Der Frankfurter Dialekt mit seinen nasalen und undeutlichen Zwischenlauten eignet sich sehr schlecht für die Wiedergabe mittels Radio. Hingegen ist der Berliner mit seiner hellen, scharfen Artikulation ein besonders guter Rundfunker."

40. R. Murray Schafer, *The Soundscape: Our Sonic Environment and the Tuning of the World* (Rochester, Vt: Destiny Books, 1994), 90–91.

41. For additional resources on the relationships between language differentiation and notions of authority see James Milroy and Lesley Milroy, *Authority in Language: Investigating Language Prescription and Standardisation* (London: Routledge, 1991), and Deborah Cameron, *Verbal Hygiene* (London: Routledge, 1995). I am grateful to Holly R. Cashman for helping me to clarify these ideas about the uses of dialect in radio broadcast. It is interesting to note here that the emergence of one of the first pirate radio stations in West Germany in 1977, Radio Dreyeckland, around the antinuclear movement, also saw the resurgence of regional dialects being broadcast, given the station's location in the borderlands of West Germany, Switzerland, and France. These ideas are discussed more in depth in chapter 4 of this study.

42. Hans Flesch, "Die kulturellen Aufgaben des Rundfunks," *Der Deutsche Rundfunk* 4, no. 12 (1926): 798–801, here 798. It also appears in Hans Bredow, *Aus meinem Archiv*, 93–97, here 94–95. "Betrachtet man rückblickend die Entwicklung, die die deutschen Rundfunkprogramme seit Anfang durchgemacht haben, so kann man ganz bestimmte Perioden unterscheiden. In der allerersten Zeit läßt sich, wenn das Wort Richtung hier angebracht ist, von einer instrumentalen

oder experimentellen Richtung sprechen. Ein völlig neues Instrument wurde dem Leiter in die Hand gegeben. Niemand kannte etwas von diesem Instrument als seine physikalischen Formeln und seine rein tatsächlichen Auswirkungen. Dem Publikum gegenüber genügte das an und für sich völlig. Der Hörer war dankbar für jeden Ton, für jedes Wort, das er vernahm, gleichgültig, was und wie er es vernahm, wenn er nur Empfang hatte."

43. Jonathan Sterne, *The Audible Past: Cultural Origins of Sound Reproduction* (Durham, N.C.: Duke University Press, 2003), 219. For an early history of sound fidelity, see his chapter 5, "The Social Genesis of Sound Fidelity."

44. Gebühreneinzugszentrale der öffentlich-rechtlichen Rundfunkanstalten in der Bundesrepublik Deutschland, "Geschichte des Rundfunks in Deutschland," www.gez.de/docs/geschichte_rundfunk.pdf (accessed February 12, 2006), 1. PDF. "In 1923, dem Jahr der Inflation, beträgt die Jahresgebühr 350 Mrd. Papiermark (1 Brot kostete 2 Mrd. Papiermark)." The Papiermark, or paper mark, preceded the Rentenmark, which was introduced in November 1923 to help stabilize the hyperinflation, and this was soon replaced by the Reichsmark in 1924. In her study *Feminine Frequencies*, Kate Lacey mentions that the number of registered listeners was most assuredly higher than reported, "given the practice of communal listening [and] because of the thousands of unofficial home receivers." She later continues that "few people could afford such a luxury — the license alone cost 350 million paper marks at a time when the average cost of living was 657 million paper marks — so most of the early listeners were *Schwarzhörer,* running the risk of a hefty fine by tuning in 'on the black' on homemade sets" 32.

45. Braun, *Achtung, Achtung, Hier ist Berlin!* 80–81. Braun lists the first transmission of advertising spots (September 1924), the first broadcast of the Berlin Philharmonic from inside a concert hall (October 1924), the first broadcast of an opera, Mozart's *Die Zauberflöte,* from the Berlin *Staatsoper* (mid-October 1924), and the first broadcast of an operatic sound play, Mozart's *Figaros Hochzeit* (November 1924), as important broadcasting milestones in the latter part of 1924.

46. Hans Flesch, "Zur Ausgestaltung des Programms im Rundfunk," *Die Besprechung (Beilage der "Radio-Umschau"),* no. 1 (1924): 3–4; *Die Besprechung,* no. 2 (1924): 11–13, here 3–4. Many thanks to members of the Women in German discussion forum for assistance in translating tricky aspects of this passage. "Das Kino war, als es begann, das Theater ersetzen zu wollen, folgerichtig Ersatz geworden, und niemals kann Ersatz Kunst sein. Als es später wieder einer Eigenart zustrebte und ... sich nun bewußt vom Theater losmachte und da einsetzte, wo das Theater in seinen Möglichkeiten mit der Versenkung und der Windmaschine erschöpft war, da begann es uns wieder zu interessieren. Hier war kein Ersatz mehr, denn diese Dinge ließen sich nicht auf das Theater zurückübertragen oder gar auf der Bühne verbessern. Hier war nicht die Maschine als Träger des ganzen kinematographischen Seins schamhaft verhüllt, sondern keck als solche genommen und sogar dem Theater gegenüber ausgespielt. Die Maschine wurde nicht verborgen sondern aufs Banner gesetzt, und wir glauben, daß aus der Maschine Künstlerisches entstehen kann — aber nur, wenn sie selbständiger Ausgangspunkt, nie, wenn sie versteckt werden [sic]: Alle Eigenart kann Kunstwerte schaffen."

47. Ibid., 4. "auch im Radio ist die Maschine Zwischenträger und nicht zu beseitigender Vermittler zwischen Darbietung und Ohr. Darum wird auch beim Rundfunk-Konzert niemals künstlerisch Wertvolles herauskommen, wenn der Rundfunk seine Aufgabe darin sieht, lediglich gute Konzerte zu übertragen. Es bleibt dann beim unkünstlicherischen Konzertersatz."

48. In a later essay from February 1927, written in honor of Thomas Edison's eightieth birthday, Flesch also draws connections between Edison's gramophone and the radio in bringing "Kunst ins Haus" (art into the house) and "uns gemeinsam das Odium anhaftet, am Untergang der guten alten Hausmusik mitzuwirken" (were stuck with the odium of having mutually contributed to the demise of the good old family-style music). Hans Flesch, "Grammophon," *Südwestdeutsche Rundfunk-Zeitung*, no. 8 (1927): 4.

49. Flesch, "Zur Ausgestaltung des Programms im Rundfunk," 4. "Wir wollen hier an das Grammophon als Lehrer denken. Im Konzertsaal läßt uns das Gefühl nicht dazu kommen, Musikstücke zu studieren. Die Kunst eines großen Sängers, in allen Nüancen aufzunehmen, dazu bietet uns das Grammophon zu Hause die beste Gelegenheit. Eine gute Caruso-Platte kann uns Nüancen dieses genialen Sängers so im einzelnen wiedergeben, daß wir durch die Erinnerung an das wirklich schon Gehörte oder, wenn wir ihn noch nie gehört haben, durch den Gedanken daran, daß es so etwas gibt, erschüttert werden können."

50. Golo Föllmer, "Audio Art," Medien Kunst Netz, www.medienkunstnetz.de/themes/overview_of_media_art/audio/4/ (accessed October 30, 2006).

51. Flesch, "Zur Ausgestaltung des Programms im Rundfunk," 4. "erlebt im Konzertsaal alle jene Wirkungen der Musik, die man in tausend Gedichten beschrieben findet: bessere Regungen werden im Menschen erweckt, freudige Stimmungen erzeugt, heldische Empfindungen, schmerzvolle Trauer, kurzum der Mensch wird in seinem Innersten gepackt und, wie es immer wieder heißt, 'in höhere Sphären gehoben.'"

52. Ibid., 4. "Diese Wirkung hervorzubringen, kann und darf durch das Radio hindurch nicht gelingen und, wenn es zu gelingen scheint, so muß es unecht und sentimental sein, denn in höhere Sphären hebt uns nur Unmittelbarkeit und keine Maschine!"

53. Ibid. "Durch den Gedanken daran: Es handelt sich also um einen rein geistigen, um einen intellektuellen Vorgang, den uns die Maschine des Grammophons vermittelt. Auf dem Umweg über das Gedankliche können wir gefühlsmäß erschüttert werden. Dieses Umwegs aber müssen wir uns sowohl beim Grammophon als auch beim Rundfunk stets bewußt bleiben. Es wäre darum falsch, ein Programm nach den Gesichtspunkten zusammenzustellen, nach denen im Konzertsaal gewöhnlich die Programme zusammengestellt sind. Die gedanklichen Komponenten müssen in den Vordergrund gestellt werden."

54. For additional information on these public listening venues, see Carsten Lenk, "Medium der Privatheit? Über Rundfunk, Freizeit und Konsum in der Weimarer Republik," in *Radiozeiten: Herrschaft, Alltag, Gesellschaft (1924–1960)*, ed. Inge Marßolek and Adelheid von Saldern (Potsdam: Verlag für Berlin-Brandenburg, 1999), 206–17. Lenk mentions that Ernst Ludwig Voss's idea of the *Saalfunk* was

prevalent into the early 1930s, when many households began to outfit themselves with radio receivers. Until then it was common for many listeners to access radio in common spaces such as pubs, at neighbor's houses where a radio-hobbyist lived, and at amusement parks, which wanted to cash in on the rarity of the device and the listening experience. See especially his pages 207–8.

55. Lacey, "Öffentliches Zuhören: Eine alternative Geschichte des Radiohörens," in *Politiken der Medien*, ed. Daniel Gethmann and Markus Stauff (Zurich: Diaphenes, 2005), 195–208, here 197. Lacey cites William Boddy's essay "Archaeologies of Electronic Vision and the Gendered Spectator," *Screen* 35 (1994): 105–22, as an example of an approach that sets up this type of binary between active and passive listening along gender lines. "Angefangen bei den frühen berauschenden Tagen, in denen junge Männer sich aus der Eintönigkeit des Alltagslebens in die Dachkammern zurückziehen, um ihre eigenen Sender zu bauen, zu verbessern und sich mit exotischen Fremden über den magischen Äther in Verbindung zu setzen, bis zu den gefürchteten Jahren der passiven, isolierten Unbeweglichkeit in der domestizierten und daher feminisierten Massenkultur. Diese Fassung der Geschichte bietet übrigens auch eine mögliche Erklärung für die Verherrlichung von 'Interaktivität', welche die eifrige Annahme neuer Computer-Technologien durch eine neue Generation hauptsächlich männlicher Enthusiasten umgeben hat."

56. Ibid., 202–7.

57. Flesch, "Zur Ausgestaltung des Programms im Rundfunk," 4. "Das Gefühlsmäßige im Rundfunk muß zweite Linie, indirektes Resultat sein. Auf die Denkarbeit kommt es an, und so ist das Radio-Konzert-Programm im eigentlichsten Sinne intellektuell."

58. I am making reference here to Brecht's short essay "Suggestions for the Director of Radio Broadcasting," first published in 1927 and translated into English in *Bertolt Brecht on Film and Radio*, ed. Marc Silberman (London: Methuen, 2000), 35–36. The essay forms a part of Brecht's radio theory and is discussed in more detail in chapter 3.

59. Hans Flesch, "Wie kommt ein Rundfunkprogramm zustande?" *Die Besprechung (Beilage der "Radio-Umschau")*, no. 3 (1925): 17–18, here 17. "Musikstück an Musikstück gereiht, ergibt noch kein Programm. Häufungen von Produkten größter musikalischer Genies kann eine Form oder vielmehr eine Unform annehmen, die rohe Menschen zu dem häßlichen Ausdruck "Gulasch" hinreißt. So lernen wir als zweiten Punkt den Formwillen als programbeeinflussendes Instrument kennen. Rechnen wir noch einen für den Leiter unbedingt notwendigen Radioinstinkt dazu, so können wir uns schon vorstellen, daß ein Programm zustandekommt. So weit wäre alles schön und gut."

60. Ibid., 17. "Tradition, Geschmack, und Musiklexikon belehren, was gut und böse sei, und, wohl ausgerüstet mit diesen drei Dingen, insbesondere mit dem Musiklexikon, schöpft nun der Leiter frohgemut aus besagtem Born."

61. Ibid., 17–18. "Eigentlich ist er bedauernswert. Er leidet an einer idée fixe. Er hat es sich in den Verlegerkopf gesetzt:... (a) stets ein Programm für eine ganze Woche (sprich ganze Woche) zu drucken, (b) besagtes Wochenprogramm bereits 10 Tage vor Beginn bezeichneter Woche in seinen Händen zu haben. Wer jemals

von Formwille und Gestaltungsvermögen gehört hat, der weiß, wie schwer eine Einigung zwischen diesen beiden wesentlichen aber schwierigen Mitbürgern unter diesen Umständen ist."

62. Kate Lacey suggests that sustained audience research was not widely performed until after the Nazis came to power, which accounts for the meager data available pertaining to the Weimar period. See *Feminine Frequencies*, 104–9.

63. Hans Flesch, "Ein Jahr Frankfurter Programm: Vortrag gehalten im Frankfurter Sender am 1. April 1925 von Dr. Hans Flesch," *Die Besprechung (Beilage der Radio-Umschau)*, no. 15 (1925): 154–7, here 154.

64. Ibid., 155. "Ich habe in früheren Vorträgen oft genug darauf hingewiesen, warum der Rundfunk diese Wege der Erziehung und nicht der Unterhaltung gehen muß;...weil der Rundfunk kaum Kunst an sich sein kann. — Das Fehlen des Unmittelbaren, die Dazwischenschaltung der Maschine, wird den Rundfunk immer als Vermittler und nie als Ding an sich erscheinen lassen. Wenn man das ausspricht, so schädigt man nicht etwa den Rundfunkgedanken, sondern man hebt ihn, indem man ihn auf sein eigenes Postament setzt. Der Rundfunk als Kunstersatz wird stehts mit Recht Ablehnung finden; der Rundfunk als Kunstgattung für sich liegt zwar im Bereiche der Möglichkeit, scheint aber nur einen begrenzten Umfang zu besitzen. Der Rundfunk als Vermittler, als Führer zur Kunst, als Führer zu den schönen und guten Dingen der Wissenschaft, der Bildung, mit einem Wort, der Rundfunk als geistiger Helfer wird immer eine hervorragende Rolle spielen."

65. Hans Flesch, "Mein Bekenntnis zum Rundfunk," *Funk* 2, no. 36 (1925): 445. "Das Rundfunk-Hören ist eine Art Partiturlesen für jedermann, d. h. es vermittelt dem Laien dieselbe Art von Kenntnissen — natürlich nicht im gleichen Maße und auf ganz anderm Wege! — , die der Musiker durch die Lektüre der Partitur erwirbt. Deshalb bin ich gegen die vielverbreitete Ansicht, den Rundfunk als eine Bequemlichkeits-Einrichtung zu feiern: die alles hübsch bis ins Haus bringt, bis in den weichen Klubsessel, daß man nur zuzugreifen braucht und die Unbequemlichkeiten der Theater- und Konzertbesuche erspart. Nein, der Rundfunk ist dazu da, die Bequemen und Unentschlossenen zu solchem Besuch anzureizen!"

66. Magnus, "Gedenken an Hans Flesch und seine Freunde," 413, quoted in Wolfgang Schivelbusch, *Intellektuellendämmerung: Zur Lage der Franfurter Intelligenz in den zwanziger Jahren* (Frankfurt am Main: Insel, 1982), 65. The nine regional stations organized in the year following the introduction of public radio reception in 1923 were located in Berlin (October 1923), Leipzig (March 1924), Munich (March 1924), Frankfurt am Main (March 1924), Hamburg (May 1924), Stuttgart (May 1924), Breslau (May 1924), Königsberg (June 1924; the capital of the former German province of East Prussia, now Kaliningrad, Russia), and Münster (October 1924; moved to Cologne in 1927). "Modern bis in die Fingerspitzen, allem Neuen zugewandt und keiner irgendwie gearteten Form verhaftet."

67. Schivelbusch, *Intellektuellendämmerung*, 66 (original emphasis). "Was er dabei selber als Autor schuf, ist nicht besonders aufregend und beeindruckend, wie z.B. die 1924 gesendete kabarettistische Spielerei "Zauberei auf dem Rundfunk," die alle technischen und dramaturgischen Tricks des Mediums vorexerzierte. Seine eigentliche Leistung lag in der Auswahl der Mitarbeiter und den Möglichkeiten, die

er ihnen gab. Hier zeigte Flesch tatsächlich ein "bis in die Fingerspitzen modernes" Gespür für Begabungen und Innovationen. Die Mitarbeiter und Autoren, die den Sender Frankfurt in den zwanziger Jahren zu einem Innovationszentrum für die Rundfunk-Genres der *Reportage,* der *neuen Musik,* des *Hörspiels* und des *freien Streitgesprächs* machten, konnten sich hier besonders frei entfalten, weil die Organisationsstruktur dieses Unternehmens entsprechend beschaffen war."

68. Since recording technologies were not yet available in 1924, there is no recording of the original 1924 broadcast. However, the script of the play was published shortly after its broadcast in the first volume of the journal *Funk* and has been republished since in various German radio play anthologies. See Hans Flesch, "Zauberei auf dem Sender: Versuch einer Rundfunkgroteske," *Funk* 1, no. 35 (1924): 543–46; and Hans Flesch, "Zauberei auf dem Sender: Versuch einer Rundfunkgroteske" in *Zauberei auf dem Sender und andere Hörspiele,* ed. Ulrich Lauterbach and Günther Rühle (Frankfurt am Main: Verlag Waldemar Kramer, 1962), 24–35. In addition, the play was reproduced and broadcast by the Hessischer Rundfunk in 1962, and a recording of this broadcast is available in .mp3 format: Hans Flesch, *Zauberei auf dem Sender: Versuch einer Rundfunkgroteske* (Hessischer Rundfunk, 1962), 22 min., 9 sec.; *MediaCulture-online,* mp3 audio file www.mediaculture-online.de/Hoerspiele.811 +M517b0cdfebd.0.html (accessed March 29, 2007). Finally, a recording from a new production of the play in June 1974 is available from the Deutsches Rundfunkarchiv: Hans Flesch, *Zauberei auf dem Sender: Neuinszenierung anläßlich der Wilhelmsbader Produktionen 1974,* (Hessischer Rundfunk, 1974) 28 min., 43 sec.; Deutsches Rundfunkarchiv, 5901561. mp3 audio file. For purposes of this study, I will be using the 1924 script and the recording from the 1962 radio broadcast, which most closely resembles the 1924 script.

69. Flesch, "Mein Bekenntnis zum Rundfunk," 445. "Einmal habe ich den Versuch unternommen, ein rundfunk-charakteristisches Hörspiel zu schaffen, schrieb — als Nichtschriftsteller, als Theoretiker eigentlich — die "Zauberei auf dem Sender," um durch den Zusammenklang der Geräusche eine rundfunkeigentümliche Kunstgattung anzudeuten; diese Groteske wäre nie auf die Bühne oder in den Konzertsaal übertragbar, und das ist das Entscheidende."

70. M. H. "Der Sender ist verrückt: Ein Versuch am 24. Oktober auf Welle 467," *Die Besprechung (Beilage der "Radio-Umschau"),* no. 6 (1924): 44. "Punkt ½9 Uhr beginnt es. Mit einer "höllischen" Fra Diavolo-Ouvertüre. Alle Rundfunkteilnehmer fahren entsetzt in die Höhe. Aber was ist das? Dr. Flesch, der Herrscher des Sendereiches, wird in seinem Programm gestört. Tatsächlich gestört. Von der Märchentante. Die auch einmal abends Märchen erzählen will. Und während noch gütlich mit ihr verhandelt wird, ertönen Zahlen, nichts als Zahlen. Nein: schon werden Soprantöne laut, schon beginnt das Orchester zu spielen, schon werden philosophische Probleme erörtert. Gleichzeitig. Alles gleichzeitig. Der Sender ist verrückt! Chaos, Stimmengewirr, Trommelfellangst. Bis sich eine tiefe Stimme herausschält, machtvoll, suggestiv, die Stimme des Zauberers, der sein Werk der Zerstörung und Verwirrung lobt. Vergebens bittet Dr. Flesch sein Orchester, den Donauwalzer zu spielen. Ein Trauermarsch wird daraus. Unordnung scheint über

Ordnung zu siegen. Bis Dr. Flesch mit dem Mahnruf an den Willen des Menschen, der Zauberei Herr wird. Frei und klar ertönt der Donauwalzer. Ernsthaftes Wollen hat den Spuk besiegt."

71. Flesch, "Zauberei auf dem Sender," 543. "Jeder macht, was ihm einfällt! Der Sender ist verrückt geworden."

72. Ibid., 543. "ein Rundfunkteilnehmer, der war mit allem zufrieden, was der Sender ihm bot — das ist lange, lange her...."

73. Ibid., 545. "Warum erlaubten Sie mir nicht, den Leuten meine Kunststücke im Sender vorzumachen; harmlose, fröhliche Zaubereien, die die Leute erfreut hätten, ich bat Sie doch dringend genug, mir zu glauben, daß die Rundfunkhörer kraft meiner Macht Funkzuschauer werden könnten. Sie haben mich ausgelacht! Die Leute hätten alle diese lustigen Dinge in ihren Elektronenröhren, in ihren Detektoren gesehen, gesehen, ja, Herr Doktor, gesehen, so wie Sie mich hier vor sich stehen sehen. (Zum Apparat) Meine Damen und Herren, sehen Sie fest — ganz fest in Ihren Apparat, in die Glühfarben Ihrer Verstärkerröhren, auf das Krystall Ihres Detektors — ich zähle bis drei — auf drei sehen Sie mich alle...."

74. Friedrich Bischoff and Werner Milch, *Hallo! Welle Erdball. Hörspiel — Zwei Szenen* (November 11, 1929), 18 min., 54 sec.; Deutsches Rundfunkarchiv, 2600339-06. mp3 audio file.

75. W. Roller, *Tondokumente zur Kultur- und Zeitgeschichte 1888–1932: Ein Verzeichnis,* ed. Deutsches Rundfunkarchiv (Potsdam: Verl. für Berlin-Brandenburg, 1998), 196. "Bei dem Hörspiel "Hallo! Welle Erdball" handelt es sich um eine auf Schallplatten aufgezeichnete veränderte Version des Hörspiels "Hallo! Hier Welle Erdball!" von Fritz Walter (Friedrich) Bischoff und Werner Milch; diese "Hörspielsymphonie" wurde am 4. 2. 1928 in der Schlesischen Funkstunde uraufgeführt, eine Tonaufnahme von dieser Fassung ist nicht erhalten."

76. Reinhard Döhl, "Neues vom Alten Hörspiel," *Rundfunk und Fernsehen* 29 (1981): 127–41, here 128. "Es handelt sich um eine Sequenz aus einer anderen Produktion, vielleicht nicht einmal von Bischoff handelt, die noch zu ermitteln wäre."

77. Bischoff and Milch, *Hallo! Welle Erdball,* audio transcript [00:18.17– 00:18.53]. "Sie hörten eine Szene aus "Hallo! Welle Erdball" von F. W. Bischoff. Sie wurde mit Hilfe von vier Schallplatten wiedergegeben. Der Übergang von einer Platte zur anderen sollte unmerklich vor sich gehen. Der Versuch wurde durchgeführt, um festzustellen, ob eine solche Wiedergabe der vollwertige Ersatz eines Originalhörspiels ist."

78. Hans Tasiemka, "Film ohne Bild: 'Hallo — hier Welle Erdball!' wird vertonfilmt," *Der Deutsche Rundfunk* 7, no. 49 (1929): 1547. "Es ist also ein Tonfilm ohne bewegte Bilder, ein Photophonogramm aus Ton und Laut."

79. "Film Sound History," at www.mtsu.edu/smpte/twenties.html (accessed April 10, 2007). Additional information about the Tri-Ergon company and its optical sound recording process can be found in Douglas Gomery, "Tri-Ergon, Tobis Klangfilm, and the Coming of Sound," *Cinema Journal* 16 (1976): 51–61.

80. Hans Flesch, "Hörspiel Film Schallplatte," in *Rundfunk Jahrbuch 1931,* ed. Reichs-Rundfunk Gesellschaft (Berlin: Union Deutsche Verlagsgesellschaft,

1931), 31–36, here 35–36. "Der Hörspielregisseur von heute arbeitet…noch zu sehr vor dem Mikrophon und nicht aus dem Mikrophon heraus.…Will er aber aus dem Mikrophon schaffen, so führt ein Weg dazu, seinerseits zwischen Künstler und Maschine (das Mikrophon) ein Medium einzuschalten, das die seelische Äußerung, die Produktion des Künstlers der Maschine adäquat macht. Wir glauben, daß dieses Medium der Tonfilm ist.…Das Hauptmerkmal der Maschine ist die Präzision. Soll aus einer Maschine etwas Künstlerisches herauskommen, so darf diese Haupteigenschaft nicht verletzt werden. Niemals aber kann etwa ein Hörspiel mit der Präzision ausgeführt werden, wie sie die Maschine verlangt. Dies ist möglich, wenn der Film als Mittler eingeschaltet wird, der alle Eventualitäten, alle Störungen, alle Improvisationen ausschließt.…Bei einem auf Tonfilm aufgenommenen Hörspiel kann nach Abhören durch Schneiden, Überblenden, Ansetzen, usw. ein Gebilde geschaffen werden, das der Regisseur als vollständig gelungen betrachtet und nunmehr abends dem Hörer darbietet."

81. Tasiemka, "Film ohne Bild," 1547. "Es ist zu hoffen, daß die Reichs-Rundfunk-Gesellschaft ihr Hörspiel-Archiv auf diese Weise so schnell wie möglich erweitert. Auch wäre es gut, beizeiten an den Ausbau des Archivs aktueller Reportagen zu denken. Bischoff machte den ersten Schritt wie beim Hörspiel. Wer wird ihm folgen?"

82. Döhl, "Neues vom Alten Hörspiel," 129. He uses the term "Sensationshysterie."

83. Bischoff and Milch, *Hallo! Welle Erdball!* audio transcript [00:08.25–00:09.46]. "Der Tag der Sensationen! Der Tag der Sensationen! / Fred und Erna erringen die Meisterschaft im 66-Stunden-Tanzen. / Fred Groggi läuft in sechzehn Monaten, zwei Tagen, drei Stunden, einundzwanzig Minuten, siebzehneinhalb Sekunden um die Welt. / Die berühmte Koloratursängerin Maria Polodi erschießt in der Theatergarderobe ihren Gatten und vergiftet sich mit Lippenschminke. / Sensationen! Sensationen! / Die Welt besteht aus nichts, nur aus Sensationen! // Der Tag der Katastrophen! Der Tag der Katastrophen! / Riesiges Erdbeben in Japan! Zwanzigtausend Menschen obdachlos! / Ein Blizzard verwüstet die blühende Stadt Georgia in New Mexiko! / Bei den Bob-Meisterschaften in St. Moritz zerknacken bei einem Unglücksfall eins, zwei, drei, vier, fünf, sechs, sieben, zehn Köpfe. / Katastrophen! Die Welt besteht aus Katastrophen! / Die Welt besteht aus nichts, nur aus Katastrophen!"

84. See Dieter Daniels, *Kunst als Sendung: Von der Telegrafie zum Internet* (Munich: Beck, 2002), 150–52.

85. Bischoff and Milch, *Hallo! Welle Erdball!* [00:17.56–00:18.14]. "Plumpsack" is a children's game similar to "Duck Duck Goose." "Aufhör'n! Aufhör'n! Wir verstehen uns nicht! / Wir wollen das Leben, Sie das Gedicht. / Wir verzichten auf Lyrik, süchtig, zärtlich und schmal. / Wir wollen, jawohl, wir wollen die Wahrheit, nackt und kahl! / Da ist sie! / Wo? / Hier! / Hilfe! / Hunger, Hunger, Hunger! / Erbarmen! / Im Namen des Gesetzes: zum Tode verurteilt! // Umschalten! Umschalten! / Das Leben in tausend Gestalten, /Die Wahrheit in tausend Systeme gespalten! / Was sollen wir tun? / Umschalten! / Schaltet Euch um, dann seid Ihr im Spiel. / Eins, zwei, drei, der Plumpsack geht rum."

86. Friedrich Wolf, *SOS rao rao Foyn — "Krassin" rettet "Italia" (Mai bis Juli 1928)*. *Hörspiel in 20 Szenen* (November 5, 1929), 64 min., 8 sec.; Deutsches Rundfunkarchiv, 53.895. mp3 audio file. The text of the play appears as Friedrich Wolf, "SOS...rao rao...Foyn — 'Krassin' rettet 'Italia,'" in *Frühe sozialistische Hörspiele*, ed. Stefan Bodo Würffel (Frankfurt am Main: Fischer, 1982), 41–66.

87. Wolf, *SOS...rao rao...Foyn — "Krassin" rettet "Italia,"* audio transcript [00:01.51–00:02.51]. This text comprises the lead-in element for the radio play, ostensibly read by the announcer and attributed by Würffel in his volume to Friedrich Wolf. The spoken text in the broadcast deviates markedly from that provided in Würffel's volume, leaving out an entire sentence, which I highlight here in the note. "Nicht der Impuls eines Übermenschen, nicht das "Ethos" eines Religions- oder Staatsgedankens hat dies Rettungswerk ermöglicht, sondern die von der Technik beflügelte Solidarität der Völker. Sie schloß an diesem lebendigen Beispiel den Ring von dem einsamen Radiobastler an der Murmanküste bis zu der großen Funkstation in Rom, bis zum roten Zelt der Eisscholle und dem Flieger Tschuchnowski. *Es ist eine Tatsache, ohne eine Tat zu zögern hat ein politisch völlig anders gerichtete System dem gegnerischen System brüderlich geholfen.* Und diese Hilfe wurde nur möglich durch das modernste Nachrichtenmittel: durch das Radio!"

88. See Stefan Bodo Würffel, *Das deutsche Hörspiel* (Stuttgart: Metzler, 1978), 32–33.

89. Hans Flesch, "Das Studio der Berliner Funkstunde," *Rundfunk Jahrbuch 1930*, ed. Reichs-Rundfunk Gesellschaft (Berlin: Union Deutsche Verlagsgesellschaft, 1930), 117–20, here 117–18. "Für den Rundfunk, diese wundervolle Synthese von Technik und Kunst auf dem Weg der Übermittlung, gilt der Satz: Im Anfang war das Experiment. Nicht auf den technischen Teil beschränkt, außerhalb der Gesetzlichkeit physikalisher Formen, jenseits der maschinellen Gruppe Empfänger–Sender–Verstärker–Mikrophon, eroberte sich das Experiment, die Freude am Probieren, auch die Darbietung selber. Nicht nur das übermittelnde Instrument, auch das zu Übermittelnde ist neu zu formen; das Programm kann nicht am Schreibtisch gemacht werden. Eine gewisse Erfahrung mag den Programmleiter dies oder jenes voraussehen lassen, aber ebenso wie die Technik verlangt, daß Stellung des Orchesters, des Chors, der Solisten zum Mikrophon nicht schematisch festgelegt, sondern stets neu versucht werden, ebenso muß das Programm erstarren, wenn nicht ständig neue Möglichkeiten ausprobiert werden."

90. For additional information regarding this transition, see Lerg, *Rundfunkpolitik*, 438–536; and Lacey, *Feminine Frequencies*, 99–101; and for specifics related to Hans Flesch, see Weil, "Hans Flesch — Rundfunkintendant in Berlin," 234–39.

91. Eugen Hadamovsky, *Schluss mit dem Korruptionsskandal im deutschen Rundfunk*, 25 min., 10 sec.; Deutsches Rundfunkarchiv, 00-2590240. mp3 audio file. "Mit den letzten Vorgängen, die sich innerhalb der Funkhäuser und um den Rundfunk herum abgespielt haben, endet die demokratische Epoche des Rundfunks. Und damit endet zugleich die Epoche der Rundfunk-Liliputaner, jene Männer, die im Rundfunk nur einen einzigen Horizont kannten und sahen, nämlich den Horizont

ihres persönlichen Wohlergehens und den Horizont innerhalb ihres Portemonnaies. Zehn Jahre Systemrundfunk haben uns zehn Jahre verkalkten Liberalismus beschert, zehn Jahre geistloser, sich aber geistig dünkender Perversitäten.... Für uns ist, kurz gesagt, der Rundfunk das Heiligtum unseres Volkes, und er soll das Braune Haus deutschen Geistes werden!"

3. Don't Touch That Dial

1. The poem appears in Bertolt Brecht, "Auf den kleinen Radioapparat," in *Werke. Gedichte 2. Sammlungen 1938–56,* ed. Werner Hecht, Jan Knopf, et al., Bd. 12. (Frankfurt a. M: Suhrkamp, 1988), 109.

2. While Bertolt Brecht is known in the United States primarily as an insightful dramatist and for his theoretical works about theater, his writings about the media of radio and film are of equal importance. Likewise, Alfred Andersch's work has been characterized primarily by his several novels, short stories, and literary cultural essays rather than his work with radio. In addition to their work with radio, Bertolt Brecht (1898–1956) and Alfred Andersch (1914–80) shared an affiliation with the German Communist Party (KPD) and an engagement with Marxist thought, although this involvement led to very different outcomes, with Brecht returning to East Germany following the war, and Andersch's affiliation ending in 1933–34 with his arrest by the National Socialists and subsequent short-term internment in Dachau concentration camp for his work with the Communist Youth League of Bavaria.

3. Bertolt Brecht, "Radio — An Antediluvian Invention?" in *Bertolt Brecht on Film and Radio,* trans. and ed. Marc Silberman (London: Methuen, 2000), 36–38, here 37.

4. Ibid.

5. Ibid.

6. Bertolt Brecht, "Suggestions for the Director of Radio Broadcasting," *Bertolt Brecht on Film and Radio,* trans. and ed. Marc Silberman (London: Methuen, 2000), 35–36, here 36.

7. Kurt Weill, "Über die Möglichkeit einer Rundfunkversuchsstelle," *Musik und Theater. Gesammelte Schriften. Mit einer Auswahl von Gesprächen und Interviews,* ed. Stephen Hinton and Jürgen Schebera (Berlin: Henschelverlag Kunst und Gesellschaft, 1990), 243–45, here 244. "Die erste und vornehmste Aufgabe, an die eine Rundfunkversuchsstelle herangehen müßte, besteht also darin, die Grundeinstellung zum Rundfunk auf eine andere Ebene zu heben. Der Rundfunk verlangt seine eigenen Leute, er muß mehr sein als ein willkommener Nebenverdienst für anderweitig interessierte Künstler, er kann zu einem eigenen, selbständigen Kunstzweig heranreifen, wenn jede Betätigung im Senderaum den Erfordernissen, aber auch den Möglichkeiten des Mikrophons entspricht." Weill's piece first appeared in the journal *Der Deutsche Rundfunk* in February 1927.

8. Bertolt Brecht, "The Radio as a Communications Apparatus," in *Bertolt Brecht on Film and Radio,* trans. and ed. Marc Silberman (London: Methuen, 2000), 41–46, here 43.

9. Ibid., 42.

10. These *Lehrstücke,* or learning plays, for the radio include, among others, *The Flight of the Lindberghs,* later changed to *Ocean Flight* (1929), and *The Baden-Baden Lesson on Consent* (1929).

11. For additional information see "Open Source Definition," www.opensource.org/docs/definition.php (accessed September 16, 2003).

12. Jonathan Sterne's study *The Audible Past: Cultural Origins of Sound Reproduction* (Durham, N.C.: Duke University Press, 2003) locates early twentieth-century techniques of sound telegraphy and sound telephony within nineteenth-century medical practices involving stethoscopes and listening to the patient's body.

13. Friedrich Kittler, "Wellenartillerie," Kunstradio, October 27, 1988, at www.kunstradio.at/1988B/27_10_88/drei.html (accessed September 16, 2003). "Brechts Radiotheorie gipfelte in der Forderung, den Rundfunk aus einem Distributionsapparat in einen Kommunikationsapparat zu verwandeln. Seltsam nur, daß Brecht die funktechnische Revolution ausrief, ohne die funktechnische Kontrarevolution 9 Jahre zuvor auch nur zu erwähnen. Das erst die Fernmeldegesetze von 1923 einen Kommunikationsapparat in einen Distributionsapparat umgestellt hatten, fiel ihm gar nicht mehr ein. Von der Staatssicherheit als guten Grund dieser Maßnahme ganz zu schweigen."

14. Bertolt Brecht, *Der Lindberghflug* (March 18, 1930), 19 min., 2 sec.; Deutsches Rundfunkarchiv, 53.611. mp3 audio file. The audio file includes only a portion of the full play. The text of the play is available as Bertolt Brecht, *Werke. Stücke 3,* ed. Werner Hecht, Jan Knopf, et al., Bd. 3. (Frankfurt a. M: Suhrkamp, 1988). It was written in conjunction with Elisabeth Hauptmann in 1928/29 and first broadcast in July 1929. It includes music by Paul Hindemith and Kurt Weill. The original title was *Der Flug der Lindberghs,* which Brecht changed to *Der Ozeanflug* because of Lindbergh's close relationships to the Nazis.

15. Bertolt Brecht, "Explanations [about *The Flight of the Lindberghs*]," in *Bertolt Brecht on Film and Radio,* trans. and ed. Marc Silberman (London: Methuen, 2000), 38–41, here 39 (original emphasis).

16. Braun, *Achtung, Achtung, Hier ist Berlin!* 62. "Der Aufruhr in der Stadt war beispiellos.... Es wurde Abend — und plötzlich strömten die Berliner von allen Seiten auf das Tempelhofer Feld, nach der Schätzung der Presse mehr als 100,000."

17. Kittler, "Wellenartillerie." "Brechts Hörspiel *Ozeanflug* von 1929 feierte an Lindbergs erster Atlantiküberquerung alles mögliche, das Flugzeug, die Motorengeräusche, den Rauschpegel oder Widerstand der Elemente Wind und Wasser, vor allem anderen aber natürlich den Beistand der namenlosen Arbeiterklasse, ohne die die Maschine nie gestartet wäre. In Brechts *Ozeanflug* kam der Kommunikations-apparat als Basis des ganzen Flugexperiments einfach nicht vor. Kein Wunder, daß die erträumte Verwandlung von Brechts Hörspiel vom Distributionsapparat zum Kommunikationsapparat scheitern mußte. Brechts schrecklicher Eindruck, das Radio sei eine unausdenkbar alte Einrichtung, die seinerzeit durch die Sintflut in Vergessenheit geraten war, faßte seine eigene vorsintflutliche Dramatisierung einer Weltkriegstechnologie brilliant zusammen."

18. Brecht, "The Radio as a Communications Apparatus," 45.

19. Marshall McLuhan, *Understanding Media: The Extensions of Man* (London: Sphere Books, 1968), 317. McLuhan criticizes here the work of Austrian sociologist Paul Lazarsfeld, who failed to see radio as a contributing factor to the rise of fascism in Germany. In 1933 Lazarsfeld came to the United States and directed the Radio Project at Princeton University, which also employed Theodor W. Adorno as music director. Lazarsfeld's ideas about the monopolistic effects of radio will find echoes in Alfred Andersch's claims about radio in the 1950s, discussed further on in this chapter.

20. Ibid., 319–20.

21. Figures for increases to household radios taken from Ernest K. Bramsted, *Goebbels and National Socialist Propaganda, 1925–1945* (East Lansing: Michigan State University Press, 1965), 74.

22. Mark E. Cory, "Soundplay: The Polyphonous Tradition of German Radio Art," in *Wireless Imagination. Sound, Radio, and the Avant-Garde*, ed. Douglas Kahn and Gregory Whitehead. (Cambridge, Mass.: MIT, 1992), 331–71, here 343.

23. "Richtlinien für die Neuordnung des Rundfunks (1932)" in *Dokumente zur Geschichte des deutschen Rundfunks und Fernsehens*, ed. E. Kurt Fischer (Göttingen: Musterschmidt-Verlag, 1957), 85–86. "1. Der Rundfunk arbeitet mit an den Lebensaufgaben des deutschen Volkes. Die natürliche Einordnung der Menschen in Heimat und Familie, Beruf und Staat ist durch den deutschen Rundfunk zu erhalten und zu festigen. 2. Der deutsche Rundfunk wahrt christliche Gesinnung und Gesittung und die Achtung vor der ehrlichen Überzeugung Andersdenkender. Was das Christentum entwürdigt und Sitte und Kultur des deutschen Volkes gefährdet, ist vom Rundfunk ausgeschlossen. 3. Der Rundfunk dient allen Deutschen innerhalb und außerhalb der Reichsgrenzen. Er verbindet die Auslandsdeutschen mit dem Reiche und läßt die innerdeutschen Hörer am Leben und Schicksal der Auslandsdeutschen teilnehmen. Die Pflege des Reichsgedankens ist Pflicht des deutschen Rundfunks. 4. Der Rundfunk nimmt an der großen Aufgabe teil, die Deutschen zum Staatsvolk zu bilden und das staatliche Denken und Wollen der Hörer zu formen und zu stärken. 5. Die verehrungswürdigen, aus der Vergangenheit des deutschen Volkes und des deutschen Reichs überlieferten Kräfte und Güter sind in der Arbeit des Rundfunks zu achten und zu mehren. 6. Aufgabe alle Sender ist es, das Gemeinsame der Lebensgemeinschaft des deutschen Volkes zu pflegen. Die Landessender gehen dabei von den landsmannschaftlichen Besonderheiten ihres Sendebereichs aus und vermitteln auch das reiche Eigenleben der deutschen Stämme und Landschaften."

24. Joseph Goebbels, "Radio as the Eighth Great Power," ed. and trans. Randall Bytwerk et al., *German Propaganda Archive,* www.calvin.edu/academic/cas/gpa/goeb56.htm (accessed September 23, 2003). In this and other translations of Goebbels's speeches, I have taken the liberty of enhancing the archive's versions. "Wir wollen einen Rundfunk, der mit dem Volke geht, einen Rundfunk, der für das Volk arbeitet, einen Rundfunk, der Mittler ist zwischen Regierung und Nation, einen Rundfunk, der auch über die Grenzen hinweg der Welt ein Spiegelbild unserer Art, unseres Lebens, und unserer Arbeit gibt."

25. Ibid. "Nicht, als wenn wir die Absicht hätten, lediglich Parteiprogramme zu senden. Wir wollen der Unterhaltung, der leichten Muse, Spiel, Scherz und Musik breitesten Spielraum geben; aber alles soll eine innere Beziehung zur Zeit haben. Alles soll die starke Note unserer grossen Aufbauarbeit tragen, oder es soll sich doch mindestens dazu nicht in Widerspruch befinden. Dabei ist vonnöten: eine straffe Zentralisation allen rundfunkpolitischen Schaffens, der Vorrang ihrer geistigen Aufgaben vor den technischen, die Durchsetzung des Führungsprinzips, die Eindeutigkeit der weltanschaulichen Tendenzen und die weitherzige Elastizität, mit der diese weltanschaulichen Tendenzen in die praktische Sendung übersetzt werden."

26. Jeffrey Herf, *Reactionary Modernism: Technology, Culture, and Politics in Weimar and the Third Reich* (Cambridge: Cambridge University Press, 1984), 2–3.

27. Ibid., 3. Advocates of this conservative revolution included Oswald Spengler, Ernst Niekisch, Arthur Moeller van den Bruck, Ernst and Friedrich Jünger, and to a lesser degree Martin Heidegger among others, and are referred to by Jeffrey Herf as "reactionary modernists."

28. See H. Joachim Schauss, *Tondokumente des deutschsprachigen Hörspiels 1928–1945* (Frankfurt am Main: Deutsches Rundfunkarchiv, 1975).

29. Cory, "Soundplay: The Polyphonous Tradition of German Radio Art," 345. Cory's study claims that the avant-garde practices and theories of radio production from 1920s Weimar remained unvisited until the 1960s when acoustical experimentation with radio in West Germany sought to unsettle the established notion of *Hörspiel,* moving away from text-based productions for radio and moving toward sound-based productions for radio. My study follows this same premise, but views Andersch's genre-based designs for the radio in the immediate postwar period as belonging to the same line of inquiry and experimentation practiced and theorized by Brecht.

30. Friedrich Kittler, *Gramophone, Film, Typewriter* (Stanford, Calif.: Stanford University Press, 1999), 69.

31. Andrew Stuart Bergerson, "Listening to the Radio in Hildesheim, 1923–53," *German Studies Review* 24 (2001): 83–113, here 94.

32. Kittler, *Gramophone,* xxxix.

33. Alfred Andersch, "Lebenslauf, 5. 4. 1955." TS 78.7122/1. Deutsches Literaturarchiv, Marbach, Germany. "Ihre Auffassung vom Rundfunk als Monopolinstrument wie als Instrument zur Verteidigung der Freiheit decken sich vollkommen mit den meinen."

34. Basic Law for the Federal Republic of Germany, article 5, section 1, see online at www.bundestag.de/htdocs_e/parliament/function/legal/germanbasiclaw.pdf (accessed April 25, 2007).

35. Peter Humphreys, *Media and Media Policy in West Germany: The Press and Broadcasting since 1945* (New York: Berg, 1990).

36. Süddeutscher Rundfunk, located in Stuttgart, and Südwestfunk, located in Baden-Baden, were dissolved in September 1998 to form the larger regional broadcast station *Südwestrundfunk,* with broadcasting locations in Stuttgart, Baden-Baden, and Mainz.

37. Alfred Andersch, "Mitternachtsstudio" (August 1, 1948), MS, Historisches Archiv des Hessischen Rundfunks, Frankfurt, quoted in Matthias Liebe, *Alfred Andersch und sein "Radio-Essay"* (Frankfurt am Main: P. Lang, 1990), 37. Aside from the significant archival research, Liebe's biographically grounded investigation affords an introductory glimpse into Andersch's work in broadcasting, an element of his career long overlooked by many critics. Liebe's focus on the effects of Andersch's editorial work with the radio essay sketches his role as a literary facilitator for the younger generation of postwar writers and critics. "Abzulehnen sind jene Fluchttendenzen, die mit den Begriffen des 'Ewigen' und 'Überzeitlichen' operieren; sie waren im Dritten Reich sinnvoll, weil in ihnen sich eine Distanz zum System ausdrückte, heute würden sie einen Verzicht auf die erregende Diskussion bedeuten. Das 'Ewige' muß sich daraus ergeben, daß Aktualität mit den höchsten Maßstäben gemessen wird."

38. For additional information about Andersch's earliest unpublished writing see my article, Daniel Gilfillan, "Between Ontological Landscape and Rationalized Workplace: Technology and Perception in Alfred Andersch's Early Poetry and Prose," *Seminar* 44, no. 4 (2008): 433–52.

39. Andersch, "Mitternachtsstudio," 37.

40. Ibid.

41. Alfred Andersch, "Bemerkungen zum Abendstudio," in *Gesammelte Werke. Essayistische Schriften I,* ed. Dieter Lamping, Bd. 8. (Zurich: Diogenes, 2004), 257–58. "Das Abendstudio ist eine Sendung für Hörer, die ihr Rundfunkgerät nur selten andrehen. Leute, die vom 'Abendstudio' wirklich etwas haben wollen, sollten am Dienstagabend von 21.30 bis 22.00 Uhr einen kleinen Spaziergang machen. Anschließend sollten sie sich eine Tasse Kaffee kochen, die Lampe abblenden (aber nicht zu stark) und in einem bequemen (aber nicht zu bequemen) Sessel Platz nehmen. Um 22.15 kann der Apparat eingeschaltet werden. Wenn man diese Gebrauchsanweisung beachtet, wird man sich am nächsten Morgen nicht unausgeschlafen, sondern frisch und belebt fühlen.... Das 'Abendstudio' lehrt, daß die wichtigsten Worte die spontan gesprochenen sind. Aus diesem Grunde hat es selbst kein 'Programm'; sein Programm ist, auf den Geist zu horchen, wo immer er auch wehen mag."

42. Ibid., 257. "Wenn Professor X, Publizist Y, und Dichter Z manchmal eine Stunde brauchen, um ein Problem restlos ungeklärt zu lassen, hat das *Abendstudio* seinen Zweck erfüllt. Es hat gezeigt, daß ein Problem vorlag."

43. Alfred Andersch, "Versuch über das Feature: Anläßlich einer neuen Arbeit Ernst Schnabels." *Rundfunk und Fernsehen* 1 (1953): 94–97, here 95. " 'Feature' bedeutet niemals den Inhalt einer Sache, sondern ihre Erscheinungsweise, vom 'making,' 'form,' 'appearance' über den 'facial aspect' des Menschen oder der 'fashion' bis zum 'special inducement' der Zeitungen und des Funks. Es bedeutet also die Form einer Sache, nicht die Sache selbst, wobei allerdings, wie im Erscheinungsbild des Menschen, zuweilen Form und Inhalt identisch sein können."

44. Ibid., 95. "Aus seinem ausschließlich formalen, also mittelhaften Charakter ergibt es sich, daß das Feature auf allen möglichen Arten von Sendungen übergreifen kann. Es bemächtigt sich des Berichts, der Reportage, der Darstellung sozialer,

psychologischer und politischer Fragen. Da es Form, also Kunst ist, sind seine Mittel unbegrenzt; sie reichen vom Journalismus bis zur Dichtung, von der rationalen Deskription bis zum surrealen Griff in den Traum, von der bewußt für den unmittelbaren Gebrauch bestimmten Aufhellung der Aktualität bis zu jener Art dichterischer Durchdringung menschlicher Gemeinschaft."

45. Alfred Andersch, "Radio-Essay," *Der Funkkurier: Informationen des Süddeutschen Rundfunks für Presse, Kritiker und Rundfunkfreunde* 32 (1955): 2. "Eine sehr spezielle Form, und vor allem ist er eine der wenigen echten Kunst-Formen, die sich im Funk entwickelt haben. Das Wort 'Essay' kennzeichnet ihn nach zwei Richtungen hin: es unterscheidet ihn vom Hörspiel . . . und es gibt ihm den lebendigen, allen Möglichkeiten sich offen haltenden Charakter des Versuchs. In seiner höchsten Ausprägung — die nur selten erreicht wird — ist der Radio-Essay dichterisches Dokument der Realität unserer Welt und des Lebens der Menschen in ihr."

46. Alfred Andersch to Irmfried Wilimzig, June 7, 1949. Deutsches Literaturarchiv, Marbach, Germany, quoted in Stephan Reinhardt, *Alfred Andersch: Eine Biographie* (Zurich: Diogenes, 1990), 173. Wilimzig was Andersch's successor at the U.S. approved journal *Der Ruf*. "Kulturmaschine von Presse und Funk . . . ."

47. Alfred Andersch, — . "Konv. 24 frühe Gedichte." TS 84.1747. Deutsches Literaturarchiv, Marbach, Germany.

48. Andersch, "Bemerkungen," 257. "Es [das *Abendstudio*] verhilft ihnen zu der unschätzbaren Erfahrung, daß man das Radio auch abstellen kann."

49. Copies of the typescripts from the broadcasts were provided to me by Bettina Hasselbring of *Bayerischer Rundfunk* during a research stay in the mid-1990s. The *Deutsches Literaturarchiv* in Marbach a. Neckar also has copies of five of these typescripts.

50. Andersch, "Radio-Essay," 2.

51. Alfred Andersch, "Denk-Zettel für Kulturkonsumenten," *Nachtstudio* (March 4, 1959), MS, Historisches Archiv des Bayerischen Rundfunks, Munich. Andersch, n.p. "Ich möchte bemerken, daß meine Bemerkungen nicht als Denkzettel . . . sondern als Denk-Zettel, als mit einem Bindestrich zwischen dem Denken und dem Zettel, als Zettel zum Nachdenken. Es sind richtige Schmierzettel . . . Notizen zu Fragen, über die ich mir selbst durchaus nicht im Klaren bin, Einfälle, Fragen, Entwürfe . . . ."

52. Barbara Steinherr, comp., *Findbuch: Nachtstudio* (Munich: Historisches Archiv des Bayerischen Rundfunks, 2006), www.br-online.de/br-intern/geschichte/pdf/Findbuch-Nachtstudio.pdf (accessed September 30, 2006). "Es soll nicht irgendeine Elite angesprochen werden, sondern jeder aufgeschlossene Mensch, der die Vorgänge in der Welt, in die er gestellt ist, mit Anteilnahme verfolgt. Der Rundfunk ist wie keine andere publizistische Institution in der Lage, Millionen von Menschen jedes Bildungsgrades und jeder sozialen Schicht zu jeder Stunde und an jedem Ort mit den Ereignissen und Vorstellungen unmittelbar bekannt zu machen."

53. Alfred Andersch, "Denk-Zettel für Kulturkonsumenten," *Nachtstudio* (January 29, 1959), MS, Historisches Archiv des Bayerischen Rundfunks, Munich. n.p. " . . . ein Nest in der Lüneburger Heide oder am Rande von West-Berlin."

54. Ibid., n.p. "Heute ist aus dem künstlerischen Begriff der Kultur ein soziologischer geworden; wenn das Wort Kultur gebraucht wird, so nahezu ausschließlich in zwei Bedeutungen: als gesellschaftlich verwaltete Institution und als industrieller Betrieb. Die Betrachtungsweise, in der Kunst und Kultur als identisch erscheinen, ist leider gänzlich veraltet."

55. Ibid., n.p. "Ohne Zweifel befindet sich auch im innersten Kern der Kultur als Institution und Betrieb noch immer das originale Werk, aber die moderne Kultur bedient sich seiner nicht als schöpferische Achse, aus der sie ihre Kräfte bezieht, sondern sie richtet ihre ganzen Anstrengungen darauf, das Werk in Verwaltung und Betrieb einzuschließen, seine gefährlichen Bestandteile abzukapseln, seine Wirkung zu sterilisieren und es einem Prozeß allgemeiner Nivellierung zu unterwerfen, dies alles natürlich umso stärker, je totaler die Kultur industrialisiert und verwaltet wird."

56. Alfred Andersch, "Denk-Zettel für Kulturkonsumenten," *Nachtstudio* (March 4, 1959), MS, Historisches Archiv des Bayerischen Rundfunks, Munich., n.p. "der Geist der Geschichte, des gelebten Lebens, der Originalität verschwunden ist."

57. Ibid., n.p. "erscheinen die neuen Gebäude als unpersönliche Produkte irgendeines abstrakten Organismus, der 'Wiederaufbau' heißt."

58. See Humphreys, *Media and Media Policy in West Germany*, 157–61.

4. Opening the Radio Up

1. The epigraphs appear, respectively, in William Gibson, *Neuromancer* (New York: Ace Books, 1984), 51; and Vito Acconci, "Public Space in a Private Time," *Critical Inquiry* 16 (1990): 900–918, here 914.

2. Walter Ruttmann continued working in Germany with the medium of film, collaborating with Leni Riefenstahl on an unrealized portion of her propaganda epic *Triumph des Willens*, and then working primarily in advertising film until his death in 1941. See Jeanpaul Goergen, "Walter Ruttmann — Ein Porträt," in *Walter Ruttmann: Eine Dokumentation*, ed. Jeanpaul Goergen (Berlin: Freunde der deutschen Kinemathek, 1989), 17–42.

3. See Max Horkheimer and Theodor W. Adorno, *Dialectic of Enlightenment* (New York: Seabury Press, 1972).

4. Gilles Deleuze and Félix Guattari, *A Thousand Plateaus: Capitalism and Schizophrenia*, trans. Brian Massumi (Minneapolis: University of Minnesota Press, 1987).

5. Hans Magnus Enzensberger, "Constituents of a Theory of the Media," in *The Consciousness Industry: On Literature, Politics and the Media*, ed. Michael Roloff, trans. Stuart Hood (New York: Seabury Press, 1974), 95–128.

6. See Rudolf Petersen, "Infrastructures for Globalization: Transport, Telecommunication and Energy Supply," in *Responses to Globalization in Germany and the United States: Seven Sectors Compared*, ed. Carl F. Lankowski (Washington, D.C.: American Institute of Contemporary German Studies, 1999), 147–68.

7. Enzensberger, "Constituents of a Theory of the Media," 109.

8. Jacques Attali, "Interview with Jacques Attali," *Social Text* 7 (1983): 3–18, here 12–13.

9. Jacques Attali, *Noise: The Political Economy of Music,* trans. Brian Massumi (Minneapolis: University of Minnesota Press, 1985), 135.

10. Enzensberger, "Constituents of a Theory of the Media," 110.

11. See Karlheinz Grieger, Ursi Kollert, and Markus Barnay, eds., *Zum Beispiel Radio Dreyeckland: Wie Freies Radio gemacht wird: Geschichte, Praxis, Politischer Kampf* (Freiburg i. Breisgau: Dreisam-Verlag, 1987).

12. Ibid., 18. "Von einer gemeinsamen Kultur oder Geschichte der Badener, Elsässer und Nordschweizer war wenig bekannt, als sich Anfang der siebziger Jahre Umweltschützer aus allen drei Nationalstaaten über die Grenzen hinweg zusammenschlossen, um gegen die Expansionspläne der Chemie- und Atomindustrie am Oberrhein zu kämpfen.... Im grenzüberschreitenden Kampf gegen AKWs und Chemiewerke liegen auch die Wurzeln und die Grundlage für das Überleben von Radio Verte Fessenheim/Radio Dreyeckland. Die Geschichte unseres Radios ist eingebettet in die politischen Entwicklungsprozesse der Region und kann nur so verstanden werden."

13. Christian Scholze, *Radio Grünes Fessenheim* (Frankfurt am Main: Network Medien-Cooperative, 1981), 45–46. "Gewöhnlich wird die Sendung ein bis zwei Tage, bevor sie zur Ausstrahlung kommt, hergestellt. Nur bei ganz dringenden, aktuellen Anlässen senden wir life, d. h. die Sendung geht dann direkt über das Mikrofon in den Äther. Unser Tonstudio würde jedem Runkfunkprofi die Haare zu Berge treiben: zwei simple Tonbandgeräte, zwei Kassettenrekorder, ein Plattenspieler, drei gute Mikrofone, ein Kopfhörer und ein kleines Mischpult.... Ein Telefonadapter ermöglicht uns bei eiligen Fällen noch die neueste Information direkt in die Sendung mitreinzuschneiden.... Gesendet wird nun keinesfalls aus unserem Studio. Dazu haben wir kleine, mobile Sendeanlagen, die an vielen verschiedenen Standorten eingesetzt werden. Die Reichweite eines Gerätes ist groß, fünfzig Kilometer und mehr. Dabei kommen uns die Berge von Schwarzwald und Vogesen zugute.... Eine komplette UKW-Sendeanlage ... besteht aus einem Sender, einer kleinen Batterie, einem Kassettenrekorder, einem Mikrofon für Life-Sendungen und einer UKW-Antenne. Radio Fessenheim hat jetzt insgesamt mehr als zwanzig komplette einsatzbereite Sendeanlagen, ganz kleine mit einem Watt und größere, die mit 25 Watt Sendeleistung strahlen."

14. Acconci, "Public Space in a Private Time," 908.

15. Bundesverband Freier Radios, "BFR — Was ist das?" www.freie-radios.de/bfr/ueber.htm (accessed April 23, 2007).

16. Radio Dreyeckland, "Erklärung zum Sendestart aus Freiburg," April 20, 1985. Archiv sozialer Bewegungen, Freiburg i. Breisgau, Germany. "Insgesamt ist Freies Radio also heute in der Bundesrepublik nicht Realität, sondern Utopie. Nur Radio Dreyeckland hatte das Glück, einen Teil dieser Utopie bereits ausprobieren zu können: ein Radio, das als Gesellschaftsfunk unter der Kontrolle seiner Hörer arbeitet; ein Radio, das sich nicht im Privatbesitz weniger befindet, sondern das Eigentum aller ist, die seine Existenz ermöglichen; ein Radio zum Selbermachen, das von den Hörerinnen und Hörern selbst in die Hand genommen wird; eine Radio mit freiem Zugang für alle — bisher zumindest mittels Telefon und öffentlichen Redaktionssitzungen schaubar ist — mit leicht handhabbarer Technik;

ein Radio schließlich, das Nachrichtensperren durchbricht, das aufklärt, statt einzulullen, in dem es Auseinandersetzungen und lebendigen Dialog gibt anstelle von Verlautbarungs- und Berieselungsjournalismus."

17. Peter Humphreys, "Germany's 'Dual' Broadcasting System: Recipe for Pluralism in the Age of Multi-Channel Broadcasting?" *New German Critique* 78 (1999): 23–52, here 24–25.

18. See Humphreys, *Media and Media Policy in West Germany.*

19. See Jürgen Habermas, *The Structural Transformation of the Public Sphere: An Inquiry into a Category of Bourgeois Society,* trans. Thomas Burger (Cambridge, Mass.: MIT Press, 1989), and Oskar Negt and Alexander Kluge, *Public Sphere and Experience: Toward an Analysis of the Bourgeois and Proletarian Public Sphere,* trans. Peter Labanyi, Jamie Daniel, and Assenka Oksiloff (Minneapolis: University of Minnesota Press, 1993).

20. Bündnis 90/Die Grünen, "Entwurf eines Zwischenberichts der Fraktion BÜNDNIS 90/DIE GRÜNEN. Meinungsfreiheit — Meinungsvielfalt — Wettbewerb: Rundfunkbegriff und Regulierungsbedarf bei den Neuen Medien," presented as part of the *Erster Zwischenbericht der Enquete-Kommission Zukunft der Medien in Wirtschaft und Gesellschaft — Deutschlands Weg in die Informationsgesellschaft,* Deutscher Bundestag, 13. Wahlperiode, 1996, Drucksache 13/6000, 65–91, here 84.

21. Ibid., 84.

22. Geert Lovink, "The Theory of Mixing: An Inventory of Free Radio Techniques in Amsterdam," in *Radiotext(e),* ed. Neil Strauss and Dave Mandl (New York: Semiotext(e), 1993), 114–22, here 115.

23. Information about each of these live broadcast projects can be obtained from the Kunstradio website: www.kunstradio.at, which provides an archive of materials related to the art projects it supports and produces, including, in many cases, conceptual information, correspondence, biographies, intertexts and other related material. I will provide more specific references to each individual project throughout the course of the chapter.

24. Radio Subcom, *Europa Report* 1: "In Transit," 24 min., 31 sec.; (audio-cassette), 1988; received by the author from Armin Medosch; and Radio Subcom, *Europa Report* 2: "Between the Cities," 44 min., 38 sec.; ORF Kunstradio, continuous streaming audio file www.kunstradio.at/1991A/MP3/28_02_91.m3u (accessed February 12, 2002).

25. Both the live broadcast and CD remix are available on the Kunstradio website as streaming audio files: (a) Gordan Paunović, *Other Voices — Echoes from a War Zone,* live broadcast streaming audio, ORF Kunstradio, www.kunstradio.at/ 1999A/RA/ 99_04_29.ram (accessed February 14, 2004). (b) Gordan Paunović, *Other Voices — Echoes from a Warzone,* compact disc streaming audio, ORF Kunstradio, www.kunstradio.at/2000A/RA/ 00_04_02.ram (accessed February 14, 2004). The compact disc is also available: Gordan Paunović, *Other Voices — Echoes from a Warzone* (Vienna/Belgrade, April 29, 1999), compact disc, ORF Kunstradio, © 1999.

26. Joe Milutis, *Ether: The Nothing That Connects Everything* (Minneapolis: University of Minnesota Press, 2006), ix.

27. Anthony Dunne and Fiona Raby, *Design Noir: The Secret Life of Electronic Objects* (London: August/Birkhäser, 2001), 12.

28. Ibid., 15.

29. Heidi Grundmann, "Radio as Medium and Metaphor" in *Net_condition: Art and Global Media,* ed. Peter Weibel and Timothy Druckery (Cambridge, Mass.: MIT Press, 2001), 236–43, here 239.

30. ORF Kunstradio, "Kunstradio-RadioArt Manifesto," www.kunstradio.at/TEXTS/manifesto.html (accessed February 26, 2007).

31. Kittler, "Die letzte Radiosendung," 72.

32. See Kittler, "Wellenartillerie."

33. Heidi Grundmann, "Radiokunst" in *Im Netz der Systeme,* ed. Ars Electronica at www.aec.at/en/archives/festival_archive/festival_catalogs/festival_artikel.asp?iProjectID=9039 (accessed April 25, 2007). An edited, shortened English translation is available: Heidi Grundmann, "Radio Art," in *Ars Electronica: Facing the Future: A Survey of Two Decades,* ed. Timothy Druckrey (Cambridge, Mass.: MIT Press, 1999), 90–100.

34. "Radio Subcom," n.p. "Die Klänge, die aus dem Radio kommen, sind klischiert, ihre Signifikanz ist an erlernte Hörgewohnheiten gebunden. Radio Subcom greift diese Klischees auf, verändert sie mit tontechnischen Mitteln und verschiebt sie im Kontext, so daß sie eine von der ursprünglichen Absicht völlig unabhängige Bedeutung erlangen. Das Radio wird zur Recycling-Anlage gegen mediale Umweltverschmutzung. Aus Tonkonserven, vergleichbar mit Altmaterialien wie Schrott oder Altpapier, werden ansprechende neue Produkte gemacht."

35. Ibid., n.p. "Information ist ein zentrales Thema unserer Zeit. Radio Subcom erweitert es um künstlerische Dimensionen. Networking, Koordination, die immaterielle Kunst der Kommunikation, die Aufwertung der Qualität des Datenstroms durch ein poetisches Bewußtsein. Information ist eine Verpflichtung, die Alternativen und Lösungsvorschläge der Kunst sollen auf breitester Basis Gehör finden. Die Kunst der Vermittlung und die Vermittlung der Kunst brauchen Unterstützung und Zusammenarbeit für den Aufbau ihrer Infrastruktur und ihre zukunftsweisenden Ideen."

36. Radio Subcom, *Europa Report* 1, audio transcript [24:00–24:30].

37. "Radio Subcom," ed. TDP (Vienna: Takahashi Design and Publishing, 1988), n.p. "Bisher war Radio Zeitungsjournalismus mit akustischen Einschüben. Mit der Verwirklichung der hier beschriebenen Technik-Installation beginnt die Zeit der subjektiven, komponierten Sprache, basierend auf ausschließlich authentischen Aufzeichnungen. Sprache und Klang in der Radioprogrammgestaltung verschmelzen zur unauflöslichen Einheit, die nur in ihrer Gesamtheit als signifikante Botschaft aufgenommen werden kann und somit dem Medium seine Eigentlichkeit neu zurückgewinnt."

38. Radio Subcom, *Europa Report* 2, audio transcript [11:15–11:29]. "Die Lautstärke ist wieder einmal fürs Hin- und Weghören angenommen. Der Lautstärkeregler des Hörers wäre entsprechend auf eher leise anzustellen."

39. Grundmann, "Radiokunst." I have adapted this translation from the one that appears in the shortened English version: Heidi Grundmann, "Radio Art," in

Ars Electronica: Facing the Future: A Survey of Two Decades, ed. Timothy Druckrey (Cambridge, Mass.: MIT Press, 1999), 91. "Vielfalt anderer Ansätze — auch in Mitteleuropa, u.a. provoziert von den hiesigen medienpolitischen Gegebenheiten, die den eigenständigen Zugriff von Minderheiten auf die Ätherwellen nicht vorsehen. Darauf reagieren seit vielen Jahren... in den verschiedensten Gruppierungen und entwerfen... ein Gegen-Bild zur bestehenden medienpolitischen Situation: Dieses Bild beinhaltet die Möglichkeit von Künstlern (und anderen Minderheiten), selbst senden zu können und eine den eigenen Bedürfnissen angepaßte und entsprechende Radioästhetik zu entwickeln, die eben nicht von den Regeln und Konventionen der (öffentlich-rechtlichen Monopol-) Institution Radio geprägt ist."

40. Matthew Fuller, "The R, the A, the D, the I, the O: The Media Ecology of Pirate Radio," in *Media Ecologies: Materialist Energies in Art and Technoculture* (Cambridge, Mass.: MIT Press, 2005), 13–53, here 16–17.

41. Ibid., 17.

42. Fredric Jameson and Masao Miyoshi, eds., *The Cultures of Globalization* (Durham, N.C.: Duke University Press, 1998), xi.

43. Lovink, "The Theory of Mixing," 115.

44. "Radio Subcom," n.p. "Kreative Tontechnik ist ein weiterer wesentlicher Bestandteil der von Radio Subcom vertretenen neuen Radio-Aesthetik. Oil Blo verwendet eine Mischung aus neuester digitaler Audio-Technologie und Geräten aus der Steinzeit der Radiotechnik. Stimmabmischung über einen alten Röhrenverstärker, Stimmverfremdungen auf einen Gitarren-Effektgerät aus den frühen fünfziger Jahren oder billigen Vorverstärkern, Tape-scratching und andere, 'primitive' Methoden;... Radiokunst ist keine besondere Sparte im konventionellen Radio, sondern die Kunst des Radiomachens selbst."

45. Radio Subcom, *Europa Report 2*, audio transcript [24:26–25:54].

46. Ibid. [21:33–22:58]. "Milano: 1989 wurde das besetzte Kommunikationszentrum Leoncavallo durch ein brutalen Polizeieinsatz geräumt. Die letzte Underground-Schlupflöcher Europas verschwinden. Wir als Künstler werden für die Entscheidung gestellt, ob wir uns mit der Kunst etablieren wollen, oder freiwillig in den Underground gehen."

47. Naomi Klein, *Fences and Windows: Dispatches from the Front Lines of the Globalization Debate* (New York: Picador, 2002), 227.

48. Radio Subcom, *Europa Report 2*, audio transcript [19:40–20:50]. "Die Revolution wird nicht im Fernsehen gezeigt werden, ausser das Fernsehen macht halt die Revolution — im Gegenteil Osteuropas — ein gelungener Coup des internationalen Unternehmertums."

49. Ibid. [14:39–15:44].

50. Ibid. [20:56–21:31]. "Die Rolle der Medien: das Netz hat seine Fiktion über die Wirklichkeit gestülpt wie eine riesige Glasglocke. Das Netz, das elektronische Environment, besteht nunmehr aus reiner Public Relation. Alle Begriffe — Information, Unterhaltung — kommt seit dem Begriff der Public Relation untergeordnet. Die Unterscheidung zwischen Tatsache und Fiktion ist sinnlos geworden: Geiselnahmen, Krieg, Terrorüberfälle können nicht mehr aus dem eigentlichen Sinn

politisch motiviert betrachtet werden, sondern als Nebeneffekte des Big Media Business."

51. Frederic Jameson, "Notes on Globalization as a Philosophical Issue," in *The Cultures of Globalization,* ed. Fredric Jameson and Masao Miyoshi (Durham, N.C.: Duke University Press, 1998), 68.

52. Radio Subcom, *Europa Report* 2, audio transcript [25:13–25:32].

53. Jamie Shea, "NATO Speech: Morning Briefing on Kosovo — 30. Apr. 1999," NATO: NATO's role in Kosovo: Background Briefings. www.nato.int/kosovo/press/b990430b.htm (accessed February 13, 2004). Interestingly, this was the first time since World War II that a European city had been bombed, and, for Belgrade, the fourth time in the twentieth century that it had experienced aerial bombings from an outside military force. The first had been the Austrian bombing of Belgrade in July 1914, the second came with the arrival of the German National Socialists and subsequent occupation in April 1941, and the third with Allied bombings in 1944 to regain the city at the end of the war.

54. Additional information about the history of Radio B92 and a biography of Veran Matić can be accessed at: ORF Kunstradio, "Veran Matić," www.kunstradio.at/BIOS/maticbio.html (accessed February 27, 2007). Alternately, important background information to the founding and development of Radio B92 can be found in Veran Matić and Drazen Pantic, "War of Words," *The Nation* November 29, 1999, www.thenation.com/doc/19991129/matic.

55. Although this essay will not investigate in detail the intricate connections between Vienna and Belgrade as ascertained by their economic and historic ties to the Danube, the natural course of the river across national and international boundaries serves as a telling metaphor for the types of information flow taking place over the airwaves in the production of Gordan Paunović's piece.

56. Heidi Grundmann, "But Is It Radio?" in *Anarchitexts: Voices from the Global Digital Resistance: A Subsol Anthology,* ed. Joanne Richardson (New York: Autonomedia, 2003), 157–64, here 158.

57. For additional information regarding each of the individual sources employed in the live broadcast, see the accompanying Kunstradio-produced website "Surface of the Project OTHER VOICES — ECHOES FROM A WARZONE, 29th of April 1999." ORF Kunstradio, www.kunstradio.at/1999A/ANEM_B92/index.html (accessed May 31, 2005).

58. Geert Lovink, "An Insider's Guide to Tactical Media (2001)," in *Dark Fiber: Tracking Critical Internet Culture* (Cambridge, Mass.: MIT Press, 2002), 254–74. This essay provides an interesting discussion of contemporary media activism as it relates to a history of media activism in the United States and Western Europe.

59. Veran Matić, "Schaffung des Informationsraums: 'Commando Solo,'" ORF Kunstradio, at www.kunstradio.at/WAR/VOICES/matic-commsolo.html (accessed June 1, 2005). "Der einzige Beweis, der uns als die alleinige Wahrheit angeboten wird, [ist] die Kamera im Kopf der Rakete, die ihr Ziel trifft. Die tagtägliche Wiederholung gleicher oder ähnlicher Aufnahmen, die durch diese Kameras gemacht werden, verwandelt den Journalismus in eine überflüssige Berufsgruppe,

denn die alleinige Wahrheit stammt aus dem Raketenkopf. Auf diese Art werden brutale Morde und Zerstörungen zu leicht verträglichen Videospielchen." 60. ORF Kunstradio, Other Voices CD Release Website, www.kunstradio.at/ TAKE/CD/paunovic_cd.html (accessed June 1, 2005). "Die Main Stream-Medien folgten den Richtlinien des politischen Establishments beider Seiten und verwandelten die Realität damit in das riesige Bühnenbild für ein Propagandaschauspiel. Jenseits der Potemkinschen Dörfer der großen Fernsehgesellschaften aber lief ein anderes Leben ab, das Leben von Menschen, die Jahre und Jahrzehnte damit verbracht hatten, mit ihrer Ausdruckskraft und Kreativität gegen Totalitarismus und nationalistischen Hass anzukämpfen. Doch plötzlich waren SchriftstellerInnen, SoundkünstlerInnen, Radiopersönlichkeiten, MedienarbeiterInnen, JournalistInnen und MusikerInnen nichts anderes mehr als "collateral damage" des Krieges in Jugoslawien."

61. Arsenije Jovanović, *Concerto gross balcanico,* live broadcast streaming audio, ORF Kunstradio, www.kunstradio.at/1993A/RA/concerto.ram (accessed February 14, 2004).

62. Excerpts from both Jasmina Tesanović's and Slobodan Marković's diaries used by Gordan Paunović in both the live broadcast and CD remix are reproduced on the Kunstradio project's website: ORF Kunstradio, "WAR DIARIES OF JASMINA TESANOVIĆ & SLOBODAN MARKOVIĆ," www.kunstradio.at/WAR/DIARY/ (accessed February 7, 2004). Tesanović's diary and other personal diaries from Belgrade are gathered on the "Help B92" website: Jasmina Tesanović, "Personal diaries," "Help" B92, http://helpb92.xs4all.nl/diaries/jasmina/jasmina.htm (accessed February 27, 2007). Here they can be read in English and their original Serbo-Croatian. When quoting from the diary entries employed in the live broadcast and CD remix, I will utilize direct transcriptions from the recorded audio, CD version, and provide time settings from both the CD and streaming audio versions to help the reader locate these excerpts. Also, whenever possible, I will provide page numbers for these excerpts from the 2000 Midnight Editions version of Tesanović's diary, published as Jasmina Tesanović, *The Diary of a Political Idiot: Normal Life in Belgrade* (San Francisco: Midnight Editions, 2000). This will not always be doable as the American version has edited some of the passages out which exist in the sound versions of the excerpts. I thank Azerina Began for her help in translating some of the Serbo-Croatian conversations that take place in the live broadcast.

63. Geert Lovink, "Kosovo: War in the Age of Internet (1999)," *Dark Fiber: Tracking Critical Internet Culture* (Cambridge, Mass.: MIT Press, 2002), 318–28, here, 322–23. A version of this essay appeared online in 1999, written in the midst of the Kosovo conflict, and as Lovink himself was engaging several of the diaries he mentions (among them Slobodan Marković's) through his association with the "nettime" mailing list. For the online version, see Geert Lovink, "War in the Age of Internet: Some Thoughts and Reports, Spring 1999." CRAC in Context. First Editions 1999–2000, www.crac.org/contextmapp/geert.htm (accessed June 3, 2005).

64. "About the Syndicate Network," http://colossus.v2.nl/syndicate/about.html (site now offline).

65. Frédérique Delacoste, Note from the Publisher. Tesanović, *The Diary of a Political Idiot,* 10.

66. Marković's posts to the Syndicate Mailing List were reposted to several other electronic arts and media activist lists, including nettime.org and rhizome.org, both of which continue to play primary roles in the world of electronic and digital arts.

67. For more information regarding Jasmina Tesanović's work in the Women in Black movement in Serbia, see her online essay "Women and War: A Serbian Perspective" www.geocities.com/Wellesley/3321/win23a.html (accessed June 5, 2005).

68. Tesanović, *The Diary of a Political Idiot,* 72; Paunović, *Echoes from a Warzone,* compact disc, audio transcript [10:28–11:00]; Paunović, *Echoes from a Warzone,* live broadcast streaming audio, audio transcript [54:59–55:37].

69. Paunović, *Echoes from a Warzone,* compact disc, audio transcript [11:00–11:48]; Paunović, *Echoes from a Warzone,* live broadcast streaming audio, audio transcript [55:37–56:26].

70. Jasmina Tesanović, "DIARY OF JASMINA TESANOVIĆ" ORF Kunstradio, www.kunstradio.at/WAR/DIARY/diary-2.html (accessed February 7, 2004).

71. Tesanović, *The Diary of a Political Idiot,* 89; Paunović, *Echoes from a Warzone,* compact disc, audio transcript [16:42–17:33]; Paunović, *Echoes from a Warzone,* live broadcast streaming audio, audio transcript [61:26–62:16].

72. Zygmunt Bauman, *Globalization: The Human Consequences* (New York: Columbia University Press, 1998), 86.

73. Paunović, *Echoes from a Warzone,* compact disc, audio transcript [22:25–22:41]; Paunović, *Echoes from a Warzone,* live broadcast streaming audio, audio transcript [67:09–67:24].

74. Ibid. [23:24–23:47]; ibid. [68:08–68:30].

75. Ibid. [25:39–26:12]; ibid. [70:23–70:56].

76. Baumann, *Globalization,* 77.

77. David Morley, *Home Territories: Media, Mobility and Identity* (London; New York: Routledge, 2000), 3.

78. Ibid., 9.

Coda

1. The excerpts appear, respectively, in Rudolf Arnheim, *Radio: An Art of Sound,* trans. Margaret Ludwig and Herbert Read (London: Faber and Faber, 1972), 14; and Gregory Whitehead, "Radio Play Is No Place: A Conversation between Jérôme Noetinger and Gregory Whitehead," in *Experimental Sound and Radio,* ed. Allen S. Weiss (Cambridge, Mass.: MIT Press, 2001), 89.

Index

Daniel Gilfillan is associate professor of German studies and information literacy at the School of International Letters and Cultures at Arizona State University.